Volume One
Inspired learning through great books.

Ages 5-9

Second Edition

By Jane Claire Lambert

Five in a Row Volume One

Second Edition

ISBN 978-1-888659-22-1

Copyright © 1997, 2020 by Jane Claire Lambert

Published by:
Five in a Row Publishing
312 SW Greenwich Dr.
Suite 220
Lee's Summit, MO 64082
816-866-8500

Send all requests for information to the above address.

All rights reserved. No part of this publication may be reproduced, stored in a retrieval system, or transmitted in any form or by any means—electronic, mechanical, photocopy, recording, or any other—except for brief quotations in printed reviews, without prior permission of the publisher. The activity sheets following each unit may be reproduced for use by the purchaser's own family.

To my mother, whose pure love of literature was contagious.
To my dad, who encouraged me to "read the good stuff."
And to my husband ... who reads to me.

Special thanks to the "guinea pigs" who first tried *Five in a Row*:
our daughters, Becky and Carrie,
and our dear friends, Caleb, Benjamin and Nate.

Contents

Introduction	06
About the Books Themselves	08
How to Use *Five in a Row*	10
Jane Claire's Tips for Those Beginning *Five in a Row*	20
The Story About Ping by Marjorie Flack	28
Lentil by Robert McCloskey	38
Madeline by Ludwig Bemelmans	48
A Pair of Red Clogs by Masako Matsuno	56
The Rag Coat by Lauren Mills	66
Who Owns the Sun? by Stacy Chbosky	76
Mike Mulligan and His Steam Shovel by Virginia Lee Burton	86
The Glorious Flight by Alice and Martin Provensen	96
How to Make an Apple Pie and See the World by Marjorie Priceman	103
Grandfather's Journey by Allen Say	110
Cranberry Thanksgiving by Wende and Harry Devlin	118
Another Celebrated Dancing Bear by Gladys Scheffrin-Falk	130
Papa Piccolo by Carol Talley	140
Very Last First Time by Jan Andrews	150
The Clown of God by Tomie dePaola	159
Storm in the Night by Mary Stolz	170
Katy and the Big Snow by Virginia Lee Burton	180
Night of the Moonjellies by Mark Shasha	189
Stopping by Woods on a Snowy Evening by Robert Frost (Susan Jeffers' illustrations)	197
Review Week	206
Story Disks	207
Blank Disks (Reproducible)	209
Sample Lesson Planning Sheet	210
Blank Lesson Planning Sheet	212
Choices a Writer Can Make	214
Choices an Artist Can Make	215
Literary Glossary	216
Finding the Books	218
Integrating Additional Curricula with *Five in a Row*	220
Parts of a Flag	222
Index	223

Introduction

Good books have always been the doorway to learning. That doorway leads to growth and an appreciation for the wonders around us. Come along on a learning adventure using picture books to open the door to art, history, vocabulary, geography, science, human relationships, applied math and writing!

No matter how young, children get a substantial educational head start from books. *Five in a Row* was created to bring excitement and fun to learning and to enrich children's lives through wonderful children's literature. These lesson plans are simple in concept, but rich in results. Read the chosen book in its entirety each day for a week. After each reading, choose an exercise to share with your student, and watch their world expand as you begin to show them facets of the story they would never have recognized without your purposeful guidance. As a teacher of this material, you will find that you become excited and interested in a variety of subjects too. You'll rediscover the joy of learning and you'll build a special bond between you and your student as the two of you go on a learning adventure together.

This curriculum is intended to be extremely flexible, allowing you the option to do any combination of the exercises for each story. You may elect to skip over certain lessons which do not fit the needs of your student and you may place additional emphasis on certain ones which seem appropriate. You will find more exercises than you can use in a week, so enjoy choosing just the right lesson elements for your students.

You can adjust school time to fit your needs as well. By using only one lesson element each day, you can work through *Five in a Row* in as little as 30 minutes daily, including the time to read the book. If you choose to use all of the lesson elements, field trips and follow-up exercises, you could easily spend several hours daily. Use *Five in a Row* however it best suits your needs and the needs of your students.

The technique of reading the same story for at least five days in a row is one that I have tested in teaching for many years. I continue to be amazed at the effectiveness of this technique! Each book will become very special to the children. They will remember more and more about the story, but more importantly, they will begin to think more critically (even five year olds!) as they begin wondering how certain portions of the story came to be, or how the characters solved a certain problem. These results could never be achieved in just one reading. (See page 10 for the complete teaching theory behind the concept of *Five in a Row*.)

Students will see how the illustrator accomplished certain effects and they'll be encouraged to begin exploring those techniques in their own art. You'll see your students learning about science, history and applied math through everyday discussions. Your students will have the opportunity to try new activities they read about, or to learn more about a variety of people, places or animals. You'll also discover your student asking more questions than ever before. By the end of the week, a new book will have become their friend for life.

Perhaps the most valuable benefit of using *Five in a Row* is that young students learn to fully evaluate a work (with your guidance), and that skill will serve them well as they learn to read for themselves. Your students will begin looking to see whether a book is a Caldecott or a Newbery medal winner. They'll quickly classify a new book as either fact or fiction. They'll be able to articulate the point of view from which the story has been written. They will know about a wide variety of literary techniques and learn to recognize them for themselves. You'll be delighted when your students begin to evaluate the illustrator's medium and technique.

All of this is imparted in an enjoyable learning environment. Students think you're just reading them a book, but they're learning so much every day! The more lessons you do together, the more skills your young students will acquire; skills which will benefit them through high school, college and throughout life!

Welcome to the wonderful world (and the second edition!) of *Five in a Row*. Even though our world has changed greatly since the first edition, the purpose and mission of this highly effective curriculum remain the same: to provide students with a quality educational foundation for their elementary years with "inspired learning through great books." This second edition is up to date regarding today's technology while continuing to base learning on high-quality, carefully chosen books and lessons—including all-new activity sheets following each title. You are the leader for this adventure, so gather the children around you and have a great time!

Jane Claire Lambert
May 1994; March 2020

About the Books Themselves

"The goal of our instruction is to lead children to fall in love with good books and and to embrace the joy of learning."

Sutherland and Arbuthnot write in the classic children's literature textbook *Children and Books*, "Aesthetic satisfaction comes to small children as well as to adults, and the development of their taste depends not only on their initial capacities but also on *the material they encounter and the way in which it is presented.*"* (emphasis added)

If you're like most of us, you can directly attribute a lifelong interest in at least one topic to the quality and creativity with which some particular teacher or a parent introduced the subject to you as a child. Likewise, you may well have nurtured a lifelong distaste for certain subjects for the same reason: an unpleasant early experience.

Sutherland and Arbuthnot go on to suggest that by selecting excellent children's literature and reading it together each day, children have the opportunity to "catch a new theme, savor the beauty, the subtle humor or a special meaning that eluded them at first."

"Sometimes," the authors continue, "an adult has the privilege of seeing this discovery take place. The children's faces come suddenly alive; their eyes shine. They may be anticipating an amusing conclusion or a heroic triumph. There is a sudden chuckle or breath is exhaled like a sigh. The book has moved them, perhaps even to laughter or tears; in any case there is a deep inner satisfaction and they will turn to books again with anticipation."

Sutherland and Arbuthnot conclude, "Once they have experienced the joy of reading they have acquired a habit that will serve them all their lives. It is important, therefore, that those who guide their reading select wisely."

It is within this context that the titles for *Five in a Row* have been chosen. In each case, content was of supreme importance. Books were chosen that showcase close family relationships, personal triumphs, and persevering in times of trial. There are books with people characters and stories with animal characters, but in all the stories the characters touch the reader's heart and demonstrate life's truths. Please remember, however, that our selection of a particular title by an author does *not* mean that we necessarily endorse *everything* from that author. We're aware of several cases where authors have written marvelous books and very questionable books as well. Please take the time to review any book you bring home from the library *before* reading it to your children!

In addition to content, the books also cover a wide range of artistic expression: from the beautiful portraiture of Allen Say to the hilarious pictures of Marjorie Priceman; from the warm, homey drawings of Robert McCloskey to the action-packed illustrations of Virginia Lee Burton. Each title was selected for a diversity of magnificent art, beautifully rendered for the utter appreciation and enjoyment of children. Art to appreciate, art to learn from and art to be remembered for a lifetime!

It has been said some stories must be talked over or listened to while *someone who knows and loves them reads aloud*. If *you* come to love the stories, your student will too.

With these standards in mind, we hope you and your student find a special place in your heart for these stories and for the concept of *Five in a Row*.

*Sutherland and Arbuthnot, *Children and Books*, Harper Collins Publishers, 8th ed., 1991.

How to Use Five in a Row

Select a book to study with your student. There is no right or wrong order for covering the material; even though a few books could be considered "seasonal" (such as *Katy and the Big Snow*) or holiday-related (such as *Cranberry Thanksgiving*), it's entirely up to you the order that you choose. Please also note that the books in Volumes 1-3 are interchangeable in difficulty; the books do not get "harder" as you move through these three volumes. (Volume 4, however, increases in complexity and depth and is ideal for older elementary-aged students.)

Some teachers will choose to purchase each book as a valuable addition to their permanent library. Of course, most public libraries should have (or be able to request) each of the titles in this book. (See "Finding the Books" at the end of this manual for more information.)

Important Note: Please take the time to read the book aloud to your student each day before covering the lesson material. *Five in a Row* was designed and tested to be read daily! The repetition is essential to your student's learning process, and the time you spend reading together is just as important as the lesson material itself. For more information on *why* to read the story five days in a row, and suggestions if you have a child who resists this idea, see "Reading the Stories Five Days in a Row" on page 25.

Following the story units in this manual, you will find a sample planning worksheet for *Who Owns the Sun?* You'll also find a blank worksheet which you can reproduce and use for each FIAR story that you study. The sample sheet shows how to correlate the teacher's guide suggestions and plans to the five days of the week you will study each particular book. Or, feel free to design your own worksheet. Some teachers don't care to use planning sheets at all, and just work directly from the *Five in a Row* manual. Do whatever works for you!

Notice that the sample lesson plan is outlined briefly and gives you a quick reference for the week. Not every lesson suggested in the manual under *Who Owns the Sun?* is listed on the sample lesson—there are too many lessons for one week. So you will choose the ones that are especially suited to your student and list them on the blank planning sheet. While the subjects Math, Science,

Art, etc., do not have to be used in the same order every week, remember that when planning a class week, the curriculum builds on itself. Whatever you study on Monday will be recognized by your student when you read the story again on Tuesday. When you read the story a third time on Wednesday, the lessons you introduced on Monday and Tuesday will not escape the student's notice as he hears or sees the examples again. So each lesson, except the one for Friday, gets at least one review and some lessons get four reviews. The topics you think are most important, therefore, should be scheduled toward the beginning of the week. It seems as though Art often gets tagged in the Friday slot. Try using this topic earlier in the week, perhaps on Wednesday, so your student can study the pictures for several days as he hears the story read and reread.

Also following the story units, you will find a sheet of story disks. These are quick, symbolic representations of the nineteen titles included in *Five in a Row*. They are meant to be used in conjunction with a laminated world or U.S. map. First, color the disk and put the name of the book on the back of the disk. For greater durability, laminate the disks before you cut them apart (or use clear contact paper after cutting). By placing a Velcro® dot on the disk and the other dot on the map where it goes, you can quickly take it off and put it back on each day (tacky putty will also work). Eventually you will be able to track the stories you have read all over the world. Even young students will learn some map basics. Any stories with fictitious settings can be placed in the margins of the map as the "Land of Make Believe."

There is also a page of blank disks so you can make your own pictures for these stories, or replace a lost disk. You might also like to make disks for other stories you read outside of *Five in a Row*.

Social Studies

Because there are only five subject categories (to correspond to the five days of the week), many different topics are included under Social Studies. Each story has a specific geographic area, and often the culture of that area is discussed. Making a flag is fun and informative, and you'll find flags to color in most units, as well as a "Parts of a Flag" reference sheet at the end of this manual. Geography also includes the mention of oceans, continents and geographic regions. (An excellent illustrated children's geography book is Rand McNally's *Picture Atlas of the World*, illustrated by Brian Delf. You'll find it informative and fun!) Under the topic Social Studies, you will also find lessons about cities, small town life, the homeless, adoption, occupations and running a small business. In addition, the Social Studies unit includes history. Under this heading, you will see lessons which create opportunities to discuss slavery, civil rights, the Civil War, Veteran's Day, Memorial Day, Labor Day, patriotism, various other U.S. wars and explorers like Marco Polo. Social Studies also includes many lessons about people and their relationships to one another. In this category, you'll find subjects such as fathering, self-image, stewardship, friendship, taking responsibility, envy, jealousy, forgiveness, manners, and generational ties—just to name a few. As you can see, a wide variety of subjects is included under Social Studies.

Choose the topics you'd like to discuss and either mark them in the manual or write them on the Planning Sheet under whichever day it seems best to cover them. If you use the Planning Sheets, be sure when presenting the material to tie it in to the story.

Language Arts

There are many techniques for learning Language Arts using children's literature. Increasing vocabulary, learning literary devices, learning list-making skills, composing short stories and acting out dramas are just a few of the ways. Teaching Language Arts is a natural extension of the enjoyment of children's literature.

Vocabulary is enriched by hearing new words like regatta (*Papa Piccolo*), moonjellies (*Night of the Moonjellies*) or squinting (*Who Owns the Sun?*). A child's vocabulary is much greater than just the words he can read or spell, and reading a story which contains new words five times in a row will help increase his recognition and understanding of those words.

windmill

a machine that uses wind power to grind grain, pump water and make electricity

pink

a tint of the color red, made by mixing red and white paint

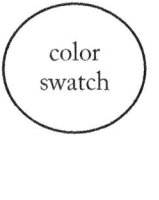

color swatch

Two methods for organizing vocabulary words are the file box and the notebook. The file box method uses four-by-six inch, unlined index cards with alphabet dividers. Either the teacher or the student can print the word at the top left of the card. Write in a short definition at the left, and either draw an illustration or or print a picture to show the word visually. Keep the words alphabetized and encourage your student to go through the cards frequently. This will help him remember which story each word was from. (To help in remembering the source, write the name of the book on the back of the card.)

A second method of keeping track of vocabulary words is to list them on a page in the Language Arts or Vocabulary section of a notebook. Print the word (large, if necessary) and illustrate with a drawing or picture as a visual reminder. Lists can be alphabetized or organized by FIAR title. Review these words from time to time while remembering your favorite incidents in the corresponding stories.

A notebook is good for more than just vocabulary words. In fact, it's a great way for a student to keep his work organized and ready for quick review and easy reference. For the grade-level student, this will likely come naturally. But for the very young student, to have his own notebook is special. For him, use colored dividers so he can find the subjects, even if he cannot yet read. In this way, he can proudly find his Science section and show someone his drawings or projects. He'll be able to look up his Vocabulary section with illustrations and share his art work with others.

List-making is another Language Arts skill that develops vocabulary, memory, associations and creativity. It is also a skill that has lifetime value in many different areas, from grocery lists, lists of people to invite to a party, "to do" lists, lists of ways to solve a problem, to descriptive lists that inform. There have been great, eloquent lists made by famous people of the things they liked, disliked, or the things they wished for. Once, while travelling together in a car, a friend's family began an oral list of methods of transportation. Many miles down the road, the list had grown to gigantic proportions with the hilarious inclusions of walking on stilts and walking on your hands added to the regular methods of riding in a car, bus or taxi. What began as a list-making exercise became entertainment. The art and skill of good list-making is included in this curriculum to provide both a learning experience and a good time.

There are many **literary devices** explained in FIAR and tied in to the lessons from children's literature. You probably will not cover them all, but they are included to remind the teacher of them and give opportunities for casual inclusion in the reading lessons. (Also see the Literary Devices section at the end of the manual.)

As you come to each new literary device, a list can be made with examples and pictures. Keep your list in the Language Arts section of the student's notebook. For instance, personification (giving human qualities to non-human things) might be defined and illustrated with a picture of the Pillsbury Doughboy® or Lightning McQueen from the movie *Cars*. Other literary devices can be illustrated, as well. Keeping a chart or list of these words makes review easy and interesting and can be used by the student as an inspirational list when he is creating his own works.

Ideas for leading your student into writing include letting them record their stories, which you then transcribe. Often the student will enjoy listening to his story in his own voice. Writing rebus stories, where pictures take the place of certain words throughout the story, is an interesting way to begin writing skills. As you follow the curriculum, you'll find lessons in what makes a good story, and ways to achieve variety. Your student will begin to appreciate the choices an author makes to create a story and the careful thought that goes into writing.

Many times in this curriculum these type of questions are asked: "How does the author make the story exciting? What words does he use? How does he…?" Eventually, as he sees these techniques modeled before him, the student will begin to include such elements in his own writing. The suggestion after every lesson to imitate an aspect of the author's work is optional, depending on the interest and abilities of the student. See if your student enjoys imitating the author's techniques. If not, just concentrate on appreciating the lesson. In time the rest will follow.

If, however, your student enjoys writing "after the manner of," imitating aspects of the author's story, he will like the suggestions to try a fable, an instructional story or a poem. He'll also begin to include a good setting, interesting characters, an exciting climax, or an important denouement (final outcome) in his own stories. Each of these is a separate lesson in the curriculum. Again, keeping a chart or a good notebook list filled with definitions and examples will give your student a ready reference when he is writing his own stories and makes review easy. Just add to the list or chart on an ongoing basis as you come to different lessons (see the Choices a Writer Can Make activity sheet at the end of the manual).

Remember, there are too many language arts topics to be covered in a single day. Choose the ones appropriate for your student and jot them briefly on the planning sheet under the day you think best. Also remember, if you are going to teach vocabulary it is a good idea to do this at the beginning of the week, perhaps on Tuesday. As the book is read and reread throughout the week, your student will see familiar vocabulary words again and again, providing a built-in review. Depending on your child's age, you may want to choose only a few words from each story.

Art

When you choose good children's literature, you will frequently discover exceptional illustrations, as well. Watercolor, pastels, charcoal, beautiful colors, active lines, funny characters and balanced compositions are all parts of fine illustrations for children. Furthermore, they can be used to introduce even young children to fundamentals and techniques of art.

Appreciating art is learning to recognize the many techniques and concepts which combine to produce effective art while learning what you like and why. Some pictures have a rhythm, balance and choice of color that combine to make them pleasing. Some illustrations are meant to evoke strong emotions or to provide information. Even young children can begin to identify great art wherever it's encountered. They'll also begin to know why they like it. By teaching about the artist and their methods, your student's taste in art will expand to include a rich and wonderful variety of work.

As you look at illustrations with your student, ask, "What do you think the illustrator used for his medium?" Sometimes it's hard to tell (check the copyright page of the book, which sometimes will provide this information). There are combinations of pen and ink with watercolor washes, etchings with strokes from oil or acrylic and the wet, transparent blends of watercolors. Look for the shading in a charcoal or pencil sketch, or the buildup of color by successive layers of colored pencils. Learn to identify the deep texture of pastels.

After you've discussed the medium, ask "why and how" questions. "Why do you think the illustrator chose this medium, color, style, viewpoint, etc.? How did the artist make it look like nighttime, etc.?" These kinds of questions will open a doorway to art appreciation for your student.

Let him study the illustrations as he tries to answer your questions. You may want to suggest some answers as you discuss the methods the artist used and how the illustrations help tell the book's story. Does the artist's work provide additional story information not included in the text? Does the choice of color palette convey the tone of the story?

Asking lots of questions will cause your student to look with a more critical eye. He will pore over the pages to find answers and he will gain a love of art based on newly-discovered information. This will lead to an emerging appreciation for great illustrations. Don't ask all the questions at the same time. Bring them up conversationally from time to time as you study each book.

One of the best techniques for teaching art fundamentals is to imitate a particular technique from the painting or drawing of a known artist. In *Five in a Row*, the lessons attempt to identify and single out a specific artistic element and to encourage imitation. Your student will be invited to mimic specific styles, colors and designs. Remember that appreciation usually precedes imitation. Therefore, look for examples of the element you are studying in other books or online. Let him examine and enjoy these additional examples before he begins experimenting with the technique himself.

In order for you to be ready to meet your student's needs, you may want to have certain supplies on hand:

Kneadable eraser

Drawing pencil or #2 lead pencil

Charcoal - (**Teacher's Note:** Supervise the use of charcoal, since it can get messy!)

Oil Pastels - The favorite medium of many young students. They don't smear as much as chalky pastels. (**Adult supervision required**.)

Markers

Colored pencils - Look for good colored pencils. They make a difference.

Crayons - Look for "name brand" crayons.

Watercolors - Prang® brand is good, or tube watercolors are extremely easy to use for mixing exercises.

Acrylics - Not necessary, but it gives your student a chance to paint layer upon layer using lighter colors on top.

Brushes - You'll need brushes with several different bristle lengths and widths. If you want to paint fine-lined tree branches, you'll need the right brush!

Watercolor paper

Canvas paper for acrylics

Drawing tablet or paper

Tracing paper

Ruler

Templates of various geometric shapes cut from cardboard or cardstock

Above all, remember that creative art is an intensely personal subject. If you wish to demonstrate a technique, do it on a separate piece of paper—never on your student's own work! Be wise with your criticism of his progress. Grant him the respect you would grant any artist. Go slowly, letting him catch the enthusiasm for the ideas you present.

Math

In many of the books chosen for this curriculum, children will enjoy finding practical ways to use the new concepts they learn in math.

For the youngest student, there are many opportunities for counting practice. It may be counting the stars in one illustration or fence pickets in another. Finding and counting all the cats in *Papa Piccolo* is fun! It will also provide a time for the teacher to see and hear the student count actual objects.

Ordinal numbers are covered in the lesson for *Very Last First Time*, and you will find an introduction to Roman numerals in *The Glorious Flight*.

The concepts of relative size, measuring, time, and money are all found in the stories of children's picture books. A book about quilts offers a chance to talk about geometric shapes. Because the concepts are linked to an enjoyable story, your student will remember them with pleasure.

If time is available, especially in the summer before school starts, make math manipulatives using ideas from the story illustrations. For instance, if you are going to read a book for a week that is about trains, make flash cards with the facts printed inside train cars. Use bright, cheerful colors and write the answers on the back. Laminating the cards will help them last. The cards can also contain any term or new concept on one side with the definition on the other.

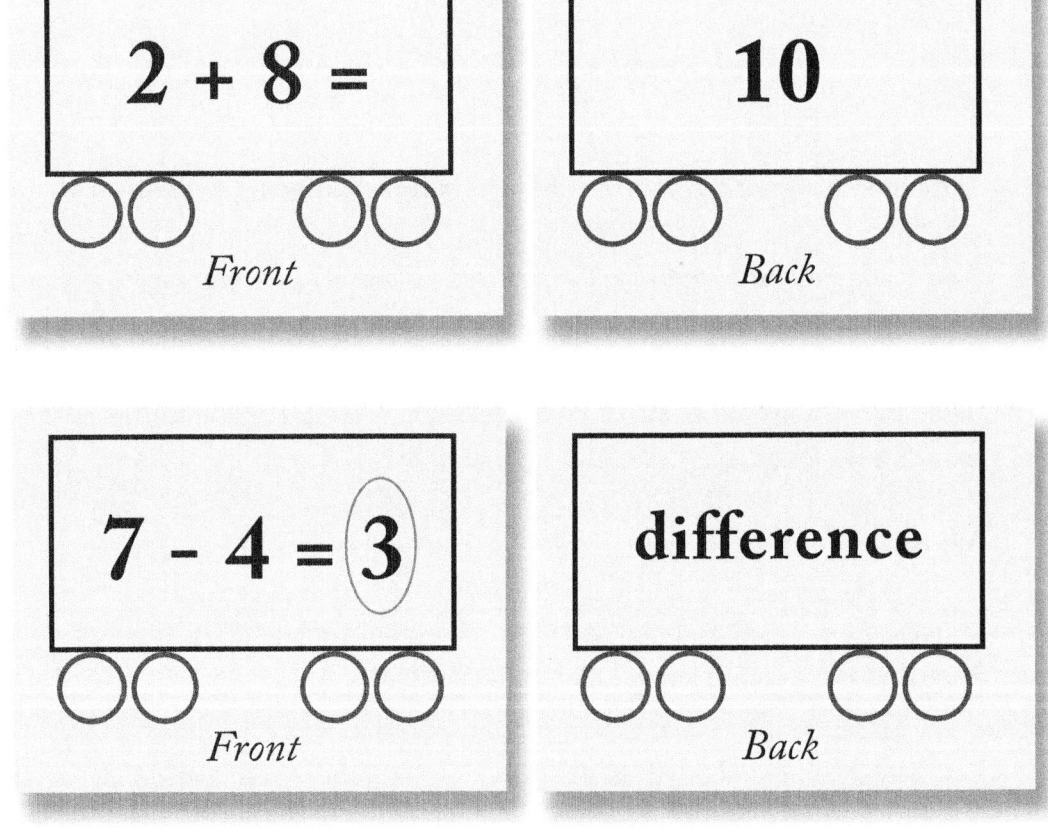

Reading the story all the way through while enjoying the closeness of the teacher and the entertainment of the book establishes a good environment for presenting a math lesson derived from the story. Even the lesson will be a shared experience. If there are more math ideas than are appropriate for one day, choose the ones you wish to cover and write them on the planning sheet for the day you wish to cover Math.

Science

Open wide the door to children's literature and find within the stories a vast array of scientific educational potential: from gazing at the stars and wondering about our sun, to discovering shadows and reflections, insect growth, how a lever works, volcanoes, pollution, seasons, nutrition, animal behavior and much more.

After reading the book for the day, bring up conversationally the science topics suggested in the lessons and other ideas that you may have. Don't try to use all the topics. *Who Owns The Sun?* for instance, includes science topics of seasons, five senses, simple machines, weather (rain and wind), stars and our sun. Just choose the ones you think are appropriate and mark them on the planning sheet on whichever day seems best.

When presenting your science lesson, *be sure to tie it into the story*. For instance, in *Night of the Moonjellies*, you might say, turning to the first page, "Remember when the boy was at the beach? What kind of things might you find at the beach?"

A science section in your student's notebook with a page for Ocean Life, a page for Simple Machines, etc., will help in reviewing lessons he's studied. If he likes, let your student illustrate the topics with his own drawings of the story. This could be part of a beloved notebook by year's end.

Note: *Five in a Row* was created to be gender-neutral and you'll find a wide variety of fascinating lessons that appeal to both boys and girls. Don't assume that a boy may not enjoy a story that has a girl as the main character, or vice versa! And, please note that we've referred to "teacher and student" in the singular. Many of you will have more than one student. Another item of note is that throughout the lessons, some words have been defined within parentheses. This is done to remind teachers of very young students that even *seemingly common* terms may have to be explained!

Jane Claire's Tips for Those Beginning
Five in a Row

If you are new to *Five in a Row*, here are some valuable thoughts from Jane Claire to help you get the most out of your experience.

There are two sections included here. One is a conversational, scripted week using some of the lessons from the *Five in a Row* manual. It will give you an idea of what a week could look like. The second is an explanation of how and why the curriculum was developed, including the educational philosophy and many tips for overcoming opposition to multiple story readings should you happen to have a reluctant student.

A Conversational Presentation of a Five in a Row Unit

There is, of course, no "absolute" way to present *Five in a Row* lessons. Each family modifies their presentation to fit a wide variety of needs. However, let me explain an effective way to use this curriculum using *The Story About Ping* for our example. There are usually several lessons for each subject category listed in your *Five in a Row* manual. In this demonstration I will not use every lesson listed but will select certain ones to illustrate the conversational teaching technique.

Whatever time in the day you choose to do your *Five in a Row* lessons, begin by cuddling up on the sofa or big chair and saying: "Let's read a book together!" Then enjoy reading a good story all the way through.

Day One

On the first day, after you've read the story through together, you simply begin conversationally, "Did you notice that our story today takes place in a foreign country? Do you remember the name of the country?" Or you could ask, "Where was it that Ping lived?" If your child doesn't remember, look in the story and find a line where it says that Ping lived in China.

Ask your student if he knows where China is. If he does, then let him show you on a world map. If he doesn't, then help him find China and the Yangtze River on a world map. The story disk (included at the end of this manual) is a wonderful manipulative which your student can use to pinpoint the setting of the story and enjoy reviewing it, on the map, each of the five days that you cover *The Story About Ping*.

Now continue by asking your student if he has ever heard of people living on boats like the one in the story? Can he see the door and windows in the illustration of the wise-eyed boat? Some of the people of China live on their boats and fish for their dinner and eat whatever they catch. Ask your student if he would like to live on a boat and never know what he was going to have for dinner till he went fishing each day. (Now, there are no right or wrong answers for this type of question. Some children will respond to this line of questioning with, "Cool! I'd love to live on a boat and fish for my dinner!" while others will say, "No way! Take me to McDonald's!" This is one of the wonderful ways that *Five in a Row* works. This curriculum helps you get to *really know* your child. And as you share with him, he will get to know you better, as well!)

Continue talking about the length of the Yangtze River and how the people of China live, using the facts listed in your manual. Please note that you do not have to use all of the information on China if you have a younger child. For some five-year-olds, for instance, just learning that there is a place called China and that it is far away is a great start!

Proceed with as much information from the lessons as you think would be interesting and enjoyable for the student you are teaching. Though the information in your manual is certainly enough, it is still fun to find a simple book or two on China at your library. The pictures are colorful and interesting. You could also search for pictures of China online.

There are many ideas in the "How to Use *Five in a Row*" section of your manual on how to help your student document what he has learned through making pages for his notebook, creating card files, or using the activity pages provided at the end of each unit. You can also visit www.fiveinarowdigital.com for Fold & Learns for several of the books in *Before Five in a Row*, *Five in a Row*, and *Beyond Five in a Row*, Notebooking Pages for use with all ages, and other helpful products.
This completes your first day of Five in a Row.

Day Two

The next day you would say (with enthusiasm!), "We're going to read *The Story About Ping* again." For most students this is exactly what they want to do! If your child is hesitant, just say, "Today we're going to read the story and we will be learning how a story is written! Marjorie Flack who wrote *The Story About Ping* has done something special with the words and we're going to see if we can hear what she has done." Then you read the story again. Your student is listening, but he will also be thinking,

Oh, Ping lives in China," and "no I wouldn't like to live on one of those boats and wow, the Yangtze river sure is long—it's longer than a trip to my grandpa's." All the things you talked about the day before will be running through his head. Reading the story again makes review easy, doesn't it?

On day two, you can ask your student if he can put the story disk on China. You can vary this prompt each day: Where did Ping live? What was the name of the country where our story takes place? What was the name of the long river in China? Can you find it?

Since you have just reread the story it is time to share how the author used a special sentence several times in the story. Read the sentence and ask your student if he can remember where else that sentence was used in the book? If he can't, just find the places in the story where the sentence is repeated and show your student how the author uses the same words in the middle of the story and again at the end. Explain that authors sometimes use an interesting sentence several times in a story to make it fun...we call that *repetition* (like repeating). An author wouldn't want to use repetition too much, but a little repetition can make a story interesting.

Ask your student if he would like to write a short story (or you can work on it together) using an interesting sentence at the beginning of the paragraph and again at the end? This story can be very simple. The idea is to give your student a chance to try using repetition as the author in *The Story About Ping* did.

If you are keeping a running chart of "Choices a Writer Can Make," (provided at the end of this manual) list repetition as one of those choices. You can add to this list each time you have a lesson on literary techniques and your list provides an easy way to review! Later, when your student wants to write a story of his own, he can go over the list and be reminded of the special ways that great authors have created stories that are interesting and enjoyable. You will see him begin to use some of these techniques in his writings, too.

Your student's writings can be illustrated and placed in the Language Arts section of his notebook. If he is too young to write, you may take his ideas or stories in dictation and let him illustrate his work and place it in his notebook under Language Arts.

Remember that *Five in a Row* does not teach "how to read." You may enjoy looking into *Reading Made Easy* for that portion of your teaching day.

Jane Claire's Tips for Those Beginning FIAR

You may stop here or go on to do another lesson from the Language section.
This is the end of day two with Five in a Row.

Day Three

On day three you'll reread the story again, this time promising some interesting art lessons to follow. (The art lessons have been placed on Wednesday so that there will be two more days of reading the book and looking at the pictures.) Today as you read the story your child will be thinking, "China… boat…oh, there's that repetitious sentence we talked about yesterday!"

After reading the story, you'll mention that Kurt Wiese was the artist who created the illustrations for *The Story About Ping*. It looks as though he may have used some colored pencils. "Let's pick a few of the pictures to look at and see how many colors he used. Do the colors look like they blend together? Why don't we use some colored pencils and paper and see how yellow over red looks and maybe some yellow over blue."

Continue with some of the other art lessons. They are easy to explain and quick to do. Again, you may want to keep a running list of "Choices an Artist Can Make" (also provided at the end of this manual) and include, as you go through the year, different mediums and other techniques. This list will serve as a point for review and allow your student to choose techniques from the list that he wants to include in his own art project of the moment.

Any art work done can be placed in the student's notebook under Art, along with illustrated examples of art techniques discussed from the book's illustrator.
This completes day three of Five in a Row.

Day Four

For Thursday, the reading of the story will have your student thinking of and recognizing all the previous lessons including a whole new look at the illustrations. Don't forget to find China on the map with the story disk. (Take the disk down each day before the lesson, so that your student can replace it on the map. Always help him cheerfully if needed.)

Proceed to the Applied Math lesson. These lessons are usually developed from the story to show children how math is used in their everyday world. *The Story About Ping* has only one math lesson and it is a counting one. It can be skipped by the older *Five in a Row* users and you can substitute additional lessons from other topic sections, if you wish. In this counting lesson the ducks can be counted, counted by two's, grouped, etc. Most of the story units will have multiple lessons for Applied Math. Remember that when your student is ready to begin a math curriculum, you need to find one even though you are doing the Applied Math lessons from *Five in a Row*. These Applied Math lessons are *not* a substitute for a regular math curriculum; they instead serve as an introduction and inspiration for ideas about math. ***This completes day four of Five in a Row.***

Day Five

On Friday, you will read the story for the last time. Imagine all the things your student is remembering as you read together! Most of the time when children read a book, they only think about the plot. Through using *Five in a Row*, they learn that a book has so much more to offer! There is often geography, history, foreign culture, character lessons, interesting ways that language is used and techniques by which great stories are written, amazing art, sometimes math, and as we'll see today there is often science in the stories that they read!

After you've read the story and put the story disk on the map for the last time, turn to the illustration of the little boy catching Ping. Ask your student why he thinks the boy has a barrel on his back. He may or may not guess that it is for his safety. (You can teach a water safety lesson here, too.) Tell him that decades ago on the Yangtze River they didn't have life preservers and water wings the way we have today and the boy's parents wanted to be sure he was safe in the water!

Ask your student, "Do you want to know how the barrel works? Well, there is a really big word—you don't have to memorize it—but I thought you'd like to hear how it sounds. The word is *buoyancy*. Isn't that a funny word? Yes, I like the sound of it, too. Anyway, buoyancy means being able to float in a liquid." Your younger student will enjoy just sounding out this unusual word, while your older student may be interested in how it's spelled, as well! Continue with the lesson in the manual and find things that can be tested in a pan of water. Enjoying seeing which things float and which things don't. Use the activity sheet at the end of the Ping unit to document your student's experiments. He can then share this page with Dad, or Aunt, etc., and explain what he learned.

All of the above is an example of "inspired learning through great books," which is the cornerstone of the conversational presentation of the lessons in *Five in a Row*. The idea is to keep your lessons light, simple, exciting—through *your* voice and *your* interest in the subjects—and to engage in discussions, back and forth together, over the various topics. Remember, too, that it is important to tie each lesson to the story through your conversation by saying things like, "Did you notice in our story today____" or "Have you ever thought of____ that happened in our story? Or, "When we read *The Story About Ping* today, I noticed that____," etc. Each lesson is included because it highlights something interesting in the story just waiting to be explored!

You may want to end your week with a meal that you make together from the *Five in a Row Cookbook* (at www.fiveinarowdigital.com). Your student can use his knowledge of the week's story to name the various menu items. You'll find ideas for this activity in the cookbook. The end of the week celebration meal is a great time to cook together and set the table with related items from your story of the week. Invite a friend or extended family members and let your student share all the things he's learned during the week. There are special places for pictures of this event and for notes in your *Five in a Row Cookbook* that make this book a special keepsake of your times together, as well.

The *Five in a Row Christian Character and Bible Study Supplement* is another way to add to your week's learning activities. These are simple lessons on character that flow easily from the week's story unit. There are many lessons for each story to choose from and these lessons can be discussed at bedtime, in the car, on the weekend or anytime you'd like to fit one or more of them into your teaching times.

Important! Just because you are having conversations doesn't mean that your students don't create entries for the notebooks that they are keeping. Having a body of work to review and share with others is important. Information on notebook entries are part of each subject covered in "How to Use *Five in a Row*" in the front of each of your manuals. Activity pages at the end of each book unit are also provided as a way of documenting some of the lessons your student has learned. And you can find many supplemental notebooking ideas in the FIAR Notebook Builder at www.fiveinarow.com.

Reading the Stories Five Days in a Row

This section explains the reasoning and philosophy that went into creating lesson plans in which the story is read over and over (five days in a row). It details benefits and what to do if there is resistance from your student.

Before you make a decision to read the selected story less than five days in a row, it may be helpful to know why the curriculum was developed this way. Then you have the background knowledge neccessary to decide how you want to use it with your student.

Some children read a story only for the plot. When they "know what has happened," they are ready for a new book. The plot is all they know to find in a book. It takes a bit of creativity and planning for these children to experience the richness of a good story—to find out how much more than just the plot can come to them through a great book!

Thus, the *Five in a Row* curriculum was designed to find many treasures in every story—across several academic topic areas—and to provide a built-in review every time you reread the story. Each day as your child hears the story again, he is saying to himself, "Oh, there is the personification!" or "Oh, I see how that artist balanced the picture...I remember that from yesterday." The *repeated opportunities* for your child to apply what he has learned as he hears the book over again is an important part of this curriculum.

In addition, each day as you read, your child will hear the sentence structure, syntax, mood and style of a story written by a great children's author. This repetitive reading of a story for five days can make a huge difference in your child's ability to read and write (at the proper time). His ear becomes used to good sentences—he may not have memorized them, but hearing them five times works almost as well. Again this will help in both reading and creative writing in the future.

Seeing the great works of art, five times in a row, in the illustrations of the *Five in a Row* selected titles, works in much the same way. Your student's eyes are being trained not to rush from one set of illustrations to another, but to observe different details each day as he listens to the book.

There truly was a great deal of thought that went into how this particular curriculum was created and structured, for the maximum benefits to occur. It isn't just a curriculum that recommends a book, has you read it once, and then moves you along.

Jane Claire's Tips for Those Beginning FIAR

Suggestions for a Resistant Student

Because there are significant benefits to reading the story over all five days, we have some suggestions for those who might have a more reluctant student. Read the story on the first day. The second day you can just say you are going to read it again, but this time you are going to leave out a part and see if they can catch you. (This technique is also good on day three or four.) Or you can add in a character or line and see if they can catch it!

Another day you can say that you are going to read the story again, but today your student can be looking for... (something in the art lesson you are going to do. For example, ask your student to look for every picture that has both orange and blue in it—since later that day you will do a lesson in complementary colors.)

You could also have your student draw something about the story while you are reading one day. This is not ideal, since they aren't looking at the pictures, but it's a good option for one day.

If you do a lesson on onomatopoeia one day, the next day have them listen for the examples and raise their hand or clap when they hear one. In this way, you are using the previous day's lessons to spur yet another reading of the book.

With the above ideas and approach, you are retaining the right to say what you will do for school in a gentle, friendly way: "This is what we are going to do," while at the same time caring for your student enough to create a helpful environment in which he can get over the hump of the problem, and learn to hear a good story for five days. Then you have a win-win situation.

I think you will find that after a few units, you won't have to do as much of this type of "leading" because your child will be used to reading the book five days in a row and he will actually be enjoying it!

All that said, you are the teacher and you will make the final decisions for your family on how to use FIAR. I just thought you might want to know why *Five in a Row* was created in this way and how this method will benefit your child's learning.

Blessings on all of your homeschool journey!
Jane Claire Lambert

The Story About Ping

Title: The Story About Ping
Author: Marjorie Flack
Illustrator: Kurt Wiese
Copyright: 1933
Category: Classic
Summary: A duck learns there are worse things than taking the consequences for one's mistakes.

Social Studies: Relationships - Discernment

Ping learns on pp. 16-18 that everything that looks good (like the rice cake trap) isn't necessarily good. Discernment is an important life skill that comes with maturity. You can discuss with your student examples of things which may look better than they really are. Discussions might include offers of candy from strangers or diving into unfamiliar ponds or streams.

Ping runs away because he doesn't want to take his punishment. He discovers that the loneliness, fear and danger he encounters are far worse than any punishment he might receive. In the end, Ping learns that family relationships and a sense of community are a vital part of life. Everyone is tempted to avoid the consequences of his mistakes. Consider sharing an example from your own life of trying to run away from consequences or punishment.

Social Studies: Geography - China

The Story About Ping takes place along the banks of China's Yangtze River. (YANG-see) Longer than any other river in the world except the Nile and the Amazon, the Yangtze is nearly four thousand miles long. Discuss with your student how long four thousand miles is by comparing it with a familiar distance. You might say, "Grandpa's house is four hundred miles away, so the Yangtze is like driving to grandfather's house ten times." You can also compare it with how far your student went on vacation last summer.

The Yangtze is so wide in places that you can stand on one bank and not see the other shore. Ask if the student has ever been to one of the Great Lakes or to the ocean. From these places you can't see the other side either. Imagine together what it might be like to live on such a long, and in some places wide, river.

Nearly one third of China's population, more than 350 million people, live on or near the Yangtze river. In fact, one of every fifteen people in the world live along the Yangtze. That's half again as many people as live in all of the United States combined. Help your student visualize how alone and frightened little Ping must have felt on such a huge, busy river. Be sure to place your story disk where Ping lived—in China, and on the Yangtze River!

Social Studies: Geography - Culture

As you read about Ping, point out the traditional clothes, hats, hair styles, houses and boats (one type of boat is called a "junk") of past Chinese culture. Wonder with your child about life on a boat! Discuss the differences and similarities between our culture and the Chinese. In America, for instance, there is a long history of people living on house boats sometimes called "shantyboats" along the Mississippi River and throughout the bayou country (a small stream that wanders through lowlands or marshes) of southern Louisiana.

You may also want to discuss the eating of duck as a delicacy in traditional Chinese cooking. Little Ping nearly becomes someone's special dinner when he leaves the safety of family and friends. Ask if your student has ever eaten at a Chinese restaurant. What sort of foods did people eat there? Did they use chopsticks? Has the student ever eaten duck? Do you think people along the Yangtze ever eat pizza or hamburgers?

If you have an older student, she could research the foods of China and help prepare a special Chinese meal. She might also look up typical mealtime customs of the Chinese and share them with the family during the meal. If you don't have an older student, you can research these things together with your student and plan a special menu featuring foods that are typically eaten in China.

Language Arts: Literature - What is a Classic Story?

This book is a classic. A "classic" is a book that generations of children have enjoyed. Ping was written in 1933. Even though the lifestyle, clothes and boats of the people in China may not be the same today as when Ping was first written (the Chinese do sometimes eat hamburgers!), the story of Ping is still as fresh today as it was in 1933.

When you begin any new book with a student, help her calculate how many years have elapsed since the story was written. You might try to identify an individual whose life dates from the early 1930s, in order to help your student comprehend how many years Ping has been in print. For example, you might say, "When Ping was written, your great-grandmother was about your age." Because Marjorie Flack wrote this story about Ping that many generations of your family could all enjoy when you were children, someday, perhaps your student's children and grandchildren will enjoy Ping, too. That's what makes Ping a "classic."

Language Arts: Literature - Fiction

Explain that fictional stories originate in the author's imagination. Point out that a fictional story often begins, "Once upon a time ...." You'll find other stories included in FIAR which also begin "Once upon a time ..." and you'll want to call the student's attention to this fictional device each time. You can even encourage your student to make up their own fictional story which begins "Once upon a time ...."

Note: There are occasional nonfiction stories that have the "once upon a time ..." beginning but they are the exception. This is most usually a fictional story starter.

Language Arts: Literary Device - Repetition

The story of Ping both begins and ends with a list of Ping's family members. Throughout the book, the author makes repeated references to Ping's family. The use of repetition as a literary device helps bring the reader "full circle" and provides both continuity and a sense of completion when the book is finished. Younger children particularly love the use of repetition. Many stories are built on repetition and children often memorize the familiar phrases and passages. Your student might enjoy creating her own story using repetition.

Art: Medium

See if your student can recognize what medium Kurt Wiese used in illustrating *Ping*. Most of the illustrations look like colored pencil or crayon. Encourage the student to try using colored pencils to do an illustration of their own. Notice how Wiese combines colors to create new tones in the sky on p. 9. At first glance, the sky appears gray, but have your student look closer and discover the variety of colors the artist has used to create the appearance of an evening sky. Similarly, notice the many colors Wiese used for the background on p. 32. Try using multiple colored pencils to create various effects.

Art: Drawing Water

Illustrator Kurt Wiese has drawn water throughout *The Story About Ping*. Discuss with your student the use of broken reflections to give the impression of water. For example, on p. 4, Wiese shows the sun's reflection in the Yangtze's surface. Cover up the reflection with your hand and see how the illusion of water is lost. Give your student a chance to try drawing her own sun and reflection to give the impression of water.

You'll also want to note the use of small, irregular blue circles to show puddles on p. 22 beneath the boy. Let your student try drawing a simple figure like the ice cube on the previous page and adding "puddles" beneath it. Note the use of ripples on p. 15 to illustrate action. Allow your student to try drawing broken, irregular circles around any object and see how it suddenly appears as if the object is surrounded by water.

On pp. 10 and 14 Wiese has used trailing, wavy lines to show motion. This pattern is repeated behind boats and ducks to create the illusion of movement. Let the student add trailing wavy lines to a simple boat drawing and discover how the boat suddenly appears to be moving. If your student can't draw a boat, draw one for her or print a picture and let her draw the background motion lines. Or try a line of ducks, each with their own wavy lines behind them!

Art: Viewpoint

The cover illustration shows Ping from a traditional viewpoint. Ping's profile, the outline of his wing, tail and bill all help to identify Ping as a duck. But, discuss with your student Wiese's use of a head-on point of view on the title page. Without the profile, bill and wing, Ping looks quite different.

Notice how the illustrator has drawn Ping from many different points of view such as "bottom up" on p. 6, "head beneath wing" on p. 9, and "swimming away" on p. 12. Have your student try drawing an egg or a football in profile. Now have her draw it again looking end-on. Point out how our **viewpoint** changes the way we see the world around us. Discuss how picking a different viewpoint adds variety and can make everyday subjects more interesting. Encourage your student to try drawing like Kurt Wiese, by exploring common subjects from uncommon points of view. In an excellent story called *Daniel's Duck* by Clyde Robert Bulla, a young artist tries an uncommon viewpoint for his handcarved wooden duck. (**Note:** *Daniel's Duck* is a featured story in FIAR Vol. 3. For now, see if you can find it for a single reading relating to this lesson in viewpoint and compare the illustrations of Wiese and Bulla.)

Art: Unity of Theme Through Subject

The illustrator has used the Yangtze River as the recurring theme which creates a sense of unity by tying the entire book together. Count the pages on which the river appears. You'll discover only three illustrations which do *not* include the Yangtze. Kurt Wiese has provided both unity and context through the repetitive theme of the water. We come away with a sense that for those 350 million people who live along the Yangtze's shores, the river is a part of everything they do. As a teacher, watch for the use of recurring themes built around a particular subject to create unity in other books you may read with your student.

Art: Composition

Every good drawing has good composition. Turn with your student to p. 9. Discuss how Kurt Wiese has created a diagonal from upper left to lower right with the foliage. This diagonal line divides the illustration into two halves. Each half includes a yellow highlight; the sun in the upper right, and Ping in the lower left. Notice how the grass fronds in the upper left create opposite diagonal lines.

Have your older student sketch some balanced compositions. Have her try pictures which are balanced diagonally, horizontally and vertically. Your student can even cut out magazine pictures or pictures found online and place them in pleasing, balanced compositions if she does not yet enjoy a lot of drawing. Encourage your student to look beyond content and think about composition whenever looking at an illustration. While good content makes an interesting picture, good composition makes for a pleasing picture.

Math: Counting Skills

Have your student count Ping's family, including: mother, father, two sisters, three brothers, eleven aunts, seven uncles and forty-two cousins. Don't forget to include Ping! To make the counting more fun, have the student draw a picture illustrating all of Ping's family surrounding Ping. Some students might prefer tracing a duck "template" on yellow construction paper and cutting out Ping's family and gluing them on a hand-painted Yangtze river. For your very young student, you might use blocks, coins or clothespins to account for each member of Ping's family. Arrange and rearrange the items as you count them together. Some children might enjoy counting *all* of the ducks or all of the boats in the book as well.

Science: Animal Kingdom

In *The Story About Ping* your student will be introduced to the animal kingdom by learning about ducks. What is Ping trying to catch when he misses the call on p. 6? Ducks search beneath the water's surface for insects, plants, small fish and snails. They look funny with their tails up. Many ducks also enjoy eating "people food." Discuss how Ping's love of rice cake crumbs on p. 15 nearly gets him in trouble.

Ask your student if she has ever "fed the ducks." Consider going to a nearby lake or park to feed the ducks corn, peas, oats, or other duck-friendly foods. Watch them dabble (poke about in the water) as they forage for food. The more time you spend observing, the more you'll learn about ducks! For more information about ducks, get *The Little Duck*, by Judy Dunn.

Science: Buoyancy

The illustrations on pp. 16 and 17 show a boy swimming with a barrel attached to his back. Ask your student why the boy is wearing a barrel. Both the wood and the air inside the barrel help the boy float, much like a life jacket helps a water skier. The barrel works on the same principle of buoyancy as fishing bobbers, inflatable pool toys, etc., since both air and wood are lighter and less dense than water.

Try finding which things float in a pan of water: a cork, penny, grape, paper clip, pencil, tennis ball, leaf, golf ball, etc. Use the activity sheet at the end of this unit to document your discoveries.

Science: Health and Safety

The boy and his barrel can also provide a good opportunity to discuss water safety. Discuss the role of lifeguards, life jackets or personal floatation devices (PFDs) and the dangers of swimming alone in unfamiliar water. Even the best of swimmers can get caught in currents and life jackets provide an added measure of safety, like wearing seat belts in the family car.

Science: Reflection of Light

See if your student can figure out why you see reflections on water. Look at the illustrations which show reflections. Discuss the fact that shiny surfaces "bounce" light, reflecting it in new directions. Take a small mirror and do some simple experiments. Try reflecting sunlight onto the ceiling or opposite wall. Now take the mirror and lay it flat on a table. Place various objects on the mirror and look at their "reflections" off the shiny glass surface. If you live near a pond or lake, go there and look at how the shiny surface acts as a mirror, reflecting the image of shoreline trees, boats, the sun, etc.

A. A. Milne wrote a poem entitled, "The Mirror." It can be found in the book of poems called *When We Were Very Young*, or in the combined volume called *The World of Christopher Robin*. One line says,

> "And there I saw a white swan make
> another white swan in the lake."

Milne's poem paints a verbal picture (imagery) of the reflection off the water's surface. Obviously, the second swan was simply the reflection of the first swan on the lake's glassy surface. Perhaps you'd like to find *The World of Christopher Robin* and read this poem while looking at the lovely illustration which accompanies it.

Teacher's Note: A. A. Milne wrote two volumes of stories about Winnie-the-Pooh titled, *Winnie-the-Pooh* and *The House at Pooh Corner*. These story books can be found in bookstores and at libraries under these titles. There is also a book with both of these volumes combined, titled, *The World of Pooh*. Milne has also written two volumes of poetry, titled, *When We Were Very Young* and *Now We Are Six*. There is also a combined book with both volumes called, *The World of Christopher Robin*. Regardless of the format, these books are treasures to be shared and enjoyed over and over! The stories and the poetry have been loved for several generations. They have brought to their readers many moments of shared intimacy, humor and poignancy. If you haven't had the pleasure of enjoying the literary world of Christopher Robin and his friends, explore some of it today!

Teacher's Note: The book *Water: Through the Eyes of Artists* by Wendy and Jack Richardson showcases twenty artists and their treatment of water. It is copyrighted 1991 by Children's Press, Chicago. If you can find it in your library, use it with the "Drawing Water" lesson by mentioning the names of the artists and just looking at their interpretations of water. You may find the information about the artists interesting for yourself, but your children will enjoy just looking at the pictures. Drawing or painting water is a fascinating subject!

Teacher's Notes

The *Five in a Row* lesson options for each unit in the manual are all you need to teach your child. The additional resource area provided below is simply a place to jot down relevant info you've found that you might want to reference.

THE STORY ABOUT PING

Date:

Student:

Five in a Row Lesson Topics Chosen:

Social Studies:

Language Arts:

Art:

Math:

Science:

Relevant Library Resources: Books, DVDs, Audio Books

Websites or Video Links:

Related Field Trip Opportunities:

Favorite Quote or Memory During Study:

The Story About Ping

Name:
Date:
Science: **Buoyancy**

The boy swam with a barrel attached to his back. The air inside the barrel made him float since it is lighter than water.

Prediction = a statement about a future event, which is usually based on knowledge or experience.

Find objects around the house or outside, make a prediction and then test it out by placing items in a bowl of water.

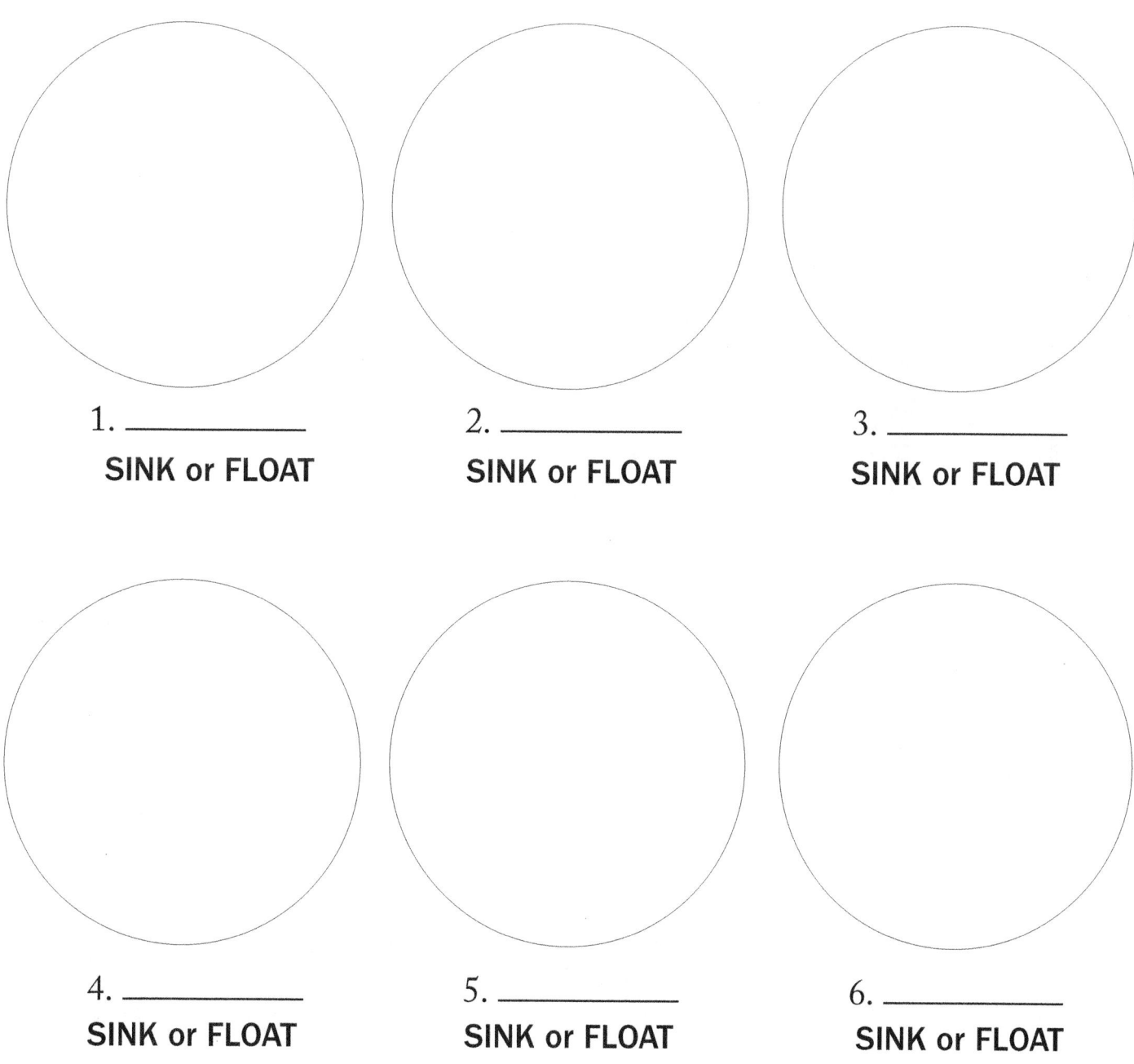

1. _____
SINK or FLOAT

2. _____
SINK or FLOAT

3. _____
SINK or FLOAT

4. _____
SINK or FLOAT

5. _____
SINK or FLOAT

6. _____
SINK or FLOAT

Five in Row Volume One

Name:
Date:
Geography: **China Flag**

The flag of China is red with five gold stars in the canton: one large star with four smaller stars in a semi-circle towards the fly. *For more information, see Parts of a Flag on page 222.*

Color in the China flag below.

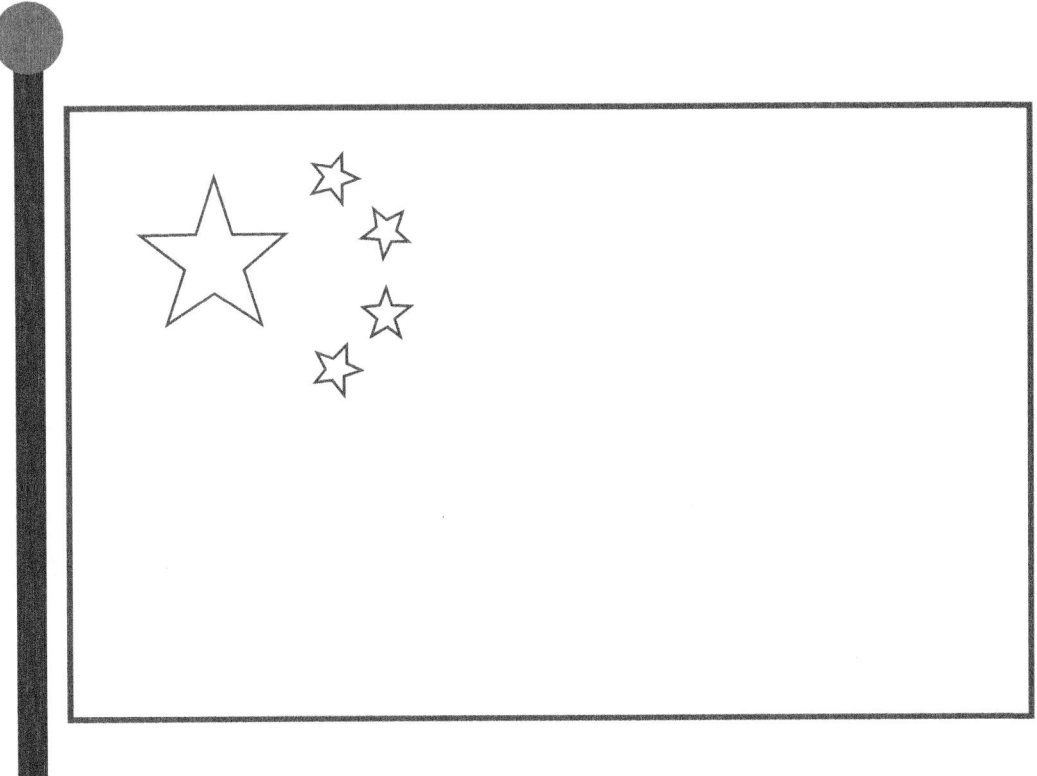

The Story About Ping

Name:

Date:

Language Arts: **Fiction**

Fictional stories originate in the author's imagination. They often begin with "Once upon a time..." Allow your student to write or dictate a fictional story in the story starter provided below.

Once upon a time...

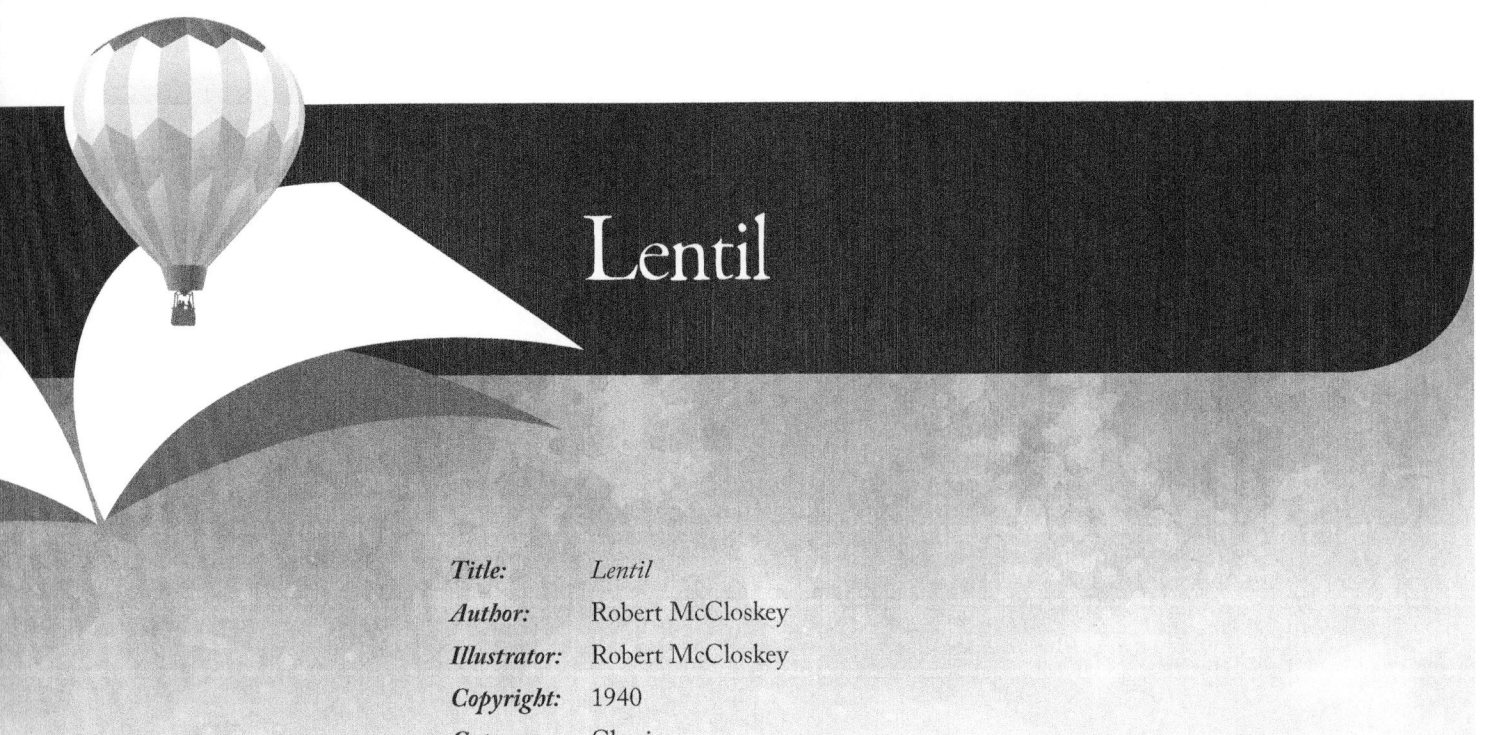

Lentil

Title: Lentil
Author: Robert McCloskey
Illustrator: Robert McCloskey
Copyright: 1940
Category: Classic
Summary: A boy discovers that he has a special talent and using it makes a difference.

Social Studies: Geography

The story of Lentil is set in the fictional small town of Alto, Ohio. Use a simple map or jigsaw puzzle of the United States and help your student locate Ohio. Have him find his own state. If your student has done some work with directions, have him determine which direction he would have to travel from his home to get to Ohio. Look at the word Ohio. It begins and ends with the letter "O" and has a "hi" in the middle. Your older student can use that association to help remember the spelling. "A friendly state with an 'O' on each end." Be sure to place your story disk on Ohio. (If your student happens to live in Ohio, find directions between Ohio and some other state of interest.)

Social Studies: Human Relationships

This story deals with Lentil's self-image and feelings. Lentil can't sing—he can't even pucker, so whistling is out of the question. Ask your student if he has ever been part of a group where the others were all doing something he was unable to do. Ask him how he felt and what he did. *Lentil* provides a great opportunity to discuss individual differences. Discuss the importance of discovering our own uniqueness. Many people go through life feeling inadequate or left out without ever discovering their own gift.

Lentil wanted to make music and he wasn't satisfied until he discovered that he could play the harmonica. In the end, it was Lentil's unique ability which proved to be so valuable. Human relationships are enriched by variety and uniqueness. In order to illustrate the importance of variety, you can have fun discussing what food your student would choose if he could only eat one food three times daily for his entire life. Even if he selects pizza or hamburgers, he would probably admit that after a month or two variety would begin to sound good. McCloskey's story can help students develop proper feelings about themselves and their own uniqueness.

Hopefully, your student will develop an appreciation for the *variety* found in his friends and neighbors. Ideally, when we encounter someone who can't do something, rather than ridiculing them, we should find ourselves asking, "What *can* they do?"

Social Studies: Human Relationships - Disagreeable People

Alto's plans are nearly ruined by Old Sneep. Ask your student why Old Sneep is so grumpy and disagreeable. Why is Sneep angry about the town's plans? Discuss how jealousy can make us miserable, unhappy people. Ask your student if he has ever been jealous of someone else's accomplishments. Ask if he has ever known anyone like Sneep. Why doesn't Sneep's plan affect Lentil? (Because he can't pucker, Lentil's problem has become his advantage.) When Lentil uses his talents, the town celebrates in such a grand way that even Old Sneep is included in the events!

Social Studies: Life in a Small Town

Discuss the small town of Alto, Ohio. Contrast Alto with your student's own town. Is it larger or smaller? Have your student use building blocks to lay out the town of Alto on the floor. Alternatively, have them draw the town on a large piece of paper or poster board. Help your student label each of the buildings named in McCloskey's story. Let your student draw each of the streets and alleys. (You may need to define *alley* for him, since many towns today no longer have alleys.) Take a toy train or make one from blocks or cardboard and let the student act out the story of Lentil using clothespin characters.

Initiate a discussion about what life is like in a small town. Interesting topics might include shopping, restaurants, recreation, entertainment, schools and traffic. Compare and contrast these differences of life in a small town versus a big city.

Social Studies: History

Lentil walks past the Soldiers and Sailors Monument in Carter Memorial Park. Ask your student why people might build a monument to soldiers and sailors who have fought to protect their country. If you know of similar war monuments, cannons or statues in your own area, take your student on a field trip. You can discuss Veterans Day and Memorial Day and their importance to us as Americans. (Veterans Day [November 11th] commemorates the end of World War I and honors all United States veterans, while Memorial Day [May 30th, but celebrated the last Monday in May] commemorates all United States soldiers killed in combat.) If appropriate, you can discuss some of the important wars in American history including the Revolutionary War, Civil War, World Wars I and II, Korea, Vietnam, the Gulf War, etc. Consider driving by an area recruiting office to allow your student to see someone in uniform and pick up a poster or brochure showing contemporary men and women serving today as soldiers and sailors.

Social Studies: Patriotism

Notice the American flags flying all over Alto when the town decorates for Colonel Carter's celebration. Show your student an American flag and discuss its symbolism. Count the stars which represent each of the fifty states. Count the thirteen stripes which represent the original thirteen colonies. Patriotism is knowing the country you live in, its unique cultural characteristics and identity, and knowing the reasons why you can be proud of it. Ask the student if he can think of any reasons he's proud of his citizenship. (Answers might include, "We're free. We help other countries with food and medicine. We protect other countries.")

Social Studies: History

Lentil was written in 1940. Look through McCloskey's illustrations with your student and discuss how things have changed in more than three-quarters of a century. Pay particular attention to the old-fashioned automobiles, school desks, cash register, nail barrels, bathroom sink, steam locomotive, passenger trains and horse drawn carts. Ask your student which of those old-fashioned experiences sound like fun even today.

Language Arts: Literature - Elements of a Good Story

Setting the Stage	Lentil begins by introducing the location and characters and building excitement in anticipation of the Colonel's visit.
Conflict	Old Sneep's jealousy of the Colonel's success unfolds.
Rising Action	McCloskey lets the reader learn more about the town's eagerness to greet the Colonel and Old Sneep's plan to disrupt the celebration.
Climax	Sneep sets his plan in motion and everyone holds their breath as Lentil saves the day.
Denouement	(day new MAHN) it is the final revelation and outcome; the Colonel is happy and honored and Sneep has a change of heart.

Help your student write a simple story of his own, incorporating these five basic principles of good storytelling. You can write the story down on paper, act it out as a play or record it as a movie if you wish. (**Note:** For your younger student, concentrate on only one element, such as the climax. Try writing a story together emphasizing that particular element of a good story.) Use the activity sheet at the end of this unit to map out the story based on the five principles.

Art: Medium

Ask your student to examine Robert McCloskey's illustrations and see if he can guess what McCloskey used to draw them. Your student may answer "pencil," but in fact McCloskey used charcoal. Draw the student's attention to the subtle shadings the artist used to give his characters a rounded, three-dimensional form. Notice the use of shadows. Take a look at the faces. Notice how much personality each individual seems to have. The artist has used exaggerated eyebrows and mouth shape to help bring each character to life. If you have a small piece of drawing charcoal, let your student try this new medium on a piece of paper (supervise your student's use of charcoal—it's messy!). If no charcoal is available, use a soft pencil to experiment with shading, shadows and facial expressions.

Art: Every Picture Tells a Story (Detail)

While covering the illustrations with your hand, read the page where Lentil attempts to sing and only strange sounds come out. Your student will discover that both the words and the pictures contain part of the story. The detail in McCloskey's illustrations helps convey how strange Lentil's sounds must have been. Point out the dogs and cats running away (this action is not mentioned in the text). Notice Lentil's own expression of surprise and dismay. Good illustrations *help tell* the story, adding more detail than is included in the text. Encourage your student to illustrate a simple story of his own with drawings that help tell the story.

Art: Architecture

Take a close look at Colonel Carter's house. Have your student point out the unique and unusual features of the Colonel's mansion, including the lightning rods, shutters, peculiar roof line, weather vane, round-windowed cupola, decorative trim brackets beneath the eaves and canopied entryway. The Colonel's house was probably built in the late 1800s in a style known as Second Empire, referring to a French architectural style of the 1800s. The unique roof shape is called a mansard roof, named after the French architect François Mansart during the time of Louis XIV. Consider driving through an older area of your own town and looking for Second Empire homes or homes with mansard roofs. Use the activity sheet at the end of this unit to take a virtual field trip to New York to discover a famous American building that has a mansard roof.

Look at other unique architectural styles and discuss how design has changed over the years. For your older student, there are several good children's books available on architecture including:

Old House, New House by Michael Gaughenbaugh
I Know That Building by Jane D'Alelio
Under Every Roof by Patricia Brown Glenn

If your student has a considerable interest in architecture, check for these or other books at the library and discuss them in more detail. Consider having your student draw a simple floor plan or exterior drawing of a house in which he'd like to live. Your older student may want to draw several elevations (front view, side view, etc.), as well as a floor plan. If you happen to have access to a real set of blueprints, perhaps of your own home, allow your student to examine them, comparing them to the finished structure.

Art: Musical Skill

Ask your student to identify the musical instrument Lentil decided to learn to play. McCloskey says that Lentil "decided to become an expert" at playing the harmonica. Does Lentil become an expert harmonica player overnight? Lentil practices "whenever and wherever" he can. Becoming an expert at anything requires commitment, dedication and practice. Locate a harmonica for your student and invite him to attempt playing. Ask him how long he thinks it might take to become expert at playing the harmonica.

Mathematics: Introduction to Fractions

Have your child look at the musical notes on the pages wherever Lentil plays his harmonica. If your student plays an instrument ask him if he can identify any of the notes on the page. If not, explain that musical notes come in several "sizes," including whole notes, half notes and quarter notes.

Now, using an apple or banana for a "learning snack," discuss the concept of "whole." Have your student cut the snack in half and talk about how two halves make up one whole. Cut each half in half and introduce the concept of quarters. Two quarters make up a half and four quarters make up a whole. You may want to get out a dollar bill and several quarters as well. Your student can compare a quarter dollar with a quarter apple and a quarter note. Each one is one quarter of a whole and it takes four quarters to make up a whole unit.

Science: Human Anatomy - Taste Buds

Old Sneep's plan for destroying the town's celebration includes the use of a lemon. In sucking on a lemon, Sneep causes all of the band members to "pucker up" so they can't play. Why do sour things make us "pucker up?" Discuss taste buds with your student. The human tongue has approximately five million taste buds which are capable of identifying taste. We replace approximately half of those cells every ten days with new taste buds. We primarily group tastes into four areas: bitter, salty, sweet and sour. Which one of these tastes does a lemon activate? Take a lemon and help your student cut it in half. Each of you take a half to taste or suck on. Discuss the unique sensation of our mouth "puckering up" when we taste something sour. Now that you've sliced a lemon, consider making a glass or pitcher of lemonade. For one or two servings, mix two cups of water, three tablespoons of lemon juice and six to eight tablespoons of sugar.

You may want to make the lemonade as a science "experiment" by carefully measuring each component as if you were in a laboratory. For the best flavor, boil the sugar and water for several minutes. Let it cool for a bit and then, add lemon juice and pour it all over ice. As you share a refreshing glass of lemonade together, finish by discussing why watching someone else suck on a lemon can make us "pucker up" as we remember how sour a lemon tastes.

Science: Sound and Acoustics

Find the page where Lentil plays his harmonica in the bathtub. He says "there the tone was improved one hundred percent." Ask your student why that might be. The hard porcelain, tile and vinyl of the bathroom reflect sounds back more clearly, and reverberates without being muffled by carpet, cushions and clothing commonly found elsewhere. That's why you'll often see singers cupping their hand to their ear or wearing headphones in order to be able to hear their own notes more clearly. The singer's hand reflects the sound back to the ear. Suggest your student try singing or playing an instrument in the bathroom and listen for the sound to be "improved one hundred percent."

Teacher's Notes

The *Five in a Row* lesson options for each unit in the manual are all you need to teach your child. The additional resource area provided below is simply a place to jot down relevant info you've found that you might want to reference.

LENTIL

Date:

Student:

Five in a Row Lesson Topics Chosen:

Social Studies:

Language Arts:

Art:

Math:

Science:

Relevant Library Resources: Books, DVDs, Audio Books

Websites or Video Links:

Related Field Trip Opportunities:

Favorite Quote or Memory During Study:

Lentil

Name:
Date:
Language Arts: **Writing**

Elements of a Good Story

Help your student write a simple story of his own, incorporating the five basic principles of good storytelling. After the story is complete, help him summarize the elements of that story below. For your younger student, concentrate on only one element, such as the climax.

1. Setting the Stage

2. Conflict

3. Rising Action

4. Climax

5. Denouement (day new MAHN)

Name:
Date:
Art: **Architecture**

Mansard Roof

Having internet access allows for exploration of faraway places without having to leave your house! Let's go on a virtual field trip to see one of the most famous American buildings with a mansard roof. We'll head to New York, via the internet! Search online for images of the Germania Insurance building. It's also known as the Guardian Life Insurance Company building.

Print a photo of the building and paste it below. Record any interesting facts about the building in the space provided.

Lentil

Name:

Date:

Art: **Architecture**

Create Your Own Mansard Roof

Using your knowledge of what a Mansard roof looks like,
re-create one yourself using a medium of your choice.

Drawing

LEGO®

Blocks

Popsicle sticks

Minecraft™

When you're finished, take a photo of your work and display it here.

Madeline

Title: *Madeline*
Author: Ludwig Bemelmans
Illustrator: Ludwig Bemelmans
Copyright: 1939
Category: Classic
Award: Caldecott Honor Medal
Summary: A spunky girl has her appendix out and demonstrates individuality within her world of order.

Social Studies: Geography

Madeline is set in Paris, France. Have your student locate France on a world map and place the *Madeline* story disk on the map. Refer to it each day as you read the story. As you look at the map, you'll see that Paris is located on the Seine river (pron. "sane," or sometimes "sen") which flows through the city and eventually empties into the English Channel. Have your student examine the picture of the Seine at the end of the girls' first outing. Ask her why so many cities are located on major rivers. Why was river transportation so important in years past? (Supplies were transported on the river.) Is your student's own city located on a river? If so, consider taking a field trip there to examine the riverfront, boat traffic, etc. Use this time to make the flag of France. You'll find it on the book's cover at the top of the Eiffel tower. Or you can use the activity sheet at the end of this unit.

Social Studies: Human Relationships

In *Madeline*, the twelve girls demonstrate important character traits.

"They smiled at the good ..."	They learn to recognize what is good and appreciate it.
"... and frowned at the bad ..."	They learn what is evil and to avoid it.
"... and sometimes they were very sad."	They learn what is sad and how to have compassion for others.

Madeline

To demonstrate compassion, people often take or send flowers, notes and gifts to those in the hospital or who are sick at home. The visits are appreciated by those who cannot get out themselves and the flowers, notes and gifts are a cheering reminder that people do care.

Make a list with your student of things people could do for someone who is ill or confined at home. The list might include things such as: bringing them their newspapers or mail, getting groceries, mowing their lawn, putting out their trash, taking them meals and phoning to check on them. It is never too soon to introduce children to the concept of recognizing the needs of others and knowing some ways to help.

Social Studies: History

Madeline was written in 1939. When you begin any new book with your student, help her calculate how many years have elapsed since the story was written. You might try to identify an individual whose life dates from the 1930s, in order to help her comprehend how many years *Madeline* has been in print. For example, you might say, "When *Madeline* was written, Mr. Smith across the street was about your age." By noticing the copyright date, your student will discover that some stories, like *Madeline*, were written long ago, and some were published more recently. This knowledge will help her evaluate and appreciate the stories' content and illustrations.

As you read *Madeline*, ask your student to notice the steam-heat radiator used for heating the hospital room. You may want to discover how your student's own house or apartment is heated. Look for the furnace and determine whether it uses electricity, natural gas or propane. Compare it with the use of a coal-burning steam boiler and radiators. Also, take a closer look at the old-fashioned ambulance and bus in the story. If you live near mass transit, consider a brief field trip to ride a city bus. Many students have never ridden a municipal bus before. See if you can find other old-fashioned things in the story.

Language Arts: Literary Devices

Here are some of the literary devices the author uses to make *Madeline* more interesting:

Poetry - The story text of *Madeline* is one long poem which utilizes rhyme and rhythm. Practice making up rhyming words with your student.

Repetition - Just before Madeline is hospitalized, we read the line, "In the middle of the night, Miss Clavel turned on her light and said, 'something is not right!'" This line is repeated near the end of the story to create added interest. The reader recognizes the repetition and says, "Hey! I've heard that before!"

There is also the repetition of the girls' daily discipline: " ... broke their bread, brushed their teeth and went to bed." You may wish to talk about daily routines and the order they bring to our lives.

Mention these literary devices *after* you've read the story. Encourage your student to experiment with poetry and repetition to make her own stories more interesting. Your young student should only try one technique at a time.

Language Arts: Vocabulary

appendix   A small, sac-like appendage of the large intestine.

solemn   Without any smile or silliness in facial expression.

disaster   Any sudden calamity.

Five in Row Volume One   49

Art: Architecture

The buildings shown in the illustrations of *Madeline* are real street scenes of Paris. Find a book with photographs of Paris. Together, see if you can match the illustrations to the photographs. Through this process, your student will begin to recognize that the illustrations are not photographic (fooling the eye into believing the drawing is a photograph), but rather the artist's *impression* of the streets of Paris. The artist's illustrations are easily identified as the actual scene, even though his art work is not "photographic" in style.

Be on the lookout for pictures in magazines, posters, and books of the more common Paris landmarks, such as the Eiffel Tower. Point them out to your student as you notice them. Maybe she will point out some to you. In this way, the learning process is continually reinforced as a shared experience between you and your student. One benefit of enrichment education is that someday your student will see a billboard or a poster (for example) and exclaim, "That's the Eiffel Tower!" As a teacher, it is your pleasure to introduce her to many things in the world around her.

Art: Appreciating Variety

Bemelmans has illustrated *Madeline* with a wide variety of drawings. Some are large, others are small. Some are monochromatic (one color), while others use a full-color palette. After you have read the story together, discuss with your student this variety, examining each page for size and color. The goal here is to help your student understand and appreciate the variety an illustrator can use in one book. If every illustration had been identical in size and color, the book would have been less interesting. Perhaps your student would like to try illustrating a simple story of her own using a variety of picture sizes and techniques. Bemelmans ends the story with a visual fading away as the print diminishes in size. We don't see this diminishing print ending in every book, so it makes *this* page of text more interesting.

Math: Beginning Grouping and Dividing Skills

Take 48 blocks, pennies, craft sticks or candies. Using the first twelve to represent the girls, see how many groups of girls you would have if Miss Clavel divided the girls up into groups of two to walk down the stairs. Now, using the second twelve items, see how many groups would be required if Miss Clavel makes the girls go to the sink in groups of three. Now, using the next dozen, see how many groups Miss Clavel would have if she has the girls eat in groups of four. Finally, line the "girls" up in two straight lines of six. How many groups are there?

Math: Relative Size and Degree

Madeline was the smallest of the twelve girls. With your young student, explore the concept of smaller and larger. Go one step further and discuss small, smaller and smallest, or big, bigger and biggest using whatever is handy. Finally, if you have a quantity of some household item in several sizes such as fruit, peanuts, etc., have your student sort them. Ask him to find the smallest item. Now the largest. Now put all the **large** items in this pile, the **medium** items over here and **small** items in another group.

Math: Symmetry

As you read *Madeline*, you'll discover that many of Bemelmans' illustrations are **symmetrical** (balanced from side to side). Select an illustration with symmetry. An example is the one where the girls are seated at the table. Count the girls: six on each side. Now the plates: six on each side. Find other ways in which the illustration is symmetrical. Have your student arrange common items symmetrically on the table. Now try an **asymmetrical** arrangement by having your child arrange items in random groups without being balanced from side to side. Many of the illustrations are asymmetrical as well. Look at the twelve girls standing in random clusters at the zoo and again at the ice skating rink. Have your student draw their own pictures showing symmetry and asymmetry.

Science: Health

On the final pages of *Madeline*, the other girls wish they could have their appendixes removed too. Miss Clavel responds, "Thank the Lord you are well!" It's important to protect our health. We can't prevent all illnesses and accidents, but there are many basic good habits we can develop to help preserve our health. Discuss with your student the importance of washing her hands after using the bathroom and before eating. Discuss the body's need for exercise, healthy well-balanced meals and the importance of rest. You might want to review the pages where the girls practice many of these same good health habits in the story of *Madeline*. Health habits are an area where discipline and order can pay big dividends.

Science: Human Body - Appendix

Madeline provides an opportunity to mention a part of the human body and show your child its appearance and location in a children's anatomy book or online. Madeline points to her scar and indeed the human appendix is located between the large and small intestine at the lower right abdomen. For your young child, just saying the name of the small body part and having her point to her own appendix (lower right side) is more than enough information for now and builds a platform for more facts later.

Five in Row Volume One

Teacher's Notes

The *Five in a Row* lesson options for each unit in the manual are all you need to teach your child. The additional resource area provided below is simply a place to jot down relevant info you've found that you might want to reference.

MADELINE

Date:

Student:

Five in a Row Lesson Topics Chosen:

Social Studies:

Language Arts:

Art:

Math:

Science:

Relevant Library Resources: Books, DVDs, Audio Books

Websites or Video Links:

Related Field Trip Opportunities:

Favorite Quote or Memory During Study:

Madeline

Name:
Date:
Math: **Grouping**

This activity is *not* a substitute for the hands-on activity of grouping found in the Math: Beginning Grouping and Dividing Skills lesson. The hands-on experience suggeseted in the manual is a kinesthetic learning method, while the activity sheet below is a visual learning method. Use *both* to reinforce your student's understanding of mathematic grouping and dividing skills.

Miss Clavel divided the girls into groups. How many groups can you find?

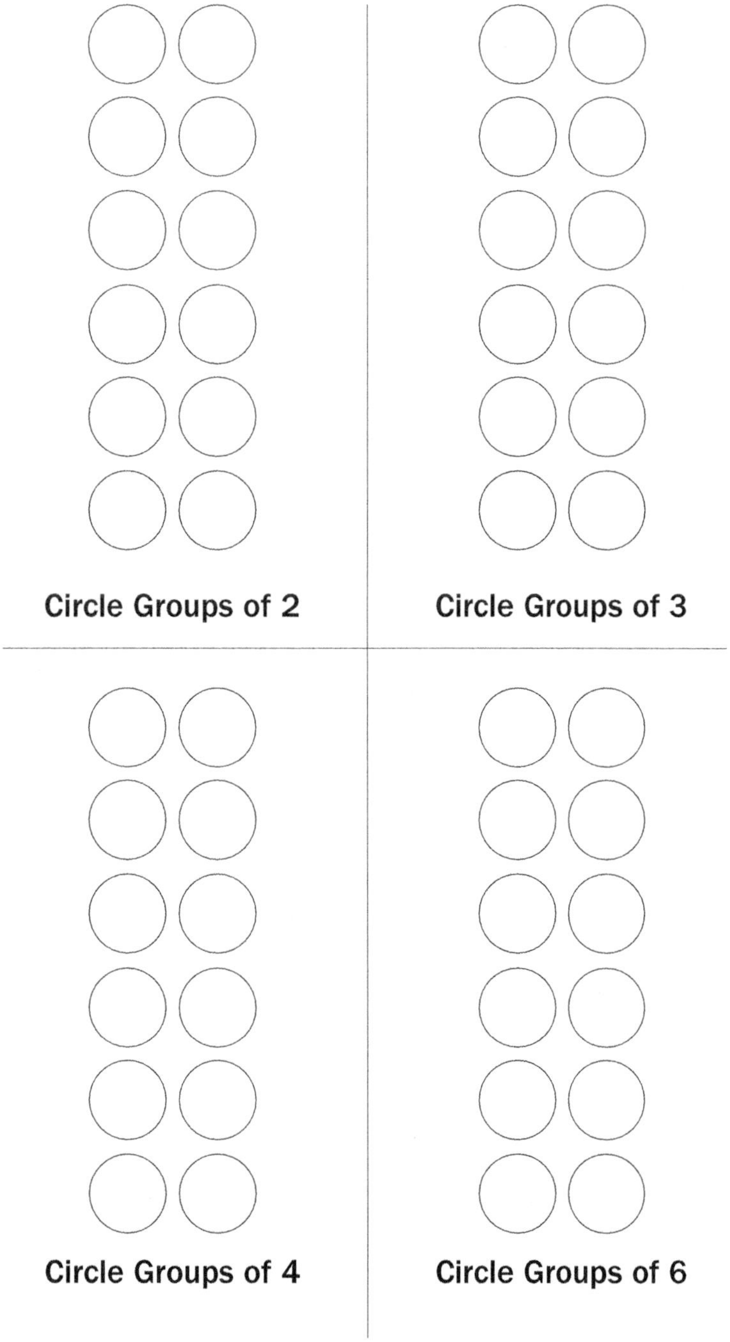

Circle Groups of 2   **Circle Groups of 3**

Circle Groups of 4   **Circle Groups of 6**

Five in Row Volume One

Name:
Date:
Geography: **France Flag**

The flag of France, (seen on the cover of the book) is a tricolor (3-color) flag of blue, (hoist side) white and red (fly). *For more information, see Parts of a Flag on page 222.*

Color in the France flag below.

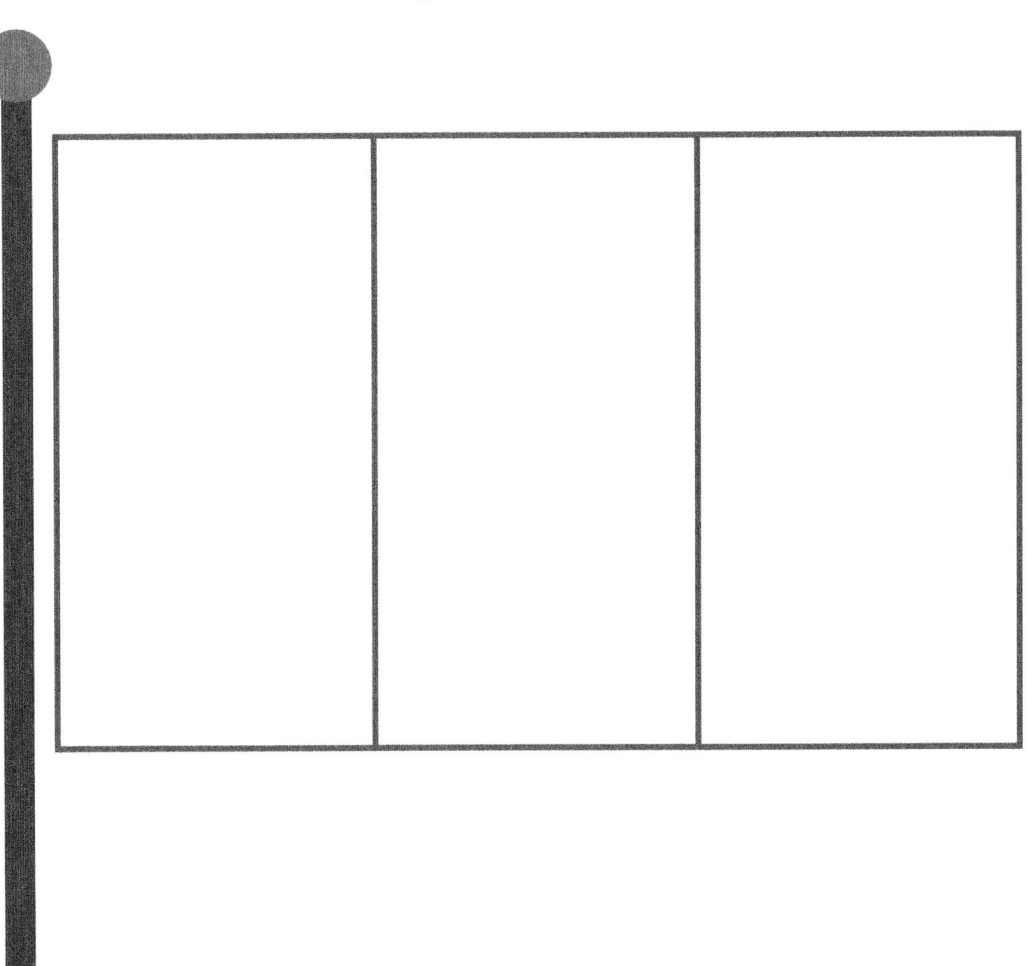

Madeline

Name:

Date:

Math: **Relative Size and Degree**

Use this activity sheet *after* completing the hands-on activities in the Math: Relative Size and Degree lesson in the manual.

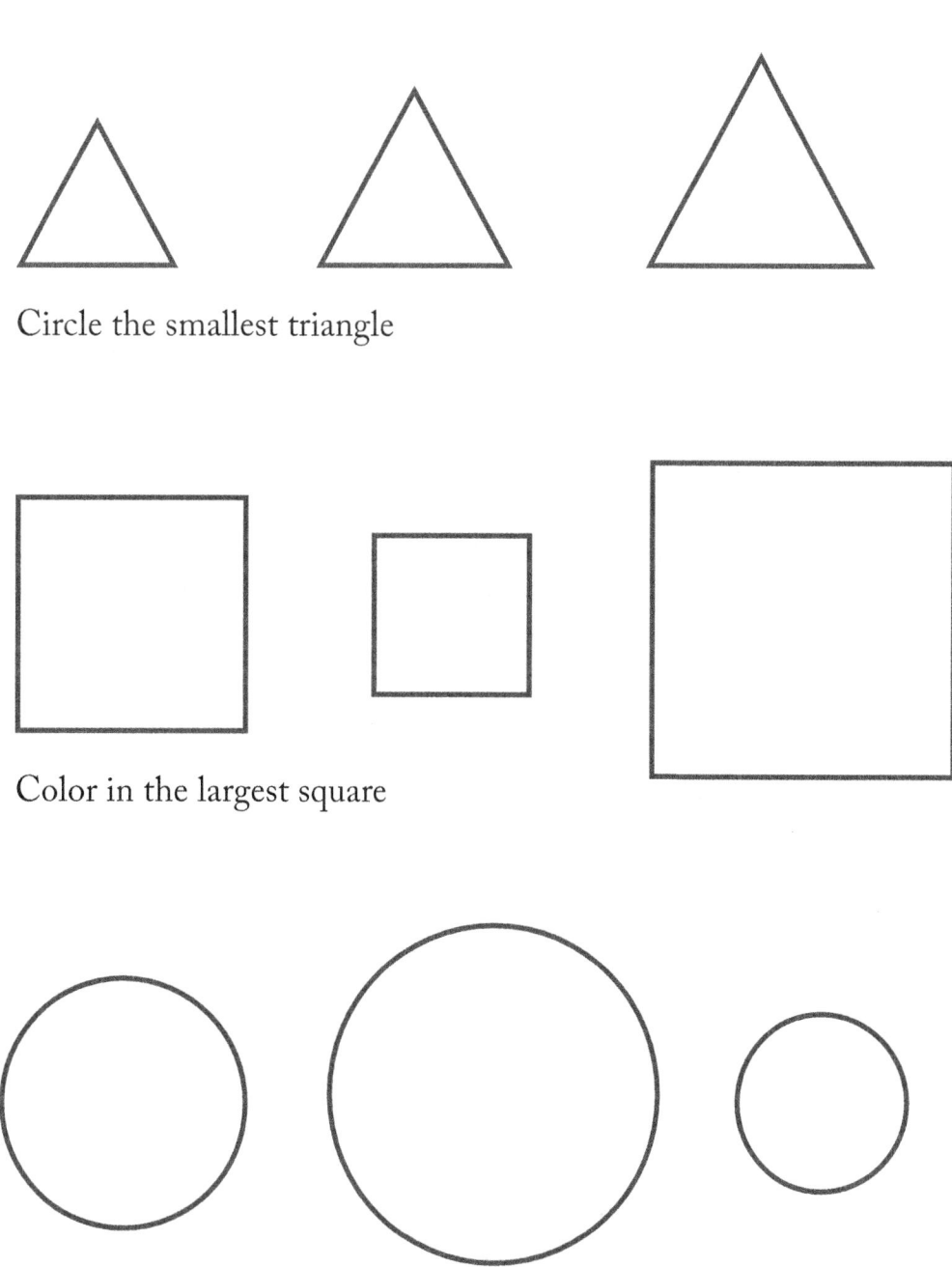

Circle the smallest triangle

Color in the largest square

Color in the smallest circle

A Pair of Red Clogs

Title: *A Pair of Red Clogs*
Author: Masako Matsuno
Illustrator: Kazue Mizumura
Copyright: 1960
Summary: Mako receives a new pair of shoes and learns the importance of honesty.

Social Studies: Geography

A Pair of Red Clogs is set in Japan. Have your student locate Japan on a world map, globe, or both. Place the story disk on the map. Japan is an island country. You may need to define the word **island** for your student (see the activity sheet at the end of this unit).

Social Studies: Japanese Culture

As you read *A Pair of Red Clogs*, your student will discover many unfamiliar and different things. He will learn about clogs, post boxes (mailboxes), markets, and weather-telling games. He will see different hair styles than he's used to and architectural styles with unusual roof lines. He will also learn about sitting around a low table at mealtime on cushions, and using chopsticks instead of silverware. Your student will see a kimono, which is a loose outer garment with wide sleeves and a sash, traditionally worn by both men and women in Japan. He may also notice Japanese writing on the shop windows and signs.

You may want to try several Japanese cultural activities. You might eat lunch sitting on cushions at a coffee table. Try using chopsticks and make your own kimono from a robe or gown and sash. These types of cultural activities enrich early learning and make books come alive!

Social Studies: Human Relationships

In *A Pair of Red Clogs*, Mako wants so much to have her clogs like new again that she decides to trick her mother into buying her a new pair. Most people would actually call this "trick" deception or lying.

What saves Mako is her family's tradition of always trying to clean an object before they buy a new one. It was, as Mako says, "what they always did." (This is an example of stewardship: taking care of what you own.) The tradition of good stewardship shown by Mako's parents, and the quiet, gentle wisdom of her mother and father, helps Mako return to the solid ground of honesty. This also gives Mako a desire to never try to trick her mother again.

Ask your student why Mako wants to trick her mother and why the trick does not work. Explore the honesty and trust we need to have with one another.

Teacher's Note: For teachers that love to learn themselves, John Cross Giblin's *From Hand to Mouth: or How We Invented Knives, Forks, Spoons, and Chopsticks & The Table Manners to Go With Them* is a book that will satisfy your curiosity and love of learning.

Language Arts: Storytelling - Reminiscing (Flashback)

The book begins with Mako, as a grandmother, preparing to send a new pair of clogs to her granddaughter. In the process of telling the story, Mako begins to recall a time many years ago when she was a little girl herself. This is a common storytelling technique called reminiscing or flashback, which you and your student can discuss. Be on the lookout for other stories that begin and then lapse into some reminiscing. Let your older student try to write a story using this technique. Encourage him to begin the story with a present time setting and then switch to a time of reminiscing. While he may not be able to remember "*many* years ago when he was young," he can certainly tell a story that has a flashback to "last summer, when on vacation...." Or try telling your student an autobiographical story (a story about yourself) using the technique of **reminiscing** (remembering) about a time long ago. He may enjoy illustrating your story as a project. Hopefully, your student will begin to ask himself whether a story is present tense, past tense or in the future, as he reads. Most stories can be told many different ways.

Language Arts: Vocabulary

lacquer   A highly polished finish for wood.

suspecting   To be distrustful or think that someone has done something wrong.

perfectly   Completely, thoroughly and without any mistakes.

Art: Colored Pencil Techniques

A Pair of Red Clogs is illustrated with a combination of pencil, pen and ink, and colored pencil. Look closely at the colored pencil portion of the illustrations. Note how Kazue Mizumura has used "cross-hatching" (coloring in more than one direction) to achieve texture. You'll also find that Mizumura uses more than one color of pencil to achieve new colors and shading. Have your student look closely at the illustration of the sunset. Notice how the yellows, reds and blues combine to give shading and new sunset colors. Let him try these techniques in a very simple drawing.

Art: Unity of Theme Through Color

Have your student find which pages do *not* have yellow in them. You'll discover that the artist has used yellow as a unifying theme on every page of the story. Only in Mako's introduction, (before the story actually begins) when she herself is a grandmother, is there no yellow. The repetitive use of one color to give a series of illustrations unity is a good technique. If he is interested, have your student draw a series of three or more illustrations using one predominately recurring color to achieve unity throughout the series of pictures.

Notice that when Mako sits before the fire warming herself, the artist combines red pencil with the recurring yellow to produce a warm, orange color. This gives the effect of heat and warmth. Explain that if your student wants to make something look warm, he can use the *warm palette colors:* yellows, oranges and reds.

Art: Action and Expression in Figures

Explore the illustrations in *A Pair of Red Clogs*, paying particular attention to the action portrayed in the character's bodies. For instance, you can tell, even without seeing Mako's face, that she is full of wonder at the things she sees in the market window. The tilt of her head portrays the emotion. In addition, look at how the artist shows Mako's pride as she wears her new clogs. Her chin is lifted, arms held out and she has a prancing step. Contrast this colorful picture to the grayed illustration of Mako walking dejectedly home under the street light. Again, we see Mako from the back. Her head hanging down, shoulders drooping. Talk about how the artist uses the bright colors to show happiness and the grayed, dull picture to show sorrow. Have your student try drawing pictures of joyful subjects in appropriate colors and of more solemn subjects in the duller colors. Choices of color and body language are other ways an artist uses to express himself. If drawing is too difficult for the student, try to find pictures in books, online or even at a gallery, which match the subject with the artists' choice of colors.

See the Body Action Sheet at the end of this unit. The "stick" figures represent the skeletal **armature** (simplest stick form) of several of Mizumura's illustrations. By matching the sketches to various drawings in the book, try to identify where each tracing came from. Now try making your own tracings of skeletal armatures. Your student will discover that even simple stick figures can express a wide range of activity and motion. Now "flesh out" your tracings with form and color. Let your student work at his own skill level, whether he is just beginning to appreciate Mizumura's action figures, or wants to try drawing some himself.

Math: Counting

A Pair of Red Clogs offers many different subjects for counting. You may want your student to count (as high as he can go) all the clogs pictured in the story. You may choose to count the children in the story or the items at the market.

Math: Playing Store

With your student, play market (or "store"), like the lady in the story who sold the clogs. Use buttons for money and find interesting items to include in your "market." For your older student, make a long list of what should be in the market. Add prices to the items and pretend to play store. Choose several items from the list, and have your student add the prices. Pay each other with actual money and make change.

Science: Weather and Weather Forecasting

What is weather? What do we mean by weather? One definition is: the general condition of the atmosphere with regard to temperature, cloudiness and moisture. In other words, what is the temperature? Are there clouds? Is there any rain, hail, sleet, snow, fog, dew, etc.? Is there any wind?

What is good weather? What do we mean when we say "good weather"? If we have an outing planned at the lake, beach or pool, we mean sunny and warm. If we want to go skiing, we mean fresh snow and lots of it. If we're farmers in the midst of a drought, we think of rainy days as "good" weather. What kind of weather does the student like? Which is his favorite season? Discuss the four seasons and the changing weather he can expect in each.

How do we predict weather? How do weather forecasters predict (tell before it happens) the weather? Mako and her friends played a weather-telling game, but it was only a game and nothing more. Meteorologists (scientists who study the weather) can and do predict the weather. They use many tools and techniques from thermometers (measuring devices which indicate the temperature) and barometers (measuring devices which measure atmospheric pressure) to photographs taken by satellites orbiting above the earth. Watch the weather forecast with your student and make notes about the meteorologist's predictions. Then, see if the predictions are accurate. You can even keep a daily chart for several weeks, recording the high and low temperature, precipitation (rain or snow), etc.

Five in Row Volume One   59

Teacher's Notes

The *Five in a Row* lesson options for each unit in the manual are all you need to teach your child. The additional resource area provided below is simply a place to jot down relevant info you've found that you might want to reference.

A PAIR OF RED CLOGS

Date:

Student:

Five in a Row Lesson Topics Chosen:

Social Studies:

Language Arts:

Art:

Math:

Science:

Relevant Library Resources: Books, DVDs, Audio Books

Websites or Video Links:

Related Field Trip Opportunities:

Favorite Quote or Memory During Study:

Body Action Sheet

These skeletal "stick" figures were made by laying tracing paper over some of the illustrated figures in the story *A Pair of Red Clogs*. Take tracing paper and trace them. Now lay your traced paper over your story book and try to find the figures that match. Trace some other figures from the story. When you come to clothing, just imagine where the body lines would actually be, according to the position of the figure.

Five in Row Volume One 61

Name:
Date:
Geography: **Japan Flag**

Japan's flag is a field of white with a red circle in the middle. The red circle represents the sun. Japan is known as the Land of the Rising Sun. *For more information, see Parts of a Flag on page 222.*

Color in the Japan flag below.

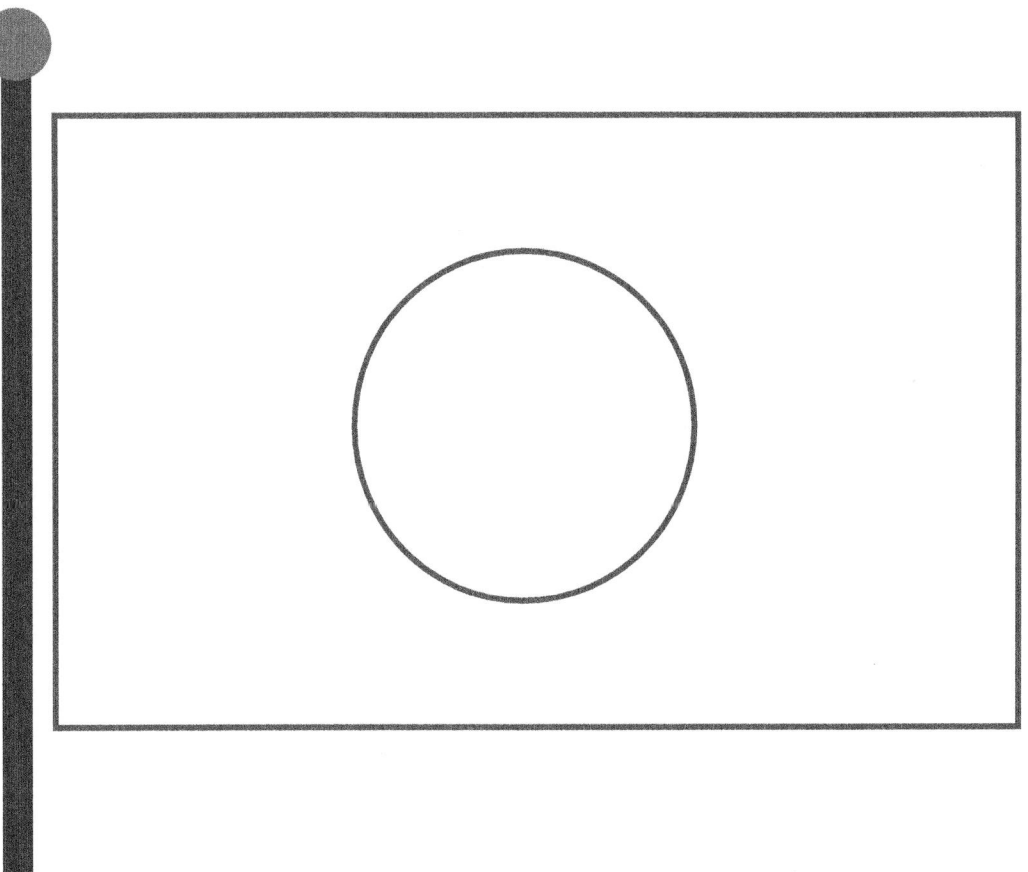

62

A Pair of Red Clogs

Name:
Date:
Science: **Weather**

Weather Vocabulary Matching Game

Sunny	Rainbow	Lightning	Cloudy
Thunderstorm	Rainy	Windy	Snowy

Copy the weather word from above into the space under the matching image.

_____   _____   _____   _____

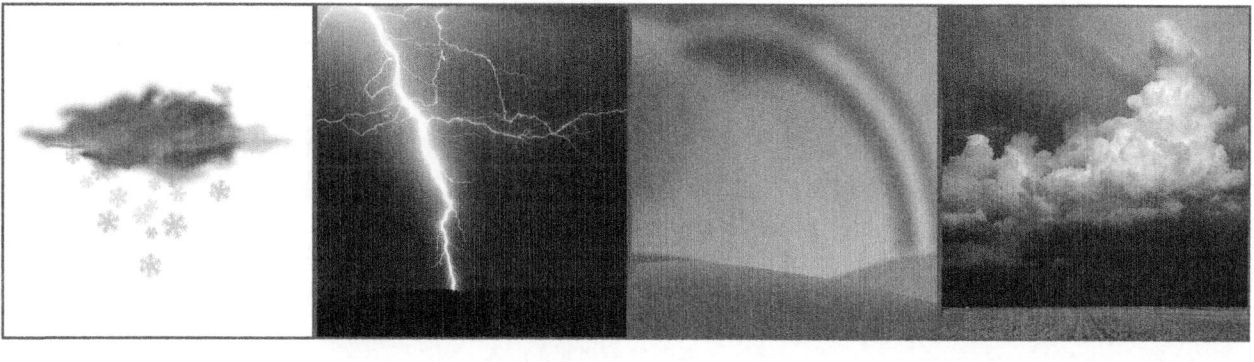

_____   _____   _____   _____

Name:
Date:
Geography: **Island**

Island - a piece of land surrounded by water.
Color the land and water surrounding it.

Map of Japan

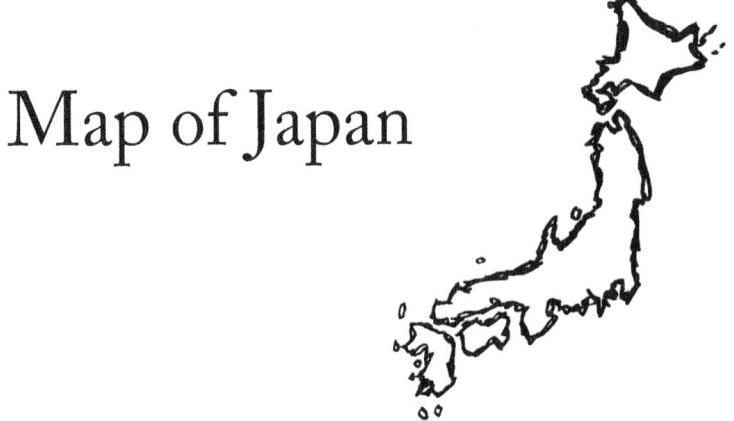

A Pair of Red Clogs

Name:

Date:

Art: **Warm and Cool Color Palettes**

Color in the "pie chart" of warm and cool colors. Use the squares provided to mix, combine, and blend colors to create different shades from the warm and cool palettes. Your student may also enjoy drawing two pictures on separate sheets of paper: one using a warm palette and one using a cool palette.

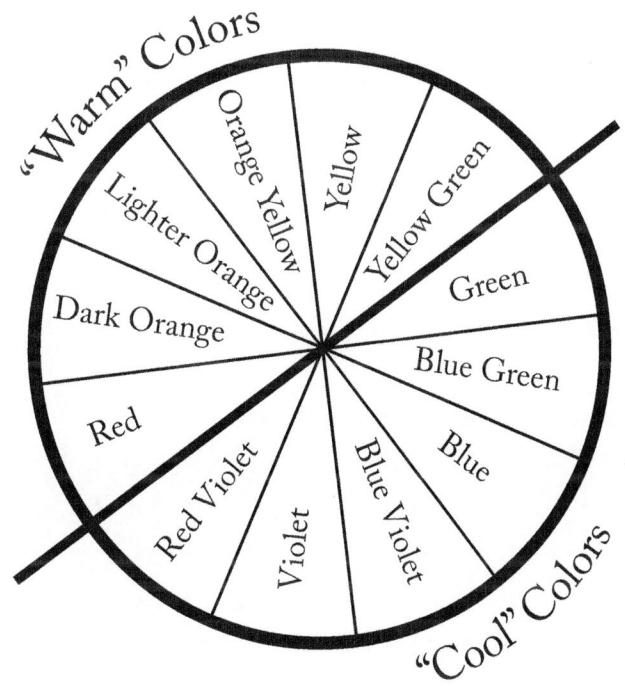

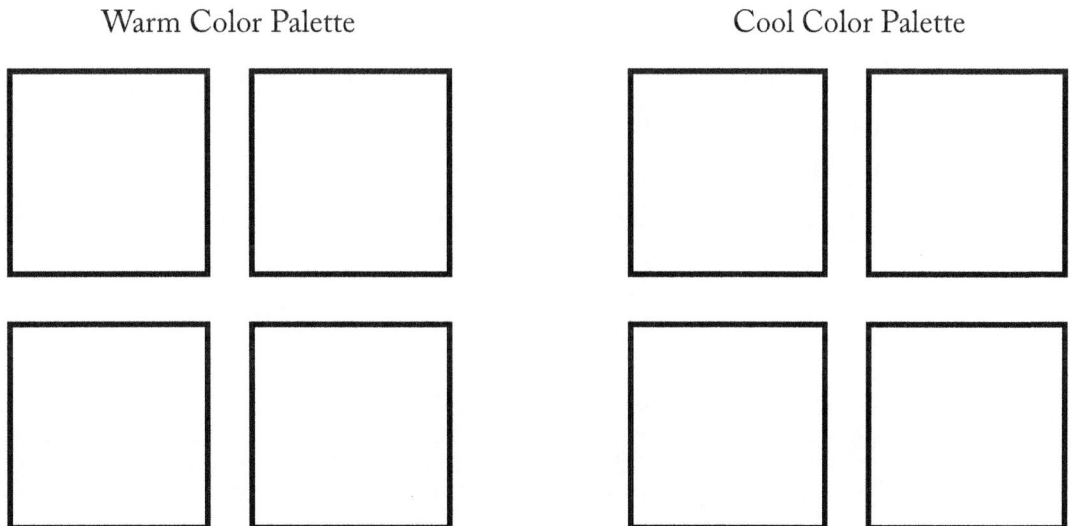

Warm Color Palette

Cool Color Palette

Five in Row Volume One

The Rag Coat

Title: *The Rag Coat*
Author: Lauren Mills
Illustrator: Lauren Mills
Copyright: 1991
Summary: Minna needs a coat for school, and finds acceptance through forgiveness and wisdom.

Social Studies: Geography

The Rag Coat is set in the eastern United States. See if your student can point to the eastern portion of the United States on a map. Discuss the four basic points of the compass and how we find each direction on a map. You may want to help your student orient her house or classroom in relation to the four compass points, as well. If you have access to a compass, talk about its use as a tool in orienting yourself (a compass always point to north).

Specifically, *The Rag Coat* is set in the Appalachian mountains, a range of highlands running from Pennsylvania to Alabama. Locate the Appalachian mountains on the map. See if you can locate other mountain ranges in the United States such as the Rocky Mountains and the Cascades in the Northwest.

Place your story disk on the Appalachian region.

Social Studies: Appalachian Culture

The Appalachian region has its own unique culture. As you read *The Rag Coat*, you'll see many items of interest. Notice the log cabin on the dedication page.

Point out the wagon, dulcimer (a mountain music instrument), the process of carding cotton, Minna's father's overalls, quilting, pot-bellied stove, one-room schoolhouse, clothes, boots, bare feet, butter churn, popcorn popper by the fireplace and the oil lamps and candlesticks. See how many other unusual items you can find.

If you'd like to learn more about Appalachian life, check out one or more of the *Foxfire* books (ed. by Eliot Wigginton). Your student might enjoy watching the movie *Christy*, which is set in the Appalachian mountains in the 1930s and is based on the Catherine Marshall novel of the same name.

Social Studies: Human Relationships

There are many relationships portrayed in *The Rag Coat*. Discuss the warm and loving relationship between Minna and her father. It seems filled with Minna's good humor and her father's wisdom.

Explore the attitude of the quilting mothers who give, even when they themselves have need. Unselfish and kind, they help Minna get a coat and keep her secret. Help your student think of times when she may have given generously, even sacrificially.

Minna dreamed of having good friends when she went to school. Instead, she found that the children taunted her and made fun of her. Obviously this was devastating to Minna. Ask your student if this has ever happened to her, not necessarily at school but anywhere. Ask her how she felt and empathize with the feelings. These are emotions that *everyone* has felt at one time or another.

Ask your student what she did about the teasing and then examine the decision that Minna bravely made. Minna, using the wisdom of her father, forgave her schoolmates and brought about a surprise reconciliation. This is a story that beautifully portrays the *power* of forgiveness.

The last important lesson of *The Rag Coat* is the truth that people do need people. When Minna was hurt by the things her schoolmates said, she went off by herself. When she remembered what her father had told her she made a decision to *return* to the classroom. This meant she had to forgive her classmates because she valued being *with people* and wasn't content to stay on the outside (isolated). There may be a place to share with your student a similar experience of your own or to talk about valuing other people.

Social Studies: Funerals and Mourning

This may be a good time to discuss funerals with your student. Ask if she has ever attended a funeral. How did she feel? Minna's father died and Minna was frightened by all the people who came to their cabin wearing black. She couldn't understand why everyone was wearing black, a color her father had hated. She didn't understand that traditionally, people have worn black to funerals to show respect and to demonstrate their own grief. It would have been helpful if someone had explained this to her. If your student has been to a funeral, there may be many things she didn't understand. Like one little boy who was totally confused when a distant relative, attending his grandfather's funeral, commented that the little boy had "his grandfather's nose." He was frightened and confused at the prospect of his grandfather having no nose in the closed casket. Death and funerals can indeed be confusing to small children.

Discuss funeral traditions in your student's family or cultural setting. Perhaps wakes are common, or keening (loud crying). She may have wondered about caskets, embalming or cremation. Go only as far as seems appropriate, but many students *will* have questions.

Minna wanted to remain close to her father, even after his death. She wanted a piece of her father's work jacket sewn into her crazy quilt coat. She also wanted the feed sack he had wrapped her in to be the lining of her coat. Pursue this topic with care and sensitivity as you discuss these important issues with your student. Dying is a natural part of living and even small children need honest answers to difficult questions.

Language Arts: Stories

Minna exclaims, "My coat is full of stories, stories about everybody here." Quilts have traditionally been used in literature to tell stories. If you have access to a quilt and know stories corresponding to the pieces, this would be a good time to have fun and discuss them.

Make a simple pieced pillow top using materials that have meaning for the student. Let her tell or write down the stories, sharing her memories of the fabric pieces.

In addition, there are several good books written around the quilt theme:

The Patchwork Quilt by Valerie Flournoy
A young girl steadfastly works on the quilt her Grandmother began.

Sweet Clara and the Freedom Quilt by Deborah Hopkinson
A creative girl helps slaves escape by hiding clues in a quilt's design.

Stories from Grandma's Attic by Arleta Richardson
Quilt pieces provide the inspiration for a grandmother to retell stories from her childhood. This series is to be heard aloud and then read over and over!

Art: Viewpoint

Nearly every one of Lauren Mills' illustrations is of traditional size and viewpoint. The exception is the illustration of Minna and her brother, cowering on a stool by the potbellied stove. The giant adult figures, seemingly out of proportion, tower in front of them. Mills' unique viewpoint helps emphasize Minna's vulnerability. Suggest that your student try drawing from an unusual viewpoint in order to emphasize an emotion, or she could print out pictures and glue them into a collage. She might have a picture with huge animals and tiny people to emphasize how dangerous the animals are. Conversely, she might have tiny animals with giant children towering over them to emphasize how vulnerable small animals feel. Have your student think of her own ideas. Learning to find an interesting viewpoint is an important lesson in learning to communicate effectively through art.

Art: Limited Palette

In the illustrations for *The Rag Coat*, Lauren Mills uses a limited, subtle palette to convey the impression of warmth, homeyness, and Minna's sensitivity. Minna is a gentle girl with a tender spirit, and Mills' choice of colors (pastels of soft blues, greens and warm browns) give the impression of gentleness and softness. Imagine how differently the illustration would make you feel if the artist had used bright oranges, purples and electric yellows to illustrate the book.

Let your student try drawing or painting with a limited palette of only two or three colors. (Additional colors can be mixed from these two or three.) What sort of colors would you use to illustrate a science fiction story about a trip to the moon? What about a story of a little girl who wanted to be a ballerina? How about an adventure story set in the jungle? Each story could use a different group of colors. As artists create, their choice of palette colors helps tell the story.

Art: Facial Expressions

Look through *The Rag Coat* with your student and try to name each of Minna's expressions. You might choose words like: hopeful, pleased, happy, intent, loving, frightened, wondering, grateful, eager, admiring, remembering, encouraging, broken-hearted, grieving, determined or quietly triumphant. Or, using the above list, ask your student to find a picture of Minna where she looks "eager," etc.

The arrangement of facial components in a drawing tells us what the person is feeling. What makes a face happy or sad? See if your student can draw an upturned and down-turned mouth. What about surprise? Try drawing the eyebrows much higher than usual. For a look of wonder, try making the eyes big and round. Let the student experiment with eyes, eyebrows and mouth and try to decide what emotion each face is expressing. See the face templates at the end of this unit.

Facial expressions are one of the primary ways we tell what someone else is feeling. Whether in life or in books, expressions are important. For excellent lessons on facial expressions, look online for *The Big Yellow Drawing Book* by Dan O'Neill.

Art: Quilts

Quilts are made like an Oreo® cookie. They have a top, a bottom and a stuffing in the middle. The bottom is usually a piece of solid fabric while the top is made up of many smaller scraps of material sewn together. In between is a soft, fluffy material called batting. Quilt tops, like Minna's coat, can be randomly assembled. They are called crazy quilts. Other tops are sewn in regular, geometric arrangements called patterns. Most quilt designs have well-known names

Five in Row Volume One 69

and have been sewn the same way for many, many generations. You can learn a great deal of history by studying quilts because the patterns are sometimes named after famous people and events. Many quilts are "pieced" (made of various pieces sewn together edge to edge). In *The Rag Coat*, the mothers piece a quilt together in a pattern called Joseph's Coat of Many Colors. This pattern was named after a story in the Bible from chapter 37 of Genesis. You'll find a pattern for this design at the end of this unit.

Let your student try making her own quilt block by using geometric shapes. She may color or paint her pattern, or use cut-out shapes from construction paper. If you want to sew a quilt block, use a variety of fabric scraps. You can try copying Joseph's Coat of Many Colors from the book's illustration, or use the the pattern found at the end of this unit. You can even make a crazy quilt pattern like the one in Minna's coat. If you actually sew quilt blocks (enlarge the pattern), use them to make a pillow top, or a small quilt (using several blocks) to snuggle under while reading with your student.

For younger children, try making a *quilt puzzle*. Cut out quilt pieces from cardstock or posterboard and color them like the illustration in the story. Have your student assemble the "quilt pieces" to duplicate the original pattern, like a jigsaw puzzle.

Mathematics: Geometric Shapes

The quilting mothers piece a quilt in a pattern called Joseph's Coat of Many Colors. Look at the illustration and see if your student can identify any of the geometric shapes used in the pattern. She should find triangles and squares of several sizes. If she is interested in geometric patterns, you may wish to introduce tangrams, which are plastic geometric shapes that can be assembled to create various patterns. You might also purchase or make a geoboard by driving short nails in a circle, like the hours on a clock face around a board, or in a square grid pattern. Then allow the student to stretch colorful rubber bands or string from nail to nail, creating geometric shapes.

Science: Coal

In *The Rag Coat*, Minna's father is a coal miner. Ask your student what she thinks it would be like to work every day in a coal mine, hundreds of feet beneath the earth's surface. Imagine the darkness and dust. Many coal miners have suffered from black lung disease, a respiratory illness caused by years of breathing coal dust. Minna's father dies from black lung disease.

Coal comes in two types: bituminous (soft coal) and anthracite (hard coal). It's possible that your student's grandparents or great-grandparents remember heating their home with coal. Watch for coal trains in your area, hauling coal to electric generating plants. You may want to check out a book from the library on coal mining and learn more about this important part of America's industry.

Try taking a small flashlight and taping it to a helmet of some sort. Use a football helmet, bicycle helmet, baseball batting helmet or even a winter hat. Tape it in place using duct tape, electrical tape or several strips of masking tape. Now let your student turn on the flashlight and wear the "miner's hat" into a dark room, basement or garage. The light will shine wherever the student looks, just like a real miner's hat!

Science: Natural Fabrics

Where did the fabric for the rag coat scraps come from? There were probably scraps of cotton, wool or linen provided by the quilting mothers. Show your student samples of each of these various fabrics and discuss their origins. Cotton comes from the cotton plant. It is grown in warm climates throughout the United States and in other similar climates worldwide. You may want to show your student a picture of the cotton gin and talk about Eli Whitney as you discuss the process of carding cotton, spinning it into thread and weaving it into fabric. Linen comes from the plant fiber flax, and wool comes from sheep.

Teacher's Notes

The *Five in a Row* lesson options for each unit in the manual are all you need to teach your child. The additional resource area provided below is simply a place to jot down relevant info you've found that you might want to reference.

THE RAG COAT

Date:
Student:

Five in a Row Lesson Topics Chosen:

Social Studies:

Language Arts:

Art:

Math:

Science:

Relevant Library Resources: Books, DVDs, Audio Books

Websites or Video Links:

Related Field Trip Opportunities:

Favorite Quote or Memory During Study:

Joseph's Coat of Many Colors
Quilt Pattern

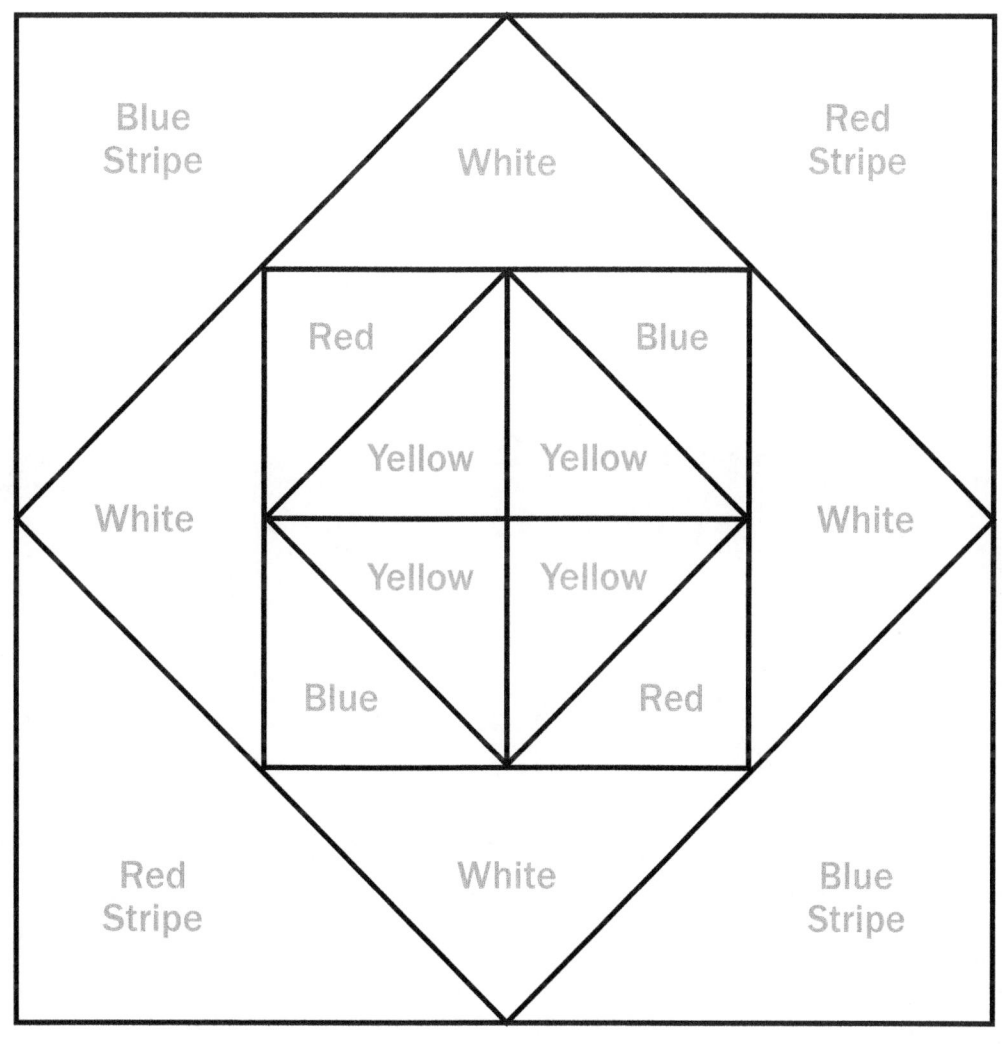

Name:
Date:
Art: **Facial Expressions**

Use the face templates below to practice drawing facial components to represent different emotions. Label the emotion on the line below the face.

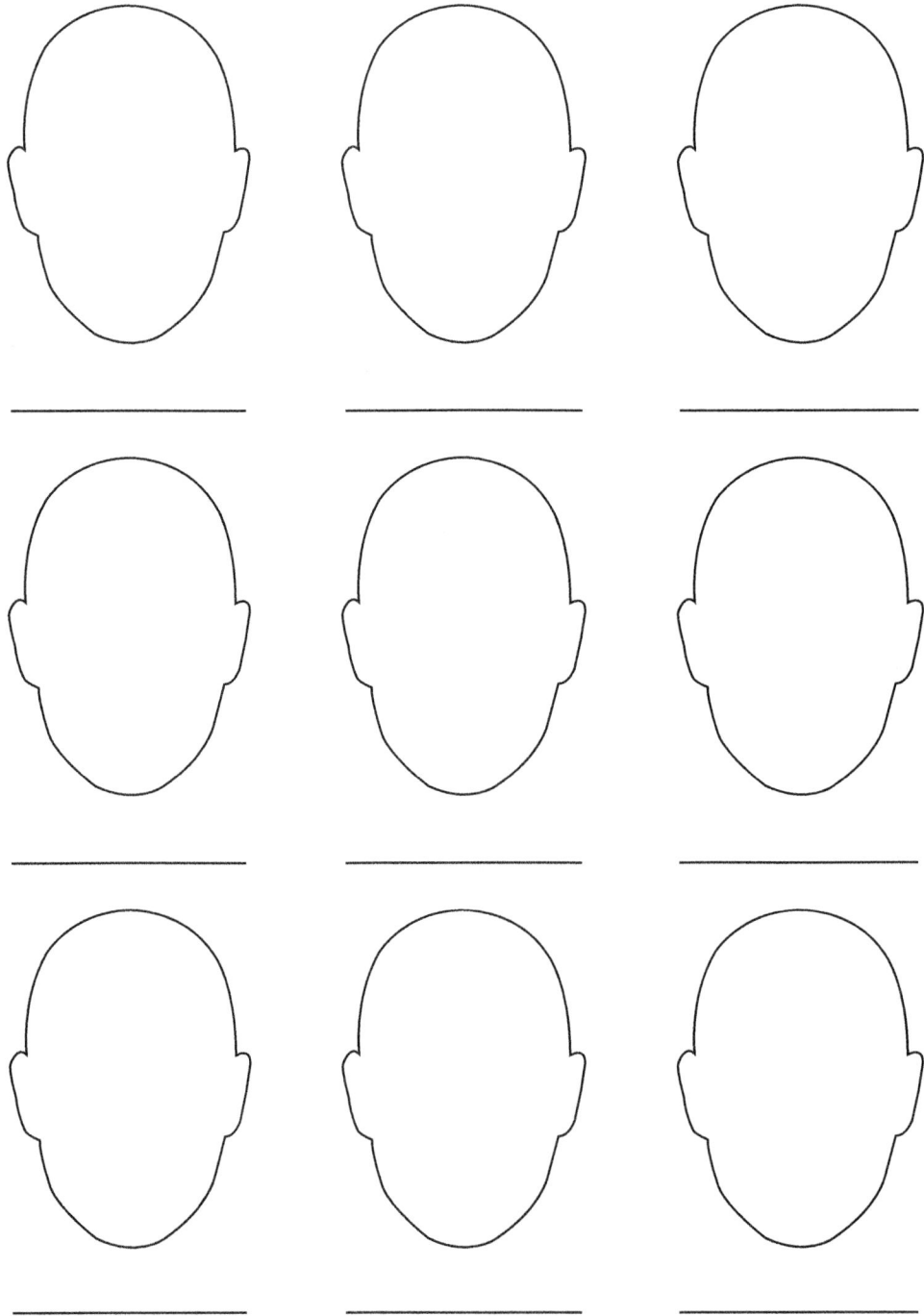

The Rag Coat

Name:
Date:
Math: **Geometric Shapes**

Circle **Triangle** **Square** **Rectangle**

1. How many sides does a triangle have? _____

2. Do a square and rectangle have the same number of sides? _____

3. Can you draw a picture below using some or all of these shapes?

Who Owns the Sun?

Title: Who Owns the Sun?
Author: Stacy Chbosky
Illustrator: Stacy Chbosky
Copyright: 1988
Award: "Written and Illustrated by ..." Award
Summary: A young boy learns a hard truth, yet perseveres.

Social Studies: History

Who Owns the Sun? may be your student's first introduction to the concept of slavery and its role in American history. This story can provide a jumping-off point to discuss slavery, the Civil War, the civil rights movement, racism, discrimination or desegregation. As the teacher, you can decide how far to go in covering these topics. As you read the story together, you'll feel the pain of both Big Jim and his son. Empathy and compassion provide a healthy gateway to difficult topics.

If you're interested in exploring a related topic, locate a copy of *The Drinking Gourd* by R. N. Monjo. This interesting children's book explores the underground railroad, a system by which slaves escaped north to Canada and their freedom. Place your story disk somewhere in the southern United States as you introduce the subject of slavery.

Social Studies: Family Relationships

Find the pages in which the son asks the father questions about the world around him. Notice that each time the father says that there are things too wonderful to be owned by anyone. Point out, too, that a measure of the son's admiration for his father is that he believes what his father says. He believes in his father's wisdom.

The son also shows a remarkable devotion to his father on p. 21 where he describes his "labor of love." Running with his father's lunch, because he knows how hungry his father is, demonstrates the depth of the son's love for his father. Talk about the many ways that we show people how much we care about them. Point out specific times that you have seen your student show extra care for someone.

The little boy in *Who Owns the Sun?* hears others praise the accomplishments of his father and he is proud of him. But the boy also hears Mr. Finley say he owns Big Jim and that is a very hard truth to discover. Ask your student how he thinks he would feel if he learned this difficult fact? What would he want to do about it? Now reread the Afterword and help your student see that in this case it seems that life went on. It was many years later that changes came to Big Jim and his son. One of the life skills demonstrated in this story is the ability to face difficulty and unfairness without becoming bitter. Sometimes we must be patiently willing to persevere and wait for change. Try talking about any of these concepts that seem applicable.

What sorts of unfair things have happened to your student? What kinds of things are people unable to change for themselves? (Answers might include being in a wheelchair, suddenly losing a job, etc.)

The son finds out that there are things that his father, no matter how great he is, cannot control. This is an important concept. Big Jim's son must decide how to relate to his father. To learn to continue loving and admiring is maturity indeed.

Language Arts: List-Making

Make a list of the qualities the author uses to describe Big Jim. You might say, "What was Big Jim like?" List the words on a sheet of paper as you and your student remember them together. You may wish to print words like "big hands" with a picture symbol beside them. Finish the list in one day or add to it each day after reading the book.

You could also try listing (with picture symbols) things too wonderful to be owned: stars, sun, flowers, rain and wind. The pictures may be drawn or printed. Think of other things too wonderful to be owned and include them in your list. This could turn out to be a long list!

Language Arts: Writing

In *Who Owns the Sun?*, the boy asks questions. In fact, it is his questioning that is the recurring thread of the story. Ask your student to make up his own story that asks repetitive questions. An example could be a story that asks several times, "How big is a ___?" or "Why ___?" or "Who told the geese it's time to fly?" or "Who told the bee where to find honey?" Have him answer the questions. In this way, perhaps you'll discover what it is your student wonders about!

You may write out the question story for your student, if necessary. You may want to include pictures after certain words or in place of some words like a **rebus** story. (A rebus is a story that uses certain picture symbols in place of specific words throughout the entire story. For instance, in a rebus story, every time the word cat would be used, a picture is used instead of the letters c-a-t.)

Language Arts: Vocabulary

There are many ways to help your student build his vocabulary. Explain the simple meaning of a word and then use it whenever it is applicable on a day-to-day basis. This helps the child assimilate the word into his vocabulary. It can be a source of togetherness and fun as you share new words with each other.

You may want to keep a chart or 3" x 5" index cards as a running vocabulary list for all the books you read together. Pictures beside the words help recall the word for young students. Go over the cards occasionally, just recalling the basic definition.

squint(ed) p. 7:   To look with eyes partly closed. Act it out.

windmill p. 13:   A mill powered by the wind blowing upon sails or vanes. Find a picture of a windmill.

wander(er) p. 13:   To travel about without plan or destination. When you and your student are outside you could aimlessly walk about and say, "Look, I'm wandering here and there." Acting out words helps students remember.

continue p. 15:   To keep going or to go on.

Language Arts: Question Mark

Who Owns the Sun? offers an opportunity to discuss the use of question marks. For your young student, start with the title and let him try to find question marks in the story after explaining their use in ending "question" sentences.

Language Arts: Poetic Prose

The style of writing that Chbosky uses is extremely poetic. She is able, with her highly descriptive phrases, to paint a specific word picture. This is called **imagery**. There is imagery in the description of the April afternoon when the son says, " ...my world, now touched by the rays of the sun, smelled sweet. The light that fell across my face felt warm and clean."

Personification, the giving of human qualities to non-human things, is used on p. 9 where it says the cricket cried itself to sleep.

Simile is the comparison of two dissimilar objects, using the word *like* or *as*. On p. 9 you read, "The black sky wrapped around us *like* a soft muffler." The black sky is being compared to a soft scarf and paints for you a word picture that helps you "feel and see" more exactly what the night is like.

There are many examples of **imagery**, **personification** and **simile** in the text of *Who Owns the Sun?* You may discuss any of these devices and even try a few in writing exercises, or it may be sufficient to simply say, "This writing is beautiful. I can almost feel the sun or smell the rain. This writing is very close to poetry which often makes the reader see, feel and hear more clearly or intensely."

Language Arts: Elements of a Story - Climax and Denouement

Ask your student if his feelings at the end of the story would be the same if the Afterword had not been included. Chbosky has ended the story at the point of **climax** (the highest point of interest or action) and, if left here, our feelings might be sad, rather hopeless or highly agitated. The afterword in *Who Owns the Sun?* serves as the **denouement** (day new MAHN) meaning final outcome or action, to let the reader down gently and leave him encouraged.

Art: The Illustrator

The author of *Who Owns the Sun?* is also the person who illustrated the book. Stacy Chbosky is unusual because she was fourteen years old when she wrote the book and painted the pictures for this story. If your student has interest in writing and drawing or painting, encourage him that *young* authors and artists are producing fine work.

Art: Subject and Symbolism

After reading the story, go back and look at each picture. The paintings of Stacy Chbosky show very simple subjects. In other words, the illustrations are simply rendered without precise details. Find a picture of a painting that is complicated in its detail to show your student the contrast to Chbosky's illustrations.

These illustrations are very simple, yet they are also strong. The bright (strong) colors, tall trees and large rocks all add the feeling of strength to the writing. Remember how the author writes of the strength of Big Jim and then shows that strength in the objects around him. That's **symbolism**! Again, the lesson is the integration of words and pictures to make a powerful story. Continue to expose your student to these ideas and someday it may become part of his work, too.

Art: Color

Chbosky has used a variety of color in her paintings for *Who Owns the Sun?* Talk about the names for the colors and introduce one or two new color names: chartreuse, pink, mauve, lavender.

Pick a picture (the ones opposite pp. 13 or 15 are good for this) and encourage the student to paint a picture after the same manner. Have him copy the colors (your student will have to try mixing paints to achieve the right color) and try to copy the types of brush strokes. Remember, when layering watercolor you must be patient and let each color dry before adding the next one. This should be fun. There is no right or wrong to this type of experimenting.

Art: Bright Light and Shadows

Study with your student the use of bright light and shadows in the illustrations. The sun is an obvious source of strong light. Examine each picture that includes the bright sun and notice the shadows of the trees, fence posts, rocks and people. Notice the strong shadows, especially the shadow of Big Jim and that of his son on pp. 19 and 21. Choose some building blocks and find a window with strong, direct sunlight. Let your student experiment with turning the blocks and seeing the shadows. Notice that in a row of blocks the shadows are all parallel (falling in the same direction.)

Talk about the direction of the light source and that the shadows of the object appear on the *opposite* side of that source. Your student may begin to point out shadows that he sees in illustrations of other books, in photographs, or that he notices himself on a sunny day.

Remind your student that he might consider the direction of the source of light in his own paintings and drawings. By thinking beforehand about the direction of light, he will know on what side of his subjects to draw his shadows! In any case, just seeing a student begin to add any shadows at all is a sign of a maturing artist.

Art: Symbolism

On p. 7 we read, "It was an April afternoon, and my world ... smelled sweet." Notice with your student the beautiful painting and especially the beautiful, tall trees. Now turn to p. 25 and read, "He bent down and put his arms around me, and then he began to cry." Look at the trees on that page. Again the words and the pictures tell the story together. The trees symbolize both the happiness and then the loss that we read about in the story.

Art: Figures

Because the illustrator has used very simple human figures without much detail, what becomes very important is the action or motion portrayed. Look at p. 19 and see the action in Big Jim's arms, back and legs as he works at moving the rock. Now see the action in the arms and legs of his son on p. 21 as he runs with the lunch. Finally, examine the great sorrow shown in the drooped shoulders and lowered head of Big Jim on p. 25. We don't need a great amount of artistic detail to see the emotion of these characters. The body language tells the story. Talk about the freedom an artist has to draw some things in detail and to draw other things with meaningful simplicity. Remind your student that he can make these kinds of choices in his art work. Add: Simplicity or Detail? to your list of Choices an Artist Can Make.

Math: Counting

Have fun counting the stars on p. 9, the pickets on the fence on pp. 7 and 21, the flowers on p. 17 and the tree stumps on p. 25. Have older students divide the stars into groups of three. See how many groups there are.

Science: Seasons

Who Owns the Sun? begins in the spring and continues into summer. You may wish to introduce the seasons, review them, or just list the descriptions of spring and summer included in this text. Add any descriptions of your own to the list. Have your student answer questions like, "To me summer is...," etc.

Science: Simple Machines

There are two simple machines included in this story. Shown on p. 19 is a **lever**. A lever is a bar used to pry, move or lift things. It is used with a fulcrum (the balancing point near the center, like a teeter-totter.)

Talk about the help a lever and fulcrum give in trying to move a heavy rock. If possible, find a large rock and try to move it without a lever and then with one. We use levers at other times to pry the lid off a can of paint, etc. (The screwdriver becomes the lever and the outer paint can edge becomes the fulcrum.) Another simple machine used in this story is a **wedge**. This is the axe head shown on p. 25. Other simple machines (not mentioned in this story) include the **wheel and axle**, the **pulley**, the **inclined plane** and the **screw** (which is really a spiral inclined plane.) Feel free to explore all six simple machines, if your student shows interest. See the activity sheet at the end of this unit.

Science: Five Senses

This story affords an opportunity to introduce the five senses: sight, smell, touch, taste and hearing. There are many descriptive phrases in *Who Owns the Sun?* to introduce a discussion about each of the five senses and what they do. See the activity sheet following this unit.

Science: Memory and Nutrition

What did the mother pack in the father's lunch? How many items can your student remember? How many can you both remember together? Look on p. 21. How many did you remember correctly?

Use the activity sheet at the end of this unit to discuss what food choices could make up a balanced, nutritious meal. Use this information to discuss whether or not the lunch packed for Big Jim was a balanced meal.

With your student, plan a balanced breakfast, lunch and dinner. Then have a balanced snack together!

Teacher's Notes

The *Five in a Row* lesson options for each unit in the manual are all you need to teach your child. The additional resource area provided below is simply a place to jot down relevant info you've found that you might want to reference.

WHO OWNS THE SUN?

Date:

Student:

Five in a Row Lesson Topics Chosen:

Social Studies:

Language Arts:

Art:

Math:

Science:

Relevant Library Resources: Books, DVDs, Audio Books

Websites or Video Links:

Related Field Trip Opportunities:

Favorite Quote or Memory During Study:

Who Owns The Sun?

Name:

Date:

Science: **Simple Machines**

1. _____ 2. _____ 3. _____

  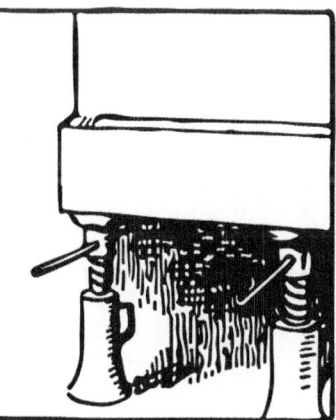

4. _____ 5. _____ 6. _____

1. Lever, 2. Wheel and axle, 3. Pulley, 4. Inclined plane, 5. Wedge, 6. Screw

Five in Row Volume One

Name:
Date:
Science: **Five Senses**

After reading the book several times, talk with your student about what the characters taste, hear, smell, see or touch in the story. List them below.

Taste	Hear	Smell	See	Touch

Who Owns The Sun?

Name:
Date:
Science: **Nutrition**

Discuss with your student which combinations of the items below could make a balanced meal.

Mike Mulligan and His Steam Shovel

Title: *Mike Mulligan and His Steam Shovel*
Author: Virginia Lee Burton
Illustrator: Virginia Lee Burton
Copyright: 1939
Category: Classic
Summary: Mike Mulligan and his steam shovel triumph in changing times.

Social Studies: History

Mike Mulligan's earth-moving shovel was steam-powered. The age of steam has been over now for more than 100 years. Talk about the important part that steam power played in industrial history. There were steam boats on the rivers; steam-powered ocean liners and fire pumpers; steam engine locomotives, tractors and threshing machines; steam-heated radiators in homes and businesses; steam calliopes in the circus, etc. The steam engine was the primary source of mechanical power for a century and a half. Today most of our machinery is powered by either electricity or internal combustion engines using gasoline or diesel fuel. That's why steam shovels like Mike Mulligan's Mary Anne are no longer in demand.

Make a list of old machines that were steam-powered (several are pictured in the book). Now make a list of modern machinery and try to determine how each one is powered. (Almost all are powered by diesel engines today, including diesel trucks, earth-moving equipment, locomotives, ships, etc.) Some students may want to learn more about steam engines. You'll be surprised to discover that steam engines date to approximately A.D. 60. You may have an old steam locomotive nearby on display. You might want to plan a field trip to explore its giant firebox, boiler, pistons, rods, etc.

As a simple history lesson just look at the pictures of the milk truck pulled by horses, the wagons for people to ride in, the old cars and the clothes people are wearing (including the ladies' hats). See what other things of days past you can find together. Place the story disk somewhere in the United States. Talk with your student about where to place it. There are many options, but you will need to choose a location that gets snow in the winter! You could also place the story disk on the margin, in the Land of Make Believe.

Social Studies: Character - Stewardship

Mike Mulligan has taken excellent care of Mary Anne. Good stewardship is taking care of the things we own and the resources we have to use. You may want to talk about the admirable way Mike cares for his steam shovel. We have many chances daily to be careful with the things around us and and use them wisely. You may also want to use this opportunity to introduce the subjects of **conservation** and **ecology**.

Social Studies: Character - Flexibility

When the basement is finished, Mike Mulligan has to come to grips with the changing world. The steam shovel is no longer in demand. Instead, the work is being done by machines powered by gasoline and diesel fuel. Mike Mulligan is willing to deal with changing times, when it is suggested that Mary Anne become the furnace for the new town hall. Rather than becoming angry or bitter because they can no longer do the same kind of work together, Mike Mulligan demonstrates the wise quality of flexibility, and accepts a different way to use their skills.

Social Studies: Human Relationships

Mike Mulligan says he and Mary Anne work faster and better when people are watching. It is fun to work before a cheering crowd, although we also need to learn diligence when no one is watching. Mike Mulligan was boasting a bit when he claimed Mary Anne could dig as much in a week as a hundred men, especially since he "wasn't quite sure." However, he did back up his boast with an agreement to forego his pay if he failed. Discuss the concept of a boast. Try to think together about times when boasting might occur.

Also, in relating to other people, there are sometimes those who seem to lack integrity. That means they may not always be completely honest and fair. Henry B. Swap had a great desire to save money. Swap was so greedy he tried to take advantage of Mike Mulligan, by asking him to dig the cellar and figuring he would get the digging done for free (notice the line, "so he smiled in rather a mean way"). As in other stories by Virginia Lee Burton, the author seems to deal with characters like Henry Swap by having the main character continue to do what is right. Often the uncharitable character begins to change for the better. The author's decision to include those figures who seem mean or unkind lends a reality of life to her stories and allows children a chance to see how others deal with some of the more difficult relationships in life. This is a good time to discuss good manners, being polite and being respectful, even when others are neither kind nor fair.

Language Arts: Story Writing - Characters

Look at all the different townspeople in *Mike Mulligan*. One way to create interest in stories is to have a variety of characters: big, little, young, old, happy, mean, imaginative, etc. Try to write a story with several types of characters. Ask the student to think of the many kinds of people she has known, read about or seen on television. Have her take a characteristic from one person and add it to something she remembers about another person and make what we call a composite character. For instance, an aunt who loves to wear blue may be combined with a neighbor who likes to play the trumpet and dance, creating a fictional, composite character: a woman that likes to wear blue, play trumpet and dance.

For your story setting, you might use a scene with a lot of people such as a movie or the circus. Try using imaginative names like Virginia Burton did in *Mike Mulligan*. She made up names like Popperville, Bangerville, Kipperville and Kopperville.

Language Arts: Elements of a Good Story

You may want to point out the elements of this story:

Setting: This is where the story takes place.

Conflict: Steam shovels are no longer wanted because they're slow.

Rising action: Mary Anne digs faster and faster.

Climax: "Then suddenly it was quiet. Slowly the dirt settled down. The smoke and steam cleared away, and …. There was the cellar all finished!"

2nd Conflict: How will they get out of the cellar?

2nd Climax: Mary Anne could be the furnace for the town hall.

Denouement: The final resolution or outcome is that Mike and Mary Anne change occupations and make a new place for themselves.

Each teacher has to know her student and present only the amount of information that is proper for that student. You may want to teach only one story element at a time. As your student progresses, it is the goal of this type of instruction to teach all the elements of a good story. In time, she will enjoy finding these elements in stories she reads and eventually will use some of this information in writing her own stories.

Language Arts: Literature - Personification

Personification is a figure of speech in which a thing, quality or idea is represented as a person. In *Mike Mulligan*, the steam shovel is named Mary Anne and given the human qualities of perseverance (sticking with a job even when it is hard) and heroism (by saving the day through extraordinary effort). You may wish only to draw your student's attention to the expressions on Mary Anne's face throughout the story and to note the way Mike relates to her with affection.

It is fun to name and give personalities to objects. Perhaps the student can already think of times he's heard the family car referred to as "Jenny Sue" or a blanket named "Buddy." Davy Crockett had a rifle named "Old Betsy," and a girl Caroline named her kettle "Maude" which meant "strong in battle."

Many people (particularly in Europe) name their houses or estates. Enjoy exploring this topic with your student. Help her think of creative names for her home, neighborhood, family car, etc. Gently encourage your student to include personification in stories she writes or that you create together. Personification can include naming objects as well as giving them certain characteristics of people.

Language Arts: Literary Classics

Mike Mulligan and His Steam Shovel was written in 1939. Generations of children and adults have enjoyed this suspenseful tale and appreciated the animated illustrations.

Have your older student look up the copyright date on *Mike Mulligan*. Explain to her that the copyright date is usually when the book was first published. Help her find the copyright in several other books which are handy, searching for other "classic" titles. Talk about the definition of copyright. If there is extreme interest help your student find out how an author obtains a copyright for a book.

Language Arts: Vocabulary

canal   A waterway dug across a narrow piece of land; there is a good picture of a canal in this story. You may also point out the Panama Canal on a map.

cellar   Another word for basement.

Art: Drawing - Trees

Turn to the page that begins, "They left the canals and the railroads..." Point out the trees on this page. They are the stick-and-ball type trees, good for aerial views and long distance views but not as good as the trees on the next page for close-ups. Explain how you can draw and paint good branching trees by starting with the bottom of the trunks and drawing upwards, forking (splitting) the branches as you go. Then you can make irregular circles, elongated ovals, etc., for the leaf effect. Your student can practice a time or two and that should be sufficient for an introduction.

Maybe you can point out unusual branched trees on an outing to help make your student aware of variety in trees. Keep a sketch pad and pencil with you to capture quick drawings of an unusual tree. Refer to this sketchbook when it is time for drawing scenes.

Additional practice, now and then, should help bring the technique to your student's memory and eventually to her work. Art can be an intensely personal subject at any age, so let your student set the pace. It is what she sees, appreciates, and picks up for herself

Five in Row Volume One

that is important. Remember to demonstrate any art technique on a separate sheet of paper and *not* on your student's own work!

Art: Motion

With your student, look at the picture of Mary Anne in her final climactic dig. See if your student can explain how the artist illustrated the extraordinary effort that Mary Anne was making. Mention the swirling circular motion of the smoke, steam and dirt that shows the funnel-like, powerful movement of the steam shovel. Take colored chalk or crayons and have fun trying to draw an action picture or just making "action" swirls like a design. Use several colors and patterns for different effects.

Math: Application in Construction

Mike Mulligan needs to know arithmetic in order to dig the cellar for the Popperville town hall. He has to dig it "neat and square." Discuss with your student the fact that construction workers and architects (those who design the buildings) need to know a lot of math. If they did not, the buildings might be crooked or possibly dangerous. When you are on outings, point out to your student areas of construction, and remind her that the people working there need to know math!

Math: Geometry

The cellar was completed: "four corners ... neat and square." The definition of a square is a polygon with four equal sides and four equal, 90-degree angles. Practice finding objects that are square (check by measuring) and draw (either freehand or by measuring) squares on paper. You can also have on hand pre-cut paper squares in various sizes and colors to make a design or a city.

Another project is to use a geoboard made by taking a square board (approx. 12 x 12 in.) and driving nails into it at the same intervals as the hours of a clock. This needs to be measured carefully. You may include a nail in the center. Colored rubber bands or string can be used to create many different geometric designs including squares.

(Squares, for example, can be created by using four rubber bands. Stretch the first from 12 o'clock to 3 o'clock, the next from 3 o'clock to 6 o'clock, and so on, or have your student try her own ideas to make a square.)

Math: Counting and Grouping

Virginia Burton has drawn many interesting things to use in counting practice such as cars, people, telephone poles and houses.

Beyond counting, try grouping. Lay a piece of tracing paper over the scene of the mountain with the pine trees. Ask your student to draw a circle around four trees and continue until all the trees are circled and count the groups.

Or you can say, "if a lumber company wants to cut six trees a day to make way for the train, how many trees could they cut in a week?" In order to figure out the problem, you could use blocks, buttons, pennies or clothespins for the trees. Arrange them in groups of six for each day you count. Then count the total number of objects.

Science: Steam Power

A teakettle of boiling water will move a pinwheel. Find the pattern and instructions for a pin wheel at the end of this unit. This shows the simple truth that steam produces power. Depending on the age of your student, you may want to go further with the topic of steam power. You can discuss the use of steam to push a piston in any of the early steam machinery or explore steam turbines. Steam can be used to turn a turbine at high speed for the production of electricity, for instance. Search your local library or online for additional information on steam power.

Science: Creative Thinking and Problem Solving

Everyone in the town argues about how to get Mary Anne *out* of the cellar, but one character looks at the problem in a different way. The little boy wonders what will happen if Mary Anne *stays* in the hole. There are many different ways to solve problems. A good beginning skill for scientific investigation is to be able to wonder "what would happen if," and to look at a problem from many directions. Gently encourage wondering by pointing out that the little boy does a good job of thinking of a *different* way to solve Mary Anne's problem. The next time a problem arises in your day, practice thinking together of different ways to solve it. Remember to look at the problem from as many different directions as possible.

Science: Road Engineering

Mike Mulligan and Mary Anne "lower the hills and straighten the curves", for roads to be built. In most parts of the country there are road cuts where the rock cliffs rise on both sides of the road. Point them out and talk about the modern machines, drills, trucks and dynamite that make the cuts today. Ask your student why highways are leveled and straightened. (The elimination of hills, valleys and sharp curves make modern highway travel faster, safer and more fuel-efficient.)

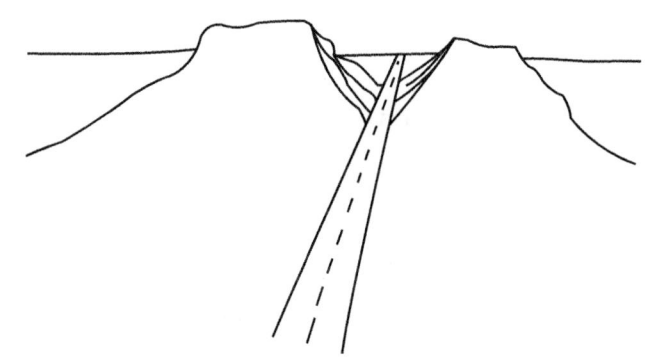

Teacher's Notes

The *Five in a Row* lesson options for each unit in the manual are all you need to teach your child. The additional resource area provided below is simply a place to jot down relevant info you've found that you might want to reference.

MIKE MULLIGAN AND HIS STEAM SHOVEL

Date:

Student:

Five in a Row Lesson Topics Chosen:

Social Studies:

Language Arts:

Art:

Math:

Science:

Relevant Library Resources:
Books, DVDs, Audio Books

Websites or Video Links:

Related Field Trip Opportunities:

Favorite Quote or Memory During Study:

Mike Mulligan and His Steam Shovel

Pinwheel Pattern

Reproduce this pattern or use a square piece of paper. Cut on dotted lines. (Do not cut all the way to the center dot!) Fold lettered corners to center and glue. Allow it to dry. Insert a straight pin through center of pinwheel and into a pencil eraser, so that the pinwheel spins on the pin. Find a teapot with a good spout which produces a solid "stream" of steam. Boil some water until the teapot steams. Hold the pinwheel near the steam adjusting carefully until the steam begins to turn the pinwheel. Yes, steam has "energy" to power your pinwheel and to do other types of work as well!

*Note - **Be careful! Steam can cause serious burns!**

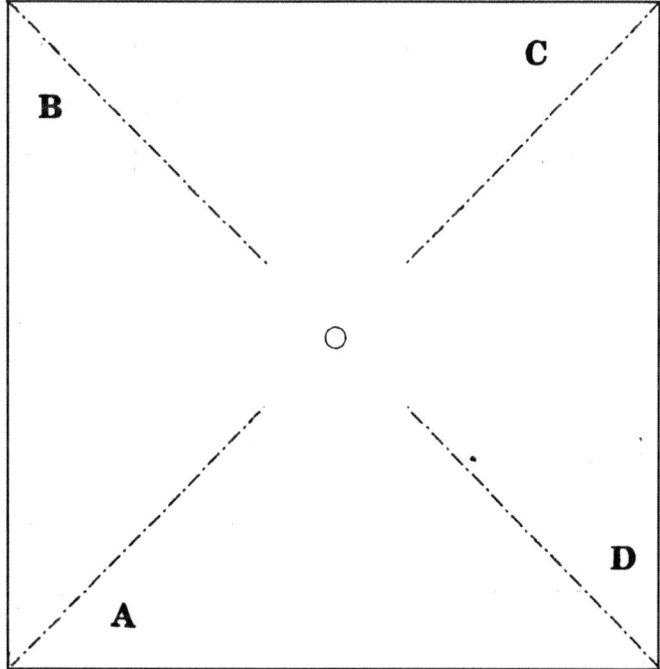

Name:

Date:

Science: **Types of Machine Power**

Steam   Diesel Engine   Electric

Find images of machines that use these types of power. Print them, cut them out and glue them in the spaces below. Label each image with the type of power it uses.

_____

_____

_____

Mike Mulligan and His Steam Shovel

Name:
Date:
Language Arts: **Personification**

Personification is a figure of speech in which a thing, quality or idea is represented as a person. It's fun to name and give personalities to objects!

Practice personifying the objects below.

Example Cloud Car

The cat grinned at me. She was proud of her new collar. Cinnamon happily greeted everyone.

The Glorious Flight

Title: The Glorious Flight
Author: Alice and Martin Provensen
Illustrator: Alice and Martin Provensen
Copyright: 1983
Award: Caldecott Medal
Summary: Papa Bleriot overcomes many obstacles in achieving his goal of flying.

Social Studies: Family Relations

Ask your student, "What can you tell me about Papa Bleriot's (BLAIR-yo) family? What kinds of things do they do together?" You may get answers like, "Papa has a wife, three girls, a boy, a cat, a dog and a cockatoo. They eat meals together, go driving, kiss each other and watch their father try to fly."

Social Studies: Human Relations - Making Reparations

Papa Bleriot has an accident in his shiny new car. Discuss how, when we hurt someone or damage their things, we need to say we're sorry, try to fix the damage and try to leave the person satisfied and not angry. This is called making amends, or reparations.

Ask your student how Papa handled the situation. If they can't remember, review this story element together. You may recall that Papa was saved by the sound of the flying machine that was a wonder to all. He then invited everyone to the cafe.

Social Studies: Geography

The Glorious Flight begins in Cambrai, France and ends just over the White Cliffs of Dover in England. Papa has successfully flown across the English Channel. This is a wonderful opportunity to introduce your student to these place names: English Channel, White Cliffs of Dover, France and England. Memorization isn't the goal. Just hearing the names is helpful. If you desire, you can place the story disk on France and use a string or narrow ribbon to connect another story disk to England, showing how the flight crossed the channel (a narrow body of water joining two larger bodies of water).

Social Studies: Geography - Culture and History

This story contains many French names: Louis Bleriot (LOO ee BLAIR yo), Alceste, Charmaine, Suzette, Jeannot (ZJON-o), Gabrielle, Minou (MEE noo), Arsene, Chloe, Cambrai (COM bray)—a city in France, Escopette, Alphonse Juvet (JOO-vay), Cesar, Achille (a SHEEL) Duval.

This true story, based on the life of Louis Bleriot, also gives us a glimpse of life in a small French town between 1901-1909. There are street scenes, shops and the furnishings inside their houses. There are outdoor cafes, vegetable carts, a steam-powered boat on p.17, and a French flag flying on p. 28. The lady on p.10 has a baguette (bag-ET) in her basket which is a long thin loaf of French bread. The conclusion of the story shows Papa in England and everyone is holding umbrellas. (You may want to mention England's reputation for rain and fog.)

The auto Papa drives was built more than one hundred years ago. Notice differences between this car and our modern ones. Answers might include: "Papa's car had no windshield. There are lanterns on the front of it instead of headlights. There do not seem to be any rear view mirrors. There is a crank in the front. (Explain how the hand crank started old cars instead of electric starters.) There are running boards and funny fenders and no doors, let alone seat belts!"

Now enjoy a baguette with butter for a treat!

Social Studies: Geography - Flags

It might be a good project to make paper flags of countries that you meet in each of the FIAR stories. They could be displayed hanging sideways on a long string or each with a small stick lined up on a styrofoam block.

The activity sheet at the end of this unit has the flag of England and the United Kingdom flag for your student to color. The flag of France can be found in the activity sheet following the lessons for *Madeline*.

Language Arts: Choosing a Title

Point out briefly that the choice of titles for stories, books and pictures is not an afterthought but a carefully thought out part of the work. Notice how the title of this story shows some of the drama and excitement of the triumph of flight. For a good creative exercise, see if you and your student can come up with other exciting title ideas for this book.

Language Arts: Literary Device - Italics

The boat on p. 32 will pick up Papa if his motor fails. The name of the boat is *Escopette* and the name appears in a different print from the rest of the story. The name of a boat or ship is written in italics. Your student may notice the difference in the print. Mention in passing that the names of ships and boats are written in that different type style. They may begin to recognize italics in other stories. If your student hand writes a story which contains the name of a boat or ship, the name of the ship should be <u>underlined</u>.

Language Arts: Descriptive Writing

Page 26 of *The Glorious Flight* describes the English Channel:

"Twenty miles wide.
Black, tossing waves.
Fog and rain.
A very cold bath.
A long swim.
It is a dangerous prospect."

You might try using any subject and having your student write or dictate to you descriptive phrases. For instance, a student might describe strawberries as:

"Round and red.
Thousands of seeds.
Sweeter than candy.
Jagged green leaves.
Funny long runners.
They are a delicious treat."

This is a prelude to the type of writing skill used in the haiku poetic form, but there is no need to count syllables. Have fun brainstorming these descriptive phrases with your student.

Language Arts: Poetic Device - Onomatopoeia

The authors of *The Glorious Flight* have written a prose story of Louis Bleriot using the poetic element **onomatopoeia** (ahna-mahta-PEA-uh): words that create the sound of the object as you say them. On p. 12 "listen" to "Clacketa, Clacketa, CLAKETA! CLACKETA!" This is the sound of the airship. Page 10 also begins with "Crump!", the actual sound of Papa's car bumping into the car of Alphonse Juvet.

Remind your student that using **onomatopoeic** devices in his stories, like writing in sound effects, is a great way to add variety.

Art: Appreciation

The paintings in *The Glorious Flight* are full of color and action, people and sky. The picture on p. 33 shows Papa's face, fully aware of the danger of his situation, and again p. 35 shows that Papa is alone in his adventure.

Art: Perspective and Viewpoint

Pages 12 and 13 are an unusual contrast to the traditional street scene of pp. 8 and 9. Many of the illustrations show people looking up at the sky while others show the viewpoint from the sky downward. If possible, try drawing a picture or two from each viewpoint.

Have fun exaggerating the view. Try to imagine what you'd see if you were high, like an eagle looking down, or very low on the ground like an ant looking up.

For a simple viewpoint project, stand up. Now look down at an apple or toy placed on the floor. Try drawing what you see. Now try sitting on the floor and looking at the same object placed on the edge of a table. Study the difference. Wonder with your student what his home or neighborhood would look like from the air. If he is interested, let him try to draw what he imagines.

Math: Ordinal Numbers

The Glorious Flight provides an opportunity to discuss the concept of "first, second, third," etc. Each time Papa tries to perfect his flying machine, you can call it the first try, the second try, etc. You might explore the difference between the numbers 1, 2, 3, and the idea of order, like standing in line and being first or second. (A number meaning quantity, like one, two, three, is called a cardinal number; a number meaning postition, such as first, second, or third, is called an ordinal number. This isn't necessary for your stuent to learn now unless you think he would be interested!)

Math: Roman Numerals

Each of Bleriot's machines is named with a Roman numeral. For a youger child, simply explain that these marks I, II, III, IV, etc. are a different way of making numbers. If there is interest, you could continue with the fact that they were used in a country called Rome a long time ago. An older student may be interested in making a list of Roman numerals and their Arabic numeral counterparts (Arabic numerals are what we use today). To ten, these counterparts are: I (1), II (2), III (3), IV (4), V (5), VI (6), VII (7), VIII (8), IX (9), X (10).

Students may also be interested in answering simple questions on paper using Roman numerals, such as, how old are you? How many siblings do you have and what are their ages? How old are your parents?

Look for children's books on this topic at your library or online if your student would like to learn more Roman numerals from I to M (1 to 1,000)!

Science: The Process of Invention

The Glorious Flight portrays a passion for invention. Every passionate inventor understands that you must try again and again until you succeed. Look with your student at how hard Papa tries. He overcomes the disappointment of flights that don't work, crashes with broken ribs, black eyes, breaks, sprains and bruises. He continues to work on his project and finally carries through the dangerous prospect of flying over the ocean. This is the process of invention that scientist and inventors must go through to reach the goals they have set. Again, notice how the title and the ending of the story lift us up to the thrill of victory, "We did it!"

If your student expresses interest, explore other inventors and their inventions. Recognize the same patterns of persistence (sticking to a project), heroism and self-sacrifice. A marvelous book on the invention of vulcanized rubber is *Oh, What an Awful Mess! A Story of Charles Goodyear* by Robert M. Quackenbush. You'll find it is easy to read, enjoyable, and it certainly reinforces the theme of perseverance.

Science: Flying

Human beings have always admired flying as they've watched the birds soar in the sky. Many attempts have been made to copy their flight. If there is interest, get a book from the library on the history of flight. This might be the time to introduce the story of Daedalus and his son Icarus. Icarus, who flew too near the sun, melted off his feathers according to Greek mythology. As your student progresses through school he will encounter allusions to the story of Daedalus in poetry and literature.

If the history of flight especially interests your student, try reading *Ruth Law Thrills a Nation* written by Don Brown, or *Lindbergh* by Chris L. Demarest, as well as beginning level stories about the Wright brothers and Amelia Earhart.

Be adventuresome and take this opportunity to design and fly paper airplanes!

This is also a wonderful time for a list. Make a list of all the different ways to travel. Include airplanes, hot air balloons, skateboards, snowshoes, buses and many more. Purchase a kraft paper roll or tape sheets of paper together to make a long scroll for your list. See if your student would like to illustrate it! You can add to it during the week as new ideas come along. Your student might also want to include ideas of travel from the future—maybe a future invention!

Teacher's Notes

The *Five in a Row* lesson options for each unit in the manual are all you need to teach your child. The additional resource area provided below is simply a place to jot down relevant info you've found that you might want to reference.

THE GLORIOUS FLIGHT

Date:

Student:

Five in a Row Lesson Topics Chosen:

Social Studies:

Language Arts:

Art:

Math:

Science:

Relevant Library Resources: Books, DVDs, Audio Books

Websites or Video Links:

Related Field Trip Opportunities:

Favorite Quote or Memory During Study:

Five in Row Volume One　　101

Name:

Date:

Geography: **Flags of England and The United Kingdom**

Color in the flags of England and The United Kingdom below.

The flag of England is derived from St. George's Cross.
It has a centered red cross on a white field.

The Union Jack is the flag for The United Kingdom (this includes England, Wales, Scotland and Northern Ireland). It incorportes the centered red cross from the flag of England.
For more information, see Parts of a Flag on page 222.

The Glorious Flight

How to Make an Apple Pie and See the World

Title: *How to Make an Apple Pie and See the World*
Author: Marjorie Priceman
Illustrator: Marorie Priceman
Copyright: 1994
Summary: An apple pie is an easy thing to make as long as you have the ingredients. If not, hang on!

Social Studies: Geography

How to Make an Apple Pie can be a springboard for many different discussions of geography. Choose one country to talk about, or chart the trip on the inside cover map or on your own map. Be sure to place your story disk on a different country each day as the story progresses.

This is a wonderful opportunity for your student to hear the place names of: Europe, Italy, France, Sri Lanka (sree or shree lanka), England, Jamaica, and Vermont. Hearing the names of famous places can spur interest when the words reappear at a later time. It makes it easier to eventually learn them. Years later your student may say, "Oh, I've heard of Sri Lanka. Cinnamon comes from there!"

Throughout the week, ask your student what the artist has chosen to include in the illustrations that show what each country is like. Talk about these choices as you look at each country's pictures.

Italy: You'll find a discussion of the Italian language (point out that different countries speak in different languages). There is also a reference to semolina (sem a LEE na), a type of wheat used for making pasta and breads. Notice the white buildings with red roofs.

France: The young baker takes the train to France. Notice the Paris sign on the train, and the *l'omlette* sign at the street cafe. Again, there are buildings to see and the Eiffel Tower peeking from in back of the buildings. If your student remembers the Eiffel Tower from the story *Madeline*, she may be able to recognize it even though the artist has chosen to show only a portion. Note that the bicycle is a common mode of transportation in rural areas.

Sri Lanka: Sri Lanka is a pear-shaped island off the southern tip of India, in the Indian Ocean. As you progress through these lessons, you may wish to introduce the names of the major bodies of water. You can point out the location of the Indian Ocean on the map and make a chart of oceans or bodies of water to be added to at different times. By doing this, the next ocean is added and the first name reviewed. This happens on a continuous basis as a built-in review. Make an ocean disk from the blank disks to place on the map.

England: Notice the country cottage, vines about the door and flowers in the yard. There are cows on the hill and a castle in the background. There is a reference to good manners and charming accents.

Jamaica: Bananas grow in Jamaica—hence the banana boat. There are palm trees and a sugar cane plantation.

Vermont: Where, in the United States besides Vermont, do they grow apples? (Washington state, Oregon, Michigan, etc.) Research different varieties of apples and let your student hear the different names. Point out the different kinds of apples at a market or orchard. Buy or pick several kinds and bring them home to compare color and taste. Mention that fall is harvest time for apples.

Geography: Memory Game

List where the apple pie baker went. After several readings, let the student try listing the locations in order from memory. If necessary, help jog her memory. She went from _____ to _____ to _____.

Language Arts: Humor in Writing

How has author Marjorie Priceman made her story funny? What are the elements of humor? (Humor is defined as the unexpected: unexpected conclusions, actions, ideas, interpretations and responses.) Ask your student what parts of the story she thinks are funny. How did the author make it funny? Explore the author's use of "traveling all over the world" to make a simple apple pie, the humor of trying to take the whole chicken or cow with you, the silliness of trying to get cinnamon from under the nose of a sleeping leopard, or milk from a "polite cow." The wild parachute jump and the frantic readying of ingredients is followed by the ridiculous way the story nearly starts over and then abruptly stops. Finally, there is the exuberance of the plantation people and the wild pie-eating party attended by the cow, chicken, dog and cat!

Humor isn't so much taught as caught and this is a good way to present "the funny story."

Language Arts: Repetition

The author uses the element of repetition in *How to Make an Apple Pie*. The use of the line, "unless, of course, the market is closed," is echoed at the end of the story, "but if the market happens to be closed." Casually ask your student if she remembers any lines that were used more than once. Briefly point out that this is another way to create interest in a story. If she hasn't already, have your student add "repetition" to her list of Choices a Writer Can Make.

Language Arts: Vocabulary

ingredients   The individual parts that make up a mixture, such as the butter, eggs, apples, etc. for the pie.

superb   Impressively excellent.

locate   To find something.

elegant   Rich and luxurious.

coax, persuade   To try to get something done by using encouraging words or arguments.

native   Native trees are trees that have always grown in a place, not those brought in from somewhere else.

plantation   A large farm, often in the southern United States.

Language Arts: Drama - Pantomime

It might be fun to act out the pages where the girl mills, grinds, boils, persuades, milks, churns, slices, mixes, bakes and even invites and eats. You could explain **pantomime** (acting without words or sounds). Have your student try it, or try the drama together and help her with actions she doesn't know.

Art: Street Scenes

You'll find a double-page picture of a street scene at the beginning of the story and again at the end. The first pages with illustrations show more of the left hand side of the street and the last scene pages show the rest of the street. The flag on the post office may help your student recognize this continuation. Find the book shop on the left side of the first picture and the locksmith and bakery on the right side of the "end of story" picture.

Call attention to the different roof lines, the different colors of each shop, the signs, the active people and the animals and flowers in the windows. (Explain that people often live above their shops.) Notice the actions of the lady holding her hat, the flag waving and the dog racing.

Take a piece of white legal size paper or long kraft paper. Fold a third of it toward the middle on the right hand side. Open the paper and have your student draw a street scene using simple square and rectangular buildings over the full width of the open paper. Have her include any people, etc. she'd like.

When the drawing is complete, fold the right side back toward the middle to hide part of the street and open it again to see all of the street. Mention that the artist of *How to Make an Apple Pie* used the continuing town (over four pages) to bring the feeling of movement and unity to her story.

Art: Humor in Art

The story's last picture is a hilarious pie-eating extravaganza. Ask your student how the illustrator was able to show the children having such a good time. Some answers might include: lots of action, feet in air, hair flying back, reaching across the table, checkered napkins everywhere and a dog balancing a plate on his nose. See if your student comments on the chicken on the table or the cow that was invited to the party! Be sure to point out the author's use of a riot of primary, active, bright colors.

Art: Contrast

The blaze of color at the pie-eating party pictured with reds, oranges, blues, greens and the use of black, is in sharp contrast to the large expanse of white table cloth. If your student recognizes this concept, have her draw a picture where there is dark color next to very light color. Let her see how this technique makes a strong statement. It helps makes objects stand out clearly.

Math: Subtraction

Subtraction surfaces in *How to Make an Apple Pie* when the girl visits Vermont to pick apples. "Pick eight rosy apples from the top of the tree. Give one to the chicken, one to the cow, and eat one yourself. That leaves five for the pie." Use this scenario to make apple subtraction math cards for learning and review. Math facts can be fun when they are tied to a story. Creative story problem scenarios could include the cow eating too many apples (choose your own numbers) and the chicken deciding she doesn't want one after all.

Math: Liquid and Dry Measure

How to Make an Apple Pie is a great story to introduce basic measuring and cooking skills. After using a liquid measuring cup to measure water (1 whole cup, 1/2 cup, 1/4 cup, etc.), and a dry measuring cup to measure flour (don't forget to demonstrate drawing a knife over the top to level it), try cooking something together. Apple pie would be perfect, but anything requiring remembering the ingredients and measuring would be fun: Jello®, pancakes, macaroni and cheese. On a subsequent day, you could teach fractional addition: 1/2 cup + 1/2 cup =1 whole cup, etc.

While you cook, take this opportunity to play a memory game. Ask how many of the apple pie ingredients your student can remember. Remind her to recall the countries and the pictures for help.

Science: Salt and Evaporation

Salt, a mineral used since ancient times to flavor and preserve food, is a combination of the elements sodium (Na) and chlorine (Cl). NaCl is the chemical symbol for salt. The source of all salt, even the underground deposits, is salt water from seas and salt lakes.

See how salt can be derived from salt water by the process of evaporation. Place two cups of hot water in a shallow pan and dissolve 1/4 cup of salt in it. Allow the water to stand (in the sun is faster) until the water evaporates—depending on weather, this may take several days! Talk about the process of evaporation. See the salt left behind!

Science: Fresh Food for Health

Taking the cow along was the girl's attempt to insure the "freshest possible results." At the sugar cane plantation, the girl flew home so that the ingredients would not spoil. This is a chance to briefly explain that we should not leave milk and meat sitting out in the heat. Microscopic bacteria cause these foods to change and become dangerous for us to eat. These lessons can be expanded if your student seems interested.

Teacher's Notes

The *Five in a Row* lesson options for each unit in the manual are all you need to teach your child. The additional resource area provided below is simply a place to jot down relevant info you've found that you might want to reference.

HOW TO MAKE AN APPLE PIE AND SEE THE WORLD

Date: _____

Student: _____

Five in a Row Lesson Topics Chosen:

Social Studies:
_____
_____

Language Arts:
_____
_____

Art:
_____
_____

Math:
_____
_____

Science:
_____
_____

Relevant Library Resources: Books, DVDs, Audio Books
_____
_____
_____
_____
_____
_____

Websites or Video Links:
_____
_____
_____
_____
_____
_____
_____

Related Field Trip Opportunities:
_____
_____
_____

Favorite Quote or Memory During Study:
_____
_____
_____

How to Make an Apple Pie and See The World

Name:

Date:

Geography: **Flags of Jamaica and Sri Lanka**

Color in the flags of Jamaica and Sri Lanka below.

- The flag of France can be found in the *Madeline* unit.
- The flag of Italy can be found in the *Papa Piccolo* unit.
- The flag of England can be found in *The Glorious Flight* unit.

For more information, see Parts of a Flag on page 222.

Grandfather's Journey

Title: *Grandfather's Journey*
Author: Allen Say
Illustrator: Allen Say
Copyright: 1993
Award: Caldecott Medal
Summary: A young man understands his grandfather's love for both his own home and a foreign land.

Social Studies: Family Relations

Grandfather's Journey spans four generations and ties each of them together. After several readings, discuss your student's ancestors. Try to identify any interests that he might have in common with them. Perhaps his grandfather enjoyed fishing too, or his grandmother also collected sea shells, etc. As the story points out on the last page, we "know" someone better if we find that we share a common experience.

Social Studies: Geography

Find the island of Japan on the map (there may already be a story disk on the map from *A Pair of Red Clogs*). This is where the "journey" begins. From Japan, the grandfather takes a steamship to the New World. (Your student might remember discussing steam-powered machines and transportation from *Mike Mulligan and His Steam Shovel*). Make a disk for the Pacific Ocean, which grandfather crosses, using the blank story disks. Talk about how your student would feel if he did not see any land for three weeks. It is hard to imagine. You might put the story disk for *Grandfather's Journey* on California, the place he liked the best. You could also use a blank disk to make a marker for the continent of North America. Explain what a continent is and that the North American continent includes Canada, the United States, Mexico and Central America. With your older student discuss the seven continents: North America, South America, Europe, Asia, Australia, Antarctica and Africa. Locate each on your map. You may wish to use blank story disks to label each of the continents.

In order to cross North America, many modes of transportation were used in this book: steam train on p. 7, riverboat also powered by steam on p. 13, and walking. If you are keeping up your list of ways to get from one place to another, begun while studying *The Glorious Flight*, then add any additional methods that come to mind: subway, scuba diving, etc.

This story portrays a love of traveling, a love of seeing things never before imagined and never thinking of returning home until Grandfather remembers his childhood. Yet this same story also emphasizes the value of one's birthplace and one's own country. It is a love that sooner or later calls us and requires our response.

Discuss with your student different places that each of you may have lived. Remember your favorite things about those places and any things that were not so good. Recalling and retaining memories is a skill that gives a sense of value and unity to one's life. It is also a great help in creative writing, as more and more details of people, places and things are stored away in memory for us to draw upon later.

Social Studies: Culture of Japan

Grandfather's Journey begins with a picture of Grandfather in his native dress, a kimono. A **kimono** is a loose-fitting outer garment with short, wide sleeves and a sash, worn by both men and women in Japan. Your student may remember this from the story *A Pair of Red Clogs*. Page 22 actually shows a pair of clogs! Page 21 shows an entire group of people wearing kimonos. Look for other examples of Japanese culture. Notice the mountains of Japan. They are pictured in many Japanese works of art. See if you can find some examples of Japanese ink drawings with mountains and share them with your student. Notice the fan held in the woman's hand on p. 23. Often, this type of folded hand fan is decorated with intricate painting. The house pictured appears to be a house with walls made of paper, a common construction in Japan. Notice the dark hair and the well-groomed hair styles.

Social Studies: History - World War II

You can discuss as much or as little of World War II history as your student finds of interest. You may want to simply say that WWII involved many of the world's major countries and was fought between 1939 and 1945, with Japan, Germany and Italy eventually losing. Or, you may want to go into more detail. You can touch on the Japanese surprise attack on the United States Navy's Pacific base in Pearl Harbor, Hawaii (December 7, 1941), the Holocaust (Nazi Germany's plan of genocide which killed more than six million Jews), the allied invasion of Europe on D-Day (June 6, 1944), the first use of nuclear power in the bombing of Hiroshima and Nagasaki, Japan (August 1945), etc. Use your judgment as teacher to determine whether your student is ready for additional, supplementary material.

Social Studies: Tolerance for Different Races and Cultures

Mention briefly that the grandfather is a reasonable and friendly man. He enjoys meeting all kinds of people. He probably learns a lot from them. Remember that the grandfather is a **foreigner** (from another country). Reread p. 12 in *Grandfather's Journey*.

Language Arts: Poetic Prose

The writing style used by Allen Say is extremely poetic. He paints particular pictures with his words alone. This is called **imagery**. Poetic prose also uses the poetic devices such as **simile**. Allen Say writes, "Bombs fell and … scattered our lives like leaves in a storm." A simile is the comparison of two unlike things using "like" or "as." Lives scattered *like* leaves in a storm presents a particular vivid picture to the reader's mind and uses the simile or comparison to accomplish that imagery. Reread the text with your student and find other examples of Say's use of simile. (Simile lessons are also found in the units for *Who Owns the Sun?*, *Cranberry Thanksgiving*, and *Storm in the Night*.) Also, with your student practice thinking of some similes.

In addition, the very sentence structure that Allen Says uses is not like the typical action stories that your student might read. It is contemplative and poetic with a gentle rhythm or cadence. There are not very many words in this story, but each word seems especially chosen to touch the reader's emotions. Yet, this story is not a poem. It is, rather, prose writing that makes some use of poetic techniques and devices. This type of writing is often called **poetic prose**. Ask your student if he enjoys how this story is written. He may already be learning to appreciate different writing styles.

Art: Reflections and Shadows

Page 6 shows the sun's reflection on the water. It reminds us of the reflections in the story *Ping*. Maybe your student will catch this point first, but if not it's a good chance for review. Page 13 pictures the reflection of the steamship in the water.

Allen Say gives us examples of shadows on pp. 5 and 24. The sun (light source) is coming from behind the boy. But on p. 7 the hat casts a shadow over part of his face showing that the light is coming from *above*. Experiment with flashlights in a dark room using blocks or apples for objects. Let the student see for himself how holding the flashlight (light source) at different angles moves the shadows to new places.

Art: Medium, Color and Contrast

Illustrations for *Grandfather's Journey* are paintings in a water medium (like watercolor or acrylic, etc.). The colors in some pictures are rich, like Grandfather's sweater on p. 18. Some are subdued such as as pp. 10 and 13, yet all are carefully rendered realistically. The strength and solidity of these illustrations are partly due to **contrast**. Notice the white collar against the black coat on p. 5, the pure white of the umbrella against the green on p. 15, the white river against the dark land on p. 11, and the married couple on p. 23. Nearly every picture is a study in contrast. Together, find more examples of contrast and keep *Grandfather's Journey* in mind as a prime example of this element of art.

To some extent, all people are artists. Before artists begin their work they think about what they want to draw or paint. They consider elements like **balance, contrast, color** and **action** (or the lack of action). Remind your student that he can make choices like these as he thinks about the kind of picture he'd like to draw or paint. If your student has not yet started a list of Choices an Artist Can Make (see the sheet near the end of this manual), now would be a good time. Make a list of the elements of art that you have studied (**viewpoint, contrast, color, unity,** etc.), and find examples of each. Choose one with strong contrast and another with extremely bright colors, etc., to illustrate the various elements. By keeping a list of these illustrated art words or concepts, then when it is time for art, these ideas will be easy to pull out and review.

Art: Symbolism - Every Picture Tells a Story

Illustrations can deepen the meaning of a story. On p. 10, ask your student why he thinks Allen Say used dark (deeply grayed) colors. Ask him how the picture makes him feel. The text says that Grandfather is bewildered, which means he is not used to such large buildings and factories and he is confused by them. Rather than using bright, clear colors, the artist uses dark gray colors to symbolize the confusion and dirtiness of the big cities. Page 11 shows a white river on dark land. Ask your student why the illustrator might have chosen white for the water. (It is possible that he was using the color white as a symbol to stand for purity. The text reads, "Rivers as clear as the sky." So the white may represent clear, clean water.)

Art: Formal Style

Allen Say has painted illustrations that are carefully posed, much like strong formal family portraits. Traditional Japanese art is formal and stable. Formality is evident both because of the formal poses and the unusual way in which each illustration is centered or balanced. In nearly every illustration, the object of interest is near the center of the picture. With your student, contrast this style of painting with the paintings of other children's books. Look at the work of Ezra Jack Keats (*The Snowy Day, Apartment 3*) or at Marjorie Priceman's *How to Make an Apple Pie and See the World*. In these books the person or object of interest is often to the left or right of center. Note also that there is very little action in Allen Say's illustrations, yet they are beautiful. Your student may come to appreciate the variety in the illustrations of Allen Say and Marjorie Priceman. He can enjoy them both and know that in his own art he has a *choice* of ways to present his subject.

Art: Intensity

Page 19 shows a good example of intensity. A lack of intensity can give the effect of distance by using less detail and less intense colors (grayed or lighter colors) for background subjects. Ask your student why the buildings look far away. How did the artist achieve this effect? Perhaps he will say that the colors are very light and there is not as much detail as the figures in the lower part of the picture. Add this element to your list of Choices an Artist Can Make. Find an illustration to print and to paste beside the word **intensity** as a visual aid. Review these techniques now and then.

Art: Origami

On the title page of *Grandfather's Journey*, you will find a painting of an origami boat. **Origami** is the traditional Japanese art of folding paper into shapes and animals. The word comes from the Japanese words "ori," meaning folded and "kami," meaning paper. Most origami uses thin, square paper which is colored on one side, but other types of paper are sometimes used. Check your local library for a book on easy origami, or look for simple patterns online. You can find origami paper in craft stores, or you can cut brightly patterned wrapping paper into squares. Have fun learning this traditional Japanese art form with your student.

Math: Days in a Week, Weeks in a Month

Grandfather did not see land for three weeks when he was traveling from Japan to the New World. Ask your student how many days that is. If necessary, explain the number of days in a week and use blocks or other manipulatives to make three groups of seven. Count the total number and the question will be answered. You may go on to teach weeks in a month if there is interest. See the activity sheet at the end of this unit for a sample calendar page and question ideas.

Math: Counting

Counting practice can be done with the smoke stacks on p. 10 or with the total number of people in the book from the beginning to the end.

Science: Different Land Types

Grandfather's Journey includes a variety of land types: mountains (both in North America and in Japan), deserts with their wind- and sand-eroded rock formations, farmland and the rocky coastline of California. Discuss the characteristics of some of these various geographic land types or regions.

Science: Factory Pollution in Cities

Sometimes factories are run in such a way that their waste and smoke seriously harm the air and water nearby. Some companies try hard to keep this from happening. They try to protect the air and water so the people and animals and plants near the factory are not injured. Page 10 shows a city full of factories. You cannot tell how these factories are managed, but this is a chance to talk about the effects of responsibility and irresponsibility. Protecting our **environment** (the natural world around us) is good stewardship and is an important issue of our time.

Science: Biology - Birds

Grandfather kept birds to remind him of the place "where he was not." Ask your student if he has ever had a bird for a pet. Encourage older students to research the origin of various pet bird species. Where do canaries come from? Parakeets? Cockatiels? Parrots? What care is necessary for a caged bird? (Birds need food, water, toys, a cage that is large enough, gravel for grit.) What are the characteristics of birds? (Birds have wings, feathers, beaks and bills, most fly, most build nests, etc.) You may want to discuss that bats have wings and a platypus has a kind of bill, even though they are both mammals. Birds can be classified (grouped) in different ways: by size, habitat (the region where they live), egg color, feather color, type of food, size, etc. (Some birds eat seeds, others insects, etc.).

Teacher's Notes

The *Five in a Row* lesson options for each unit in the manual are all you need to teach your child. The additional resource area provided below is simply a place to jot down relevant info you've found that you might want to reference.

GRANDFATHER'S JOURNEY

Date: _____

Student: _____

Five in a Row Lesson Topics Chosen:

Social Studies:
_____
_____
_____

Language Arts:
_____
_____
_____

Art:
_____
_____
_____

Math:
_____
_____
_____

Science:
_____
_____
_____

**Relevant Library Resources:
Books, DVDs, Audio Books**
_____
_____
_____
_____
_____
_____

Websites or Video Links:
_____
_____
_____
_____
_____
_____
_____

Related Field Trip Opportunities:
_____
_____
_____

Favorite Quote or Memory During Study:
_____
_____
_____

Name:
Date:
Math: **Days and Weeks in a Month**

Sunday	Monday	Tuesday	Wednesday	Thursday	Friday	Saturday
1	2	3	4	5	6	7
8	9	10	11	12	13	14
15	16	17	18	19	20	21
22	23	24	25	26	27	28
29	30	31				

Count the number of days in one week.

1. There are ____ days in one week.

2. How many days are in three weeks? ____

3. About how many weeks are in a month? ____

Five in Row Volume One

Cranberry Thanksgiving

Title: *Cranberry Thanksgiving*
Author: Wende and Harry Devlin
Illustrator: Wende and Harry Devlin
Copyright: 1971
Summary: Maggie's grandmother learns not to judge a person solely by the smell of seaweed or lavender.

Social Studies: Geography - New England

Cranberry Thanksgiving showcases a New England cranberry bog. New England, in the northeast section of the United States, includes the states of Maine, Vermont, New Hampshire, Massachusetts, Rhode Island and Connecticut. The coastal states (all except Vermont), are bordered by the Atlantic Ocean. Maine, New Hampshire and Vermont share a northern border with Canada.

New England is noted for its beautiful rural towns and villages, colonial historic sites, maple syrup, cranberries, ship building and manufacturing, and fall color. Ask your student if she's ever eaten cranberries at Thanksgiving. Did she like them? Has she ever had cranberry juice to drink? Where does she think cranberries come from? Has she ever seen cranberries being harvested?

Cranberries grow on an evergreen bush, in bogs and in damp areas beside streams in the cool regions of North America. They are harvested and marketed as fresh cranberries, as berries made into juice and jellies, and as the traditional Thanksgiving cranberry sauce.

Clams are another commonly eaten food in New England. Maggie's grandmother fumes, "Oh, a lot of people would like to get that recipe, especially Maggie's clam-digging friend, Mr. Whiskers." There is also a reference to clams in the New England area in *Night of the Moonjellies*, where they eat fried clams and clam chowder. Another children's book that mentions clams and shows clam digging is Robert McCloskey's *One Morning in Maine*. Find the New England area on your map. Place the story disk there and consider clam chowder and a glass of cranberry-apple juice for lunch.

Social Studies: Relationships

Grandparents: Maggie lives with her grandmother. This is one of several stories you will read in the *Five In A Row* curriculum that depicts special relationship between a child and a grandparent. Have your student find out special facts about her grandparents (even if they are no longer living), such as their favorite foods, hobbies, places to visit, etc.

Nicknames: "That wasn't his real name of course. It was Uriah Peabody, but Maggie had called him Mr. Whiskers ever since she could remember. Maggie was very fond of Mr. Whiskers."

Nicknames are not one's legal or real name. They are made up—sometimes based on what a person does, like "Speedy" for a runner, or based on what they look like as in the case of Mr. Whiskers.

Ask your student if she has a nickname. Do you remember a nickname you had when you were small? Share the most interesting nicknames you've ever heard.

Disagreeable people: Mr. Horace, the man who smells of lavender and carries a gold cane, is not what he appears to be. He is a thief. He is willing to take something that is not his just so he can make money. Mr. Horace is a disgrace and he is also tricky. He tricks Maggie's grandmother into revealing her recipe's hiding place.

Talk with your student about people who sometimes don't tell the truth, who are tricky and who want something so badly they are willing to steal it. These kinds of people are difficult to deal with, but there will always be some who are like this. Again, one of the things your student can do is to continue doing the right things herself and be willing to forgive the people who have wronged her.

Mr. Whiskers (and you *know* how much he wants the pie) models forgiveness valiantly, and with true character as he gives Mr. Horace the last piece!

Judging by appearance: Maggie's grandmother bases her feelings about Mr. Whiskers and Mr. Horace solely on their outward appearances. Mr. Whiskers seems to the grandmother to be less desirable because he does not smell of lavender (a plant used to scent soap) and because he does not carry a gold cane, which she considers fashionable.

While it may not be wrong to be careful about a person that may not look "right" to you, Maggie's grandmother had some clues to help her make a good judgment. Ask how Grandmother might have known what Mr. Whiskers was like. What clues did she have? Your student might infer that Mr. Whiskers has lived nearby for some time because Maggie has called him by his nickname ever since she could remember. Also, Maggie obviously likes him and he helps her with her chores. Grandmother has been able to observe him and he has given her no concrete reason to be worried. She just doesn't like the way he is dressed. Grandmother finds out that judging solely on looks can be deceptive. Ask your student how the grandmother finds out this kind of judging is wrong? Does she change her mind about Mr. Whiskers? (Yes she does.)

Social Studies: History - Thanksgiving

There are many children's books explaining Thanksgiving, its origins, and traditions. Ask your student why she thinks people celebrate Thanksgiving and what the word "thanksgiving" means. Talk about the "first Thanksgiving" and the reasons why people continue to celebrate it. Ask her what she remembers about the way her family celebrates this holiday. What are the special things they do and the special foods they eat? Does her family go to church, have grandparents or other family over, or watch the Macy's Thanksgiving Day Parade and the football games? Maggie's grandmother, in *Cranberry Thanksgiving*, suggests they all sing "We Gather Together," a traditional Thanksgiving hymn. You'll find a copy of this classic song at the end of this unit.

Each family has unique traditions that your student can begin to appreciate. It is also good for her to know that not everyone does things the way her family does them. Teaching loving tolerance for others and their traditions is a lesson in manners which should not be missed.

Holiday time is a good time to brush up on "fine manners." Remind your student that a soldier does not stand at attention all the time. In the same way your student can learn she has especially fine manners that are like standing at attention. She may not perform to the same degree all the time, but for special dinners the "at attention manners" may be in force. And a good soldier can stand at attention when necessary.

In *Cranberry Thanksgiving*, Maggie and her Grandmother know that sharing is an important part of Thanksgiving. It is not whether the spoons all match, but rather the careful preparations that make the day special. Through the decorations, food and most of all through people being together, we turn a common Thursday into a special holiday.

Molly's Pilgrim, a heart-warming story, links the Thanksgiving tradition to the Jewish feast Sukkos. Barbara Cohen writes of a girl named Molly who is cruelly teased by her classmates until they find the tradition of thanking God for the harvest began long ago with people like Molly and her family.

Language Arts: Setting

The setting for *Cranberry Thanksgiving* is concise and well-done. The first page states: "She [Maggie] and her grandmother lived at the edge of a lonely cranberry bog in New England, and the winds were cold at the edge of the sea." The action of the story actually begins on the next page. Have your student imitate this introductory setting with characters and places of her own choosing. For example: "Darcy lived with his uncle at the foot of a pine-covered mountain in Canada, where the bears roamed the woods and the sky was clear."

Language Arts: Repetition

Repetitions are found in the text of *Cranberry Thanksgiving*. Mr. Whiskers asks to sing "Sixteen Men on a Dead Man's Chest" (an old sea song about pirates) during the beginning of the dinner. Grandmother is horrified, but by the end of the story Grandmother repeats the idea by suggesting the same song, herself.

Another of Mr. Whiskers' requests is also repetitive. The rhythm (though not the words exactly) and the idea are repetitive. At the beginning of the dinner you read:

"How delicious!" said Maggie.
"How exquisite!" said Mr. Horace.
"How about some more?" said Mr. Whiskers.

and then near the end of the story:

"How delicious, " said Maggie.
"How delightful," said Grandmother.
"How about another piece?" said Mr. Whiskers.

Now you know why it isn't strange at all that Mr. Whiskers always shows up when Grandmother takes down her great yellow bowl and all the good things that go into it. He doesn't want the recipe—he wants something to eat!

Language Arts: Poetic Prose Description

"Everything was cooked with crisp edges and tender centers." These words cause your mouth to water and are descriptive in a poetic way. Alliteration helps make the words poetic with the "s" sound occurring five time in this line. Remember, alliteration is the repeated *sound* of a certain letter, not the exact letter itself; the "c" makes the same sound as "s."

Also there is a balance of the descriptive words, *crisp edges, tender centers*. Perhaps you and your student will remember these words each year at Thanksgiving, for poetic phrasing is memorable!

Language Arts: Poetic Device - Onomatopoeia

The literary device where a word makes the sound of the same object (the "snarl" of the saw or the "buzzing" of the bees) is onomatopoeia. In this story, the sounds of scuffling (Crash—clumpity!) is onomatopoeia.

Language Arts: Layout of a Manuscript

In *Cranberry Thanksgiving*, the layout of the text of the story contains wonderful variety. The words are sometimes at the top of the page, sometimes at the bottom. Sometimes they are on each separate page and other times only on one page with the rest of the picture opposite. Ask your student to follow the print with her finger as you quickly turn each page. She may say the print is at the top, bottom, the left or right. Even if she cannot read, she can see that she might find printed words in different places on each page. If your student is older, she can note the differences and remember that the text and pictures of books can be laid out in many ways. If he decides at some point to write and illustrate her own book she will make these same choices.

Language Arts: Vocabulary

aura   A faint smell.

starch   A substance that can be used to make fabric stiff.

wilt(ed)   Become damp and limp; also a synonym for defeated.

dart(ed)   To move quickly from one place to another.

turnips   (Point out this root vegetable at the market.)

peer(ed)   To look intently at something.

murmur(ed)   To speak in hushed tones and somewhat indistinctly.

exquisite   Extremely wonderful and perfect.

bog   A low-lying damp or watery area.

Language Arts: Elements of a Good Story

Discuss the elements of a good story in relation to *Cranberry Thanksgiving*:

Setting:	The setting appears on the first page.
Conflict:	The conflict becomes: is someone trying to steal the famous recipe?
Rising Action:	The tension, or rising action builds with the question: which is the thief, Mr. Whiskers or Mr. Horace? At the dinner, Mr. Horace tricks Grandmother into revealing the recipe's hiding place.
Climax:	The most exciting moment is "Oh, he's got it!" and "It's Mr. Horace!"
Denouement:	(day new MAHN) The falling action or resolution occurs when Grandmother throws Mr. Horace out, and then forgives him and offers him pie. There is also final resolution between Grandmother and Mr. Whiskers when she offers to sing "Sixteen Men on a Dead Man's Chest"!

Cranberry Thanksgiving

Language Arts: Figurative Language - Simile

"Maggie darted about like a black-stockinged bird," we read on the first page. Maggie is not a bird, but the author compares her to one. A simile is a comparison of two unlike things using the connective word "like" or "as."

In this simile, we see Maggie with long, bent, black-stockinged legs like the picture of the sea bird. The word "darting," which often describes a bird, is used in describing Maggie's actions.

Using similes in writing adds to the descriptive process and creates pictures in your mind of what the author see and wants you to see.

Have your student practice creating similes using the examples at the end of this unit.

Art: Partial View

Ask your student if she likes the picture where Maggie is peeking out the door at the recipe robber. This unusual half-face is an interesting painting to try to imitate. Take some symmetrical object, a toy animal or a ball, and put a large book or piece of cardboard in front of it to block half the view. Try drawing this "half-object." Don't forget to include in the drawing what it is that is blocking the view. Maggie's half-face would not have been so interesting without the balance of the door on the other side.

Art: Light and Dark

Contrast the picture where Mr. Whiskers is helping Maggie with her chores to the picture where Mr. Whiskers is chasing Mr. Horace around the tree. Flip back and forth, looking at each picture. Ask your student what the illustrators do to make the first picture look like day and the second picture look like night. (The artists use brighter yellows in the "chores" picture, and less yellow, except for the windows, along with more dark blues and purples in the "night" picture.) Try using dark blues and dark purples to make night scenes and remember that sources of light can be the moon, stars, lighted windows, lightning, fire, etc.

Art: Warm Palette and Silhouettes

Wende and Harry Devlin paint these pictures using a warm palette (warm yellows, oranges, reds, browns and teal blues and greens with yellow added), in keeping with the subject of Thanksgiving: a day of family togetherness and warmth. This warm color theme reaches its climax at the hearth fire scene as Maggie's family and friends eat the pie. Long a favorite illustration of children, this silhouetted picture draws you into the room and practically puts a piece of pie in your lap! The contrast of the white collars and cuffs (ask your student what these remind him of—perhaps the Pilgrims) to the black silhouettes is striking. The glow of the fire is just right for the end of the Thanksgiving dinner.

A silhouette (si luh WET) is the dark outline of a person or object shown against a lighter background. There is no detail in the two-dimensional figure and it is usually done entirely in black. Here, the white cuff and collar are the exception to a typical silhouette. Using a strong light and an easel (or board) with white paper, teacher and student may draw silhouettes of each other, and other interesting objects in profile. Be sure to use the word "profile" and explain what it means. Again, this information may not be fully grasped now but this introduction of ideas helps your student's retention later.

Math: Measuring Skills - Baking

Review what you learned in previous lessons about measuring skills in the kitchen. Then add more difficulty to it. For instance, if you introduced cups and half cups, now use quarter cups and eighth cups. Explain the equivalents: two quarter cups make a half cup, etc. Try using third cups and also make use of measuring spoons. Then use these skills to make Grandmother's Famous Cranberry Bread. You can find the recipe in the back of the story book. Many FIAR families have established a Thansgiving family tradition by making this delicious recipe each year!

Science: Seasons

In the United States, celebration of Thanksgiving takes place at the end of fall, and just before winter in the areas of the country with four distinct seasons. See if your student remembers the seasons and can name them and tell some characteristics about each one. If not, just talk about fall and the special things you associate with that season. (Rainy weather, harvesting crops, falling colored leaves, cool weather, school beginning, bluish-purple clouds, crisp apples, bonfires, Labor Day, squirrels hiding nuts, birds flying south, etc.)

Science: Starch

Starch is a substance found in the seeds of corn, rice, beans, etc. and in the stems, roots and tubers of tapioca, potatoes and arrowroot. There are different processes by which starch is removed and it has many uses. Two of the common household uses of starch are to thicken soups, for which we use cornstarch and arrowroot, and to make ironed clothes stiff and smooth.

When the story says, " ... the starch seemed to leave Mr. Horace, " the picture shows him crumpled in his clothing, but he seems to be crumpled in spirit, too. Using spray starch, you can demonstrate starching a handkerchief and ironing it. When your student has seen and felt what starch does for fabric, take a squirt bottle of water and let her lightly spray the cloth. It should "wilt" quite nicely for her, and give a wonderful visual picture of "the starch coming out of Mr. Horace!" Then talk about "wilting inside," that terrible feeling of knowing that one has done wrong, of being found out, and being shunned by people. It doesn't seem as if being deceptive is worth the emotional consequences!

Iodine test for starch: Place a drop of medicinal iodine (found at drugstores) on bread, potato, fruit, carrot, flour, and orange juice. If the item turns dark blue/black there is starch present. Try the test on laundry starch or spray a puddle of spray starch and try a drop of iodine there, testing for the presence of starch.

Begin a list of methods of testing for certain substances and add to it as you come across more. For instance, a method of testing for acid/bases uses litmus paper. There are many such tests that your student will encounter as she progresses through school. Therefore, keeping a list makes an easy review. Place the list in the science section of your student's notebook.

Science: Chemistry - Leavening and Chemical Reaction

Explain that when you bake, you need an ingredient that causes bread, cornbread, quickbreads, cakes and cookies to rise. Show your student an uncooked cake and ask her if she would like the cake if it stayed flat in the pan.

One of the things a cook might use for leavening (rising agent) is baking soda. Explain that another ingredient in the batter will react with the soda. This reaction will cause gas bubbles that make the cake rise. The second ingredient can be buttermilk, lemon juice, yogurt or vinegar. All of these are acidic and react with the alkaline soda to form gas. Have your student measure (whatever quantity you name) fresh baking soda into a bowl and set it in the sink. Then have her add some buttermilk, yogurt, lemon juice or vinegar and see if a chemical reaction takes place. It should form bubbles and possibly run over the edge of the bowl. (For your older student you can explain that the chemical reaction is releasing **carbon dioxide** gas bubbles.)

A **chemical reaction** is different from a mixture. In *The Clown of God*, also in this volume, there is a science lesson about mixtures. Mixtures occur when several compounds mix together, but each remains chemically separate, held together physically by the liquid like vegetables in a pot of soup. A chemical reaction, on the other hand, allows two or more compounds to combine and form one or more **new compounds**, different from the initial ingredients, like the chemical reaction that takes place when an acidic liquid is added to baking soda.

Teacher's Notes

The *Five in a Row* lesson options for each unit in the manual are all you need to teach your child. The additional resource area provided below is simply a place to jot down relevant info you've found that you might want to reference.

CRANBERRY THANKSGIVING

Date:
Student:

Five in a Row Lesson Topics Chosen:

Social Studies:

Language Arts:

Art:

Math:

Science:

Relevant Library Resources: Books, DVDs, Audio Books

Websites or Video Links:

Related Field Trip Opportunities:

Favorite Quote or Memory During Study:

Cranberry Thanksgiving

We Gather Together

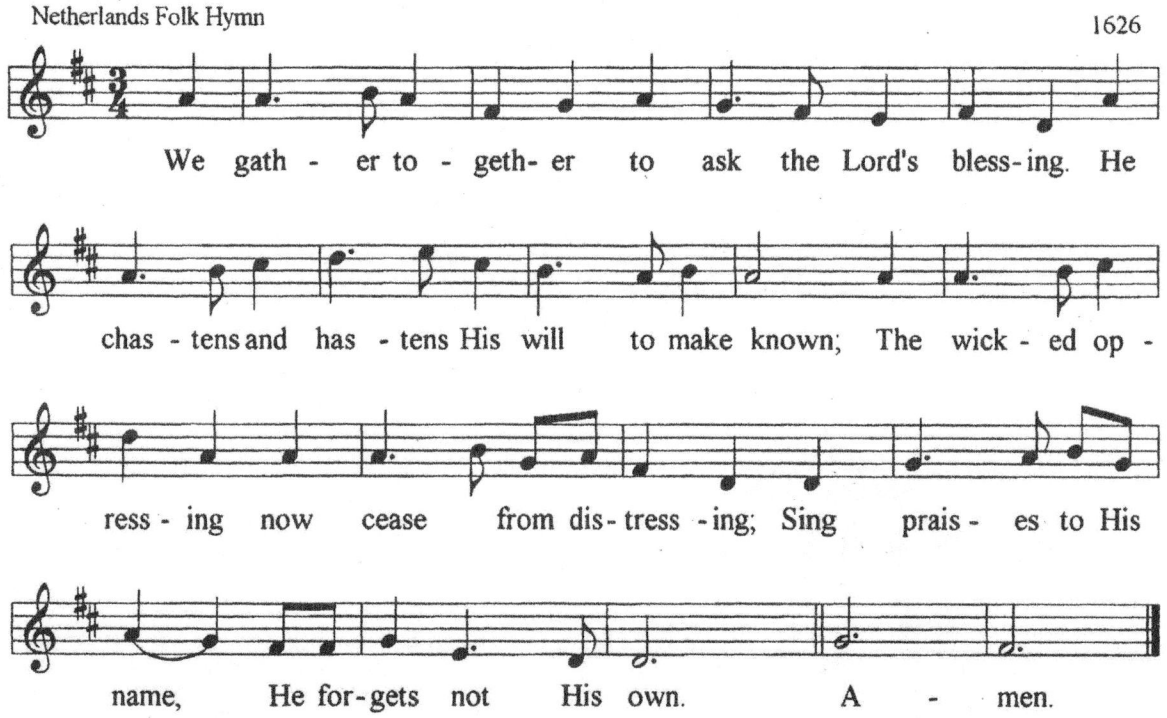

Netherlands Folk Hymn 1626

We gather together to ask the Lord's blessing. He chastens and hastens His will to make known; The wicked oppressing now cease from distressing; Sing praises to His name, He forgets not His own. A - men.

Verse 2

Beside us to guide us our God with us joining
Ordaining, maintaining His Kingdom Divine.
So from the beginning the fight we were winning
Thou, Lord, was at our side all glory be Thine!

Verse 3

We all do extol Thee our leader triumphant
And pray that Thou still our defender will be.
Let Thy congregation escape tribulation
Thy name be ever praised O, Lord, make us free.

Five in Row Volume One

Name:
Date:
Language Arts: **Figurative Language - Simile**

A simile is a comparison of two unlike things using the word "like" or "as," such as "Maggie darted about like a black-stockinged bird."

Have your student practice creating similes using the examples below. Your students' answers will vary and be based on their age and comprehension of this exercise. For a younger student you may give them two or three ideas to choose between or wait until they are older to use this activity sheet.

1. The slipper was as soft as _____ .

2. _____ was as loud as fireworks.

3. The cranberry bog was lonely like _____ .

4. The fire seemed cheerful like _____ .

5. _____ was as homey as _____ .

6. The man was as tall as _____ .

7. The wool sweater was as scratchy as _____ .

8. The hot summer day wilted the flowers like _____ .

Possible Answers:
1. The slipper was as soft as **a fluffy kitten**.
2. **The man's voice** was as loud as fireworks.
3. The cranberry bog was lonely like **an empty seat beside you at the movies**.
4. The fire seemed cheerful like **warm soup on a cold night**.
5. **The dulcimer music** was as homey as **gooseberry pie**.
6. The man was as tall as **a skyscraper**.
7. The wool sweater was as scratchy as **sandpaper**.
8. The hot summer day wilted the flowers like **a scorching furnace**.

Name:
Date:
Science: **Seasons**

Make a list of things that we associate with each season. Fill in the blanks with things that come to mind for spring, summer, fall and winter, and color in the boxes with pictures or colors associated with that season.

SPRING	SUMMER
_____	_____
_____	_____
_____	_____

FALL	WINTER
_____	_____
_____	_____
_____	_____

Five in Row Volume One

Another Celebrated Dancing Bear

Title: *Another Celebrated Dancing Bear*
Author: Gladys Scheffrin-Falk
Illustrator: Barbara Garrison
Copyright: 1991
Summary: Envy and jealousy are overcome by a true friend who shares his time and expertise.

Social Studies: Geography and Culture

Russia is extremely large—about twice the area of the United States. It has geographic extremes including cold regions (Siberia), high mountains, grassy plains and forests. Known for its caviar (a salty relish made from sturgeon or salmon roe/eggs), wheat and cotton, you can also find tigers, camels and reindeer in Russia! If you've ever heard of lemmings, you will find them there too. Russia is also known for its love of the arts. For **centuries** (groups of 100 years) they have produced **fine ballet** (such as the Bolshoi Ballet Company), excellent **authors** and **playwrights** (such as Dostoyevsky and Chekov), **art and world-class music** (such as *The Nutcracker Suite*, written by Tchaikovsky). Collectors around the world prize Russian stacking dolls, called matryoshka, and intricately painted black lacquer Russian boxes. Consider listening to a little Tchaikovsky during lunch!

There are three cities mentioned in *Another Celebrated Dancing Bear*. Although this story was set many years ago in Czarist Russia (prior to the 1917 revolution), you can still visit those cities today: Minsk, St. Petersburg and Moscow. See if you can find them on a map. Now place your story disk on Russia.

Another Celebrated Dancing Bear

From the time setting of this story when the czars ruled Russia, through the communist takeover, the Russian people did not often enjoy the freedoms we have in the United States. You may want to discuss freedoms such as voting, free business enterprise, speech, religion, etc.

With your older student you may want to discuss Russia's czarist history, the communist revolution of 1917, the formation of the Soviet Union, the role of communism in world history, the Cold War, the fall of communism in Russia, etc. Students may also be interested in the Soviet Union's early lead in the "space race" with its cosmonauts.

Social Studies: Occupations

Ask your student if he knows what is meant by "someone's occupation." If necessary, explain that an occupation is a job. When the story begins what does Boris Bear do? What does Max do? Does your student think Boris doesn't like his occupation? What seems exciting about Max's job? Can people change their jobs or occupations? (Remember Mike Mulligan and Mary Anne from *Mike Mulligan and His Steam Shovel*?) What does Boris have to do to change jobs? (He has to learn how to dance and practice a lot.) Is it hard for him? (It is both hard and enjoyable.) Point out that for some people the job of caring for the animals would be the job they would most want to do. But Boris doesn't find the joy in that job that he discovers in dancing. Finding the right job is an important concept to think about.

Have your student think of occupations he might enjoy. Some students might have strong feelings about a particular occupation already.

See the activity sheet at the end of this unit for a list-making lesson on occupations. Add to this list whenever your student recognizes another type of job and if possible have him look for pictures to illustrate the list. Sometimes libraries have stacks of used magazines that are free or nearly free, which have pictures of people engaged in various occupations. Or your student may enjoy drawing a picture to illustrate each occupation.

Social Studies: Relationships - Hospitality

Max, seeing that his friend Boris is glum, greets him with a friendly wave and invites him in for tea. Max helps him off with his jacket and hangs it in the closet. He puts the samovar on to boil. Use this excellent story to discuss ways to be hospitable. Sometimes our friends may not be happy. How can we know how they are feeling? What are the clues? (They may be quiet, withdrawn, or have a sad countenance, etc.) How can we be encouraging? (Show concern, take time to listen, etc.) Talk about manners and being polite, respectful and caring.

You and your student can plan to invite someone to share a snack that you prepare together. Talk about the ways you will greet your guest and other forms of good manners.

Social Studies: Relationships

Another Celebrated Dancing Bear presents the issues of friendship, envy and jealousy. Talk about these kind of relationships and emotions. Discuss the fact that even with good friends or family there can be many different emotions: love, anger, envy, etc. Discuss positive ways to deal with them.

How does Max handle Boris' jealousy? He loves his

friend and recognizes his sadness. Max is even willing to sacrifice his own time to help Boris learn to dance.

Language Arts: Vocabulary

czar   An absolute ruler in Russia prior to the 1917 revolution.

elegent   Rich and luxurious.

glum   Sad and miserable.

samovar   A metal urn with an internal heating tube, used in Russia for making tea.

magnificent   Fantastic, wonderful.

jealous   Envy of or anger with someone because of what they're like or what they have.

audience   Those watching a performance.

marvelous   Very good, wonderful.

embraced   Hugged.

pyramid   In a triangle shape; (find the monkeys sitting in a pyramid).

comical   Funny.

Language Arts: Characterization

"Boris was a heavy-footed brown bear whose heart was as soft as butter." "Max—short for Maximovich—was taller than Boris and always seemed quite elegant."

Descriptive language, as in the examples above, helps bring personality and life to the characters in this story. In order to learn to include such characterizations in his own writings, have your student do some descriptions patterned exactly after the above character sentence. For instance:

"Boris was a heavy-footed brown bear whose heart was as soft as butter," might become:
Sam was a lonely-hearted little boy whose clothes were as tattered as rags.

If it is too difficult for your student to think of an entire sentence, try doing one phrase at a time: "Boris was a heavy-footed brown bear ..." could become: Sam was a quick-thinking six-year-old .... And then, "whose heart was soft as butter," could be: whose hands were strong as steel, etc.

A sentence patterned after the descriptive "Max" sentence at the beginning of this lesson, might be:

Berni—short for Bernadette—was faster than Jenny and always seemed quite active.

Creating descriptive phrases will help your student learn to bring personality and life to characters. These will eventually be used by your student in his own stories.

Language Arts: Drama

Have your student act out the following action words from the story or act them out together:

applauded
bowed
beamed
drew near
giggling
chattering
mopping his brow
kicking (like the dance step)
leaping

Watch out, hilarity might be the result! Try to do a waltz together or imitate the "one—two—three—four"—glide forward then backward described in Boris' first lesson.

Language Arts: Titles

In the story by Gladys Scheffrin-Falk, the title foreshadows the plot. In the beginning of the story there is one celebrated dancing bear, and by the end of the story there are two celebrated dancing bears—***Another Celebrated Dancing Bear***! Continue to remind your student that good titles require thought. Some are just names like *Madeline*, while some are questions like *Who Owns the Sun?* Others are inspiring like *The Glorious Flight* and some are mysterious like *Very Last First Time*. Most authors carefully consider a special title for each of their stories. Creative writing includes creative titles.

Art: Etchings

The explanation of the illustrations is found on the back of the title page. It tells in detail how etchings are done.

Let the student see some story books with watercolor paintings and help him recognize the differences between watercolor illustrations and these highly detailed line etchings of Barbara Garrison.

Art: Color

Another Celebrated Dancing Bear reveals the warmth and hospitality of a hearth on a winter's night. The illustrator has chosen a burnt umber ink, a brown with a touch of warmth, and added a watercolor overwash for the color portions. The colors (the warm red-orange of the vests, the scarves and the flowers) are nearly the color of a good hearth fire. Point out that the artist thought about it and chose colors to go along with the story—to help tell the story. Remind your student that *he* can make color choices to go along with what *he* is trying to say in *his* picture.

Art: Architecture

At the top of the first page there is a picture of a Russian skyline. Ask the student what he sees in in this picture that is not familiar to him. (Perhaps he sees unusual, spiral top "onion" domes—can your studen think why they might be called that?) Trace the domes from the activity sheet at the end of this unit. Color them, cut them out and paste them on paper. Now, let your student draw rectangular buildings and towers beneath the domes. In this way he can create his own Russian styled skyline.

Art: Noticing Detail

Reading *Another Celebrated Dancing Bear* for five days in a row will give your student a chance to notice more and more detail in the pictures. The illustration on the third page has a door knocker, a mail slot, and funny handles on the umbrellas. Barbara Garrison has included many small details of Russian life and art in her etchings. Observe your student as he is able to point out new examples of illustration detail as you read the story each day.

Math: Hours on a Clock

Boris' first lessons were on Mondays, Wednesdays and Fridays from seven o'clock to eight. Take this opportunity to introduce the hours on an analog clock. Draw a very large circle on paper or cloth on the floor. Put in the numbers like the face of a clock. With your student, walk around the clock saying, "One o'clock, two o'clock, etc.," as you step on the numbers. For your older student's more advanced lesson, ask how many hours are between one o'clock and five o'clock, etc.

Math: Seven Days in a Week

Discuss the seven days of the week and their names. How many days are there in a traditional modern American working week? How many days a week does your student think his grocery store is open? His library, post office, or farmer's market? For a calendar activity sheet to use with this lesson, see the page at the end of the unit for *Grandfather's Journey*.

Science: Boiling Point and Freezing Point

Hospitable Max sets the samovar to boil. Explain that when heat is applied to water the molecules in the water begin to move around more rapidly. When the temperature of the water reaches a certain temperature (212 degrees Fahrenheit or 100 degrees Celsius), the molecules move so fast they begin to "jump out of the pan" in the form of steam! This means the water is boiling. (The freezing point of water is 32 degrees Fahrenheit and 0 degrees Celsius). Your student might enjoy drawing two thermometers showing the freezing and boiling points of water in both Fahrenheit and Celsius. (Remember, these boiling and freezing point degrees are for water; other substances have different boiling and freezing points.)

Note: After completing this lesson, you might enjoy reading *How the Tzar Drinks His Tea* by Benjamin Elkin. This is a wonderful story that shows more Russian architecture and provides further insights into Russian culture. It's a story too good to miss!

Teacher's Notes

The *Five in a Row* lesson options for each unit in the manual are all you need to teach your child. The additional resource area provided below is simply a place to jot down relevant info you've found that you might want to reference.

ANOTHER CELEBRATED DANCING BEAR

Date: _____

Student: _____

Five in a Row Lesson Topics Chosen:

Social Studies:
_____
_____
_____

Language Arts:
_____
_____
_____

Art:
_____
_____
_____

Math:
_____
_____
_____

Science:
_____
_____
_____

Relevant Library Resources: Books, DVDs, Audio Books
_____
_____
_____
_____
_____
_____
_____
_____

Websites or Video Links:
_____
_____
_____
_____
_____
_____
_____
_____

Related Field Trip Opportunities:
_____
_____
_____

Favorite Quote or Memory During Study:
_____
_____
_____

Another Celebrated Dancing Bear

Domes for a Russian Skyline

Reproduce or trace these domes and have your student color, cut and paste them along the top of a blank piece of paper, at different heights and grouping some of them together. Now draw buildings beneath them for a Russian style skyline.

Name:
Date:
Geography: **Russia Flag**

The flag of Russia is a tri-color flag with 3 equal horizontal fields. The top is white, the middle is blue and the bottom is red. *For more information, see Parts of a Flag on page 222.*

Color in the Russia flag below.

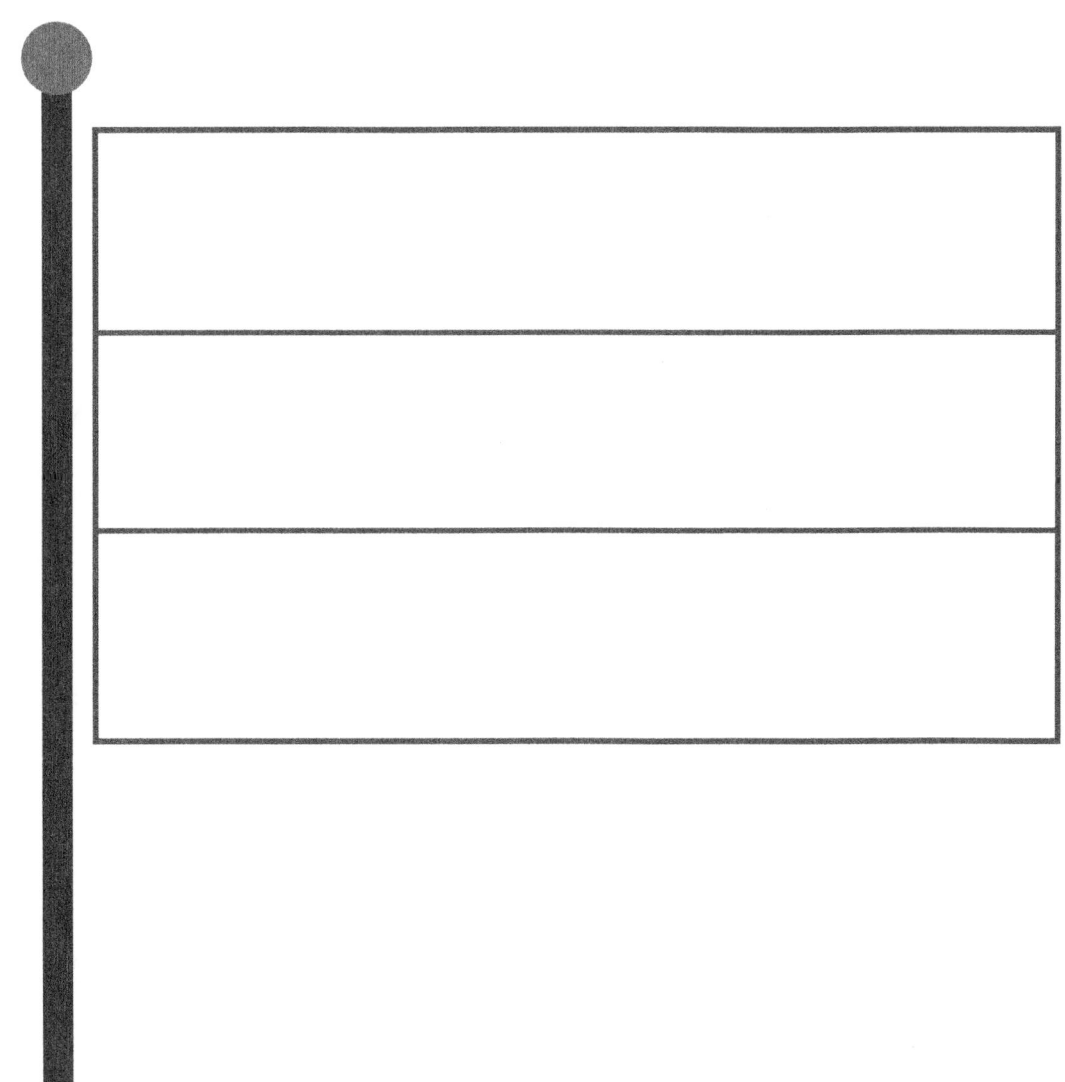

Name:
Date:
Social Studies: **Occupations**

Create an ongoing list of occupations that your student can continue adding to as they learn or discover new jobs they might enjoy.

Occupations

_____   _____

_____   _____

_____   _____

_____   _____

_____   _____

_____   _____

_____   _____

_____   _____

_____   _____

Papa Piccolo

Title: *Papa Piccolo*
Author: Carol Talley
Illustrator: Itoko Maeno
Copyright: 1992
Summary: A tomcat finds responsibilities, joys and satisfaction as he decides to adopt kittens!

Social Studies: Geography

Venice, Italy is the beautiful setting for *Papa Piccolo*. From the dedication page to the end of the story and even on the inside hard covers, you'll find information about Italy and scenes to help you remember the information. For the teacher: See if you can locate a copy of *Venice: Birth of a City* by Piero Ventura at your local library.

First, show your student where Italy is on the map and globe. Talk about the shape of the country. Many people say it looks like a tall boot with a high heel that appears to step into the Mediterranean Sea. Place the story disk for *Papa Piccolo* on Italy on your map or globe and refer to it each day you read the story.

Second, explain the streets of water and how the gondola boats take people where they need to go. Ask your student if she'd like to live where many of the streets are water. Maybe she can think of reasons why that would be fun and other reasons why it would not. (Where would you ride a bike or roller skate?)

Also, notice the architecture of the buildings, the bridges (pp. 25 and 28), the clothes of the people, and the bright colors (bright blues, yellows and reds) especially on the poles in the canals.

Social Studies: Foreign Language

There are Italian words and names used in *Papa Piccolo*. You might enjoy learning a few Italian words. Use them frequently during the week. This builds vocabulary and intimacy as you share the experience. Some of the words are: bambini (infants, children) p. 12; caro mia (my precious dear) p. 18; and buon giorno (good morning) p. 10. Some of the Italian names in this story are: Caesar, Sophia, Luigi Barbaro, Zampeta's, and the Canal Tolentini. Your student will learn to associate the "sounds" of the names and words with Italy as you use them and read them each day for five days (as she did with the sounds of the French words and names in *The Glorious Flight*). In this way you will provide your student with an introduction to another interesting country.

Social Studies: Family Relations - Fatherhood

Papa Piccolo is about fatherhood. Ask your student to describe a father. Notice on p. 8 that Papa knows what is best for the kittens though they aren't his own, and he sings lullabies to them. Even so, he doesn't want to be responsible for the kittens. What happens to change Papa's mind? (The kittens disappear and he finds himself worrying about them.) After the kittens return (notice the glad look on Papa's face, p. 25) he teaches them what they need to know, pp. 25-27. How to eat spaghetti would be a very important thing to know in Italy! You may want to use the list of what Papa taught the kittens for a memory exercise. See how many of the kittens' lessons your student can remember.

"And the three happy cats looked very much like a family." A family can be different combinations of people. Not every family has both a mother and father and children. For example, if one parent dies, the remaining parent and children are still a family, etc. Love, discipline and sacrifice are needed for any family, and Papa provides well for his kittens. Page 18 states that love, care, time, patience and a sense of adventure are needed to raise a family.

On back of the title page is a dedication (above the striped poles), "To Papas everywhere." (To *future* papas too?)

Social Studies: Flags

The inside front cover shows the flag of Italy and a smaller city flag of Venice. Using colored paper or watercolor, make flags. Include the Italian flag and the long banner-type city flag of Venice. Fly them from the window or ceiling and celebrate the fun of learning about another country!

Social Studies: History - Marco Polo

What an enjoyable way to introduce the great explorer, Marco Polo! Marco Polo was born in Venice. He traveled from Italy across Europe and Asia to China. He wrote about his adventures and let the people of Europe know about the wonders of China. Some of his descriptions were so amazing it was hard for his readers to believe. It is fitting that Papa names the kittens Marco and Polo. Like the explorer, they live in Venice and they disappear on an adventure. Remind your older student that in writing stories, she may want to choose names that have a meaning beyond a particular character.

Social Studies: Human Relationships - The Homeless and Adoption

When Piccolo presents his plan to Sophia, she just laughs. "Me? Take in two homeless kittens?" This could present an opportunity to talk about actual homeless people. Why are they homeless? There are many different answers. What does the city or town do to help them? Talk about shelters, soup kitchens, food pantries, welfare and job hunting help, etc., available in cities and towns. Often domestic animals also have no homes, which sometimes creates problems. Talk about the ways people help in this area.

Another topic for discussion is adoption. Papa Piccolo was asked if he adopted the kittens. Explain adoption and talk about what's involved, how adoptive parents and children feel, etc. You may also take this opportunity to discuss pet adoption.

Social Studies: Occupations on the Water

Page 22 tells of laundry barges that carry fresh linens to the hotels, garbage barges hauling away the city's refuse (trash), police motor boats on patrol, and water taxis transporting (carrying) eager tourists. Ask your student if she'd like to work on a boat that travels on the canals of Venice. Ask her to be on the lookout for laundry trucks, garbage trucks, police cars and taxis where s*he* lives.

Language Arts: Vocabulary

As with all FIAR vocabulary lessons, you may want to continue making index cards with these vocabulary words and add pictures to illustrate them. These cards can be filed in a box and reviewed every now and then. This will keep the words in mind and in use.

canal (p.5)   An artificial waterway for transportation (or irrigation).

trinket (p.6)   A trifle or a toy; a small piece of jewelry.

sardine (p.6)   A small fish (cats love fish!).

ledge (p. 7)   A small shelf sticking out from a window.

signora (p. 7)   Designates a married Italian woman (like Mrs.).

situation (p.8)   Condition or combination of circumstances.

chime(ed) (p.9)   The striking of bells.

carnival (p.11)   Similar to a very small circus.

regatta (p.29)   Gondola race in Venice; term now used for any boat race.

skiff, scow, barge and gondola (p.10)   Kinds of boats.

persistent (p.14)   Not giving up.

forlorn, glum (p.22)   Sad of face and expression, like one has lost something special.

gilded (p.29)   Covered with gold.

Language Arts: Matching Descriptions

On p. 8 it says, "And then Piccolo sang a little song he remembered from long ago—about stardust and moonbeams and goldfish." Papa sang a lullaby (a bedtime song to help one sleep). Have your student think of some phrases that would put a dog to sleep. For instance, "I'll sing of bones and treats, slippers and silver-lighted dog houses," etc. What phrases could your student think of to put a butterfly to sleep, or a tree, or an eagle, etc.?

Language Arts: Drama and Exercise

There is a lot of action vocabulary found in *Papa Piccolo*. Act out the words with body and facial gestures: strutting, sliding, and feasting, all from p. 12; wheeled, on p. 13; watching, begged and curled up, from p. 15; presented, on p.18; gasped, on p. 19; groaned and leaped, on p. 20; and worried and glum, from p. 22. Also find: tumbled, swung, curious, perched, awoke, prancing, ashamed and puzzled!

Language Arts: Fable - The Fox and the Sour Grapes

Read the fable of the "Fox and the Sour Grapes." (Briefly, the fox sees grapes and longs for them, but when he discovers he cannot reach them from up high, he declares they are probably sour anyway and he never wanted them at all.) Discuss the meaning of this fable. Ask your student to be ready to tell you when she hears a similar part in the story of Papa Piccolo (p.12). Talk about people using the phrase, "That's sour grapes," in their everyday speech. From now on, your student will understand the meaning of this phrase!

Art: Colors and Color Matching

From the title page (don't miss this picture!) to the end of the story, Itoko Maeno's beautiful watercolor paintings let you breathe the air of Italy and enjoy its sights, sounds, smells and tastes. It almost seems as if you have been there! Maeno's use of colors (the bright colors of the Mediterranean) makes the story come alive. Ask your student to make a list of all the colors she sees in the double-page picture that follows the title page. Be prepared to help her with the names for the more difficult ones: aqua, rose, dark violet. Note all the colors that make up the water and others that make up the sky.

With a good set of watercolors (Prang® is a good brand), help your student try to match these colors by mixing her paints. She will learn that there are blues that have a touch of red in them and blues that have a little yellow mixed in. Begin with the simple color wheel at the end of this unit. Show her how the red can have a *tiny* amount of yellow mixed in (not enough to be called orange) or the red can have a *small* amount of blue added and still be a "red."

An advanced concept for your older student is the idea of calling these colors **warm** and **cool** reds. If the red has a tiny amount of yellow added to it, it is called a warm red. Whereas if the red has a touch of blue added to it, it is called a cool red. The same warm-cool designation can apply to yellow, when red or blue is added in tiny amounts. At the end of this unit, you'll find a more advanced color wheel with secondary colors.

Art: Advanced Color Theory - Complementary Colors

By using the second color wheel with its secondary colors, you can begin to teach colors and their complement. A color's complement is sometimes called its opposite because they appear opposite one another on the color wheel. Complementary colors are used to provide contrast and make vivid artistic statements. Maeno has made use of complementary colors on p. 7. Look on the color wheel at the end of this unit and ask your student what is the opposite of red? (green) The artist has painted vivid red geraniums with dark green leaves. She could have chosen to paint pink geraniums but a stronger statement was made with the red and green. Look at the yellow and purple cushion on p. 30. There is a blue and orange picture on p. 20. Look for complementary colors in other paintings. (**Teacher Note:** Another aspect of complementary colors is that if you add equal amounts of each, as red and green, the color will become gray. Such an advanced concept isn't necessary for this lesson.)

Using complementary colors makes a bold statement. Imagine a striking green shirt with a red tie or a beautiful yellow dress that has a purple belt or scarf. People use colors and their opposites in decorating their homes inside and out. A red brick house could have green shutters, etc.

Art: Live Eyes - Highlights

The picture of Papa's face opposite the first words of the story shows a white dot in his eye. Point out to your student that this is an artist's technique. It makes the eyes look more alive. Have her look through the pages of the story and find other examples of this technique, then have her try a drawing or painting where she puts the light dot or highlight in the eye. She will discover that most of the time, rather than put white over other paint she will have to remember to *leave* that spot white. Perhaps she will notice the spot of light in the eyes of animals and people in other illustrations. Look for the highlight in good-quality photos of animals to see the "real thing" that the artist is copying.

Art: Creating the Illusion of Speed

Ask your student how the artist gave the impression the kittens are in a hurry on p.11. (The curving streaks of paint give the feeling that the kittens come from far away, swerve as they run and that they are moving so fast one can hardly see them.) Tightly tie an object (a patterned toy would be good) to the end of a 40-inch string. Now, twirl the string in a circle very quickly. Notice how the object is now just a blur and the patterns have disappeared. This is the effect Itoko Maeno was trying to accomplish in her painting of the kittens. Let your student know that she can try these speed lines and blurred images in her own art to show fast-moving objects and the paths from which they come.

Art: Use of Color for Light

On the page with the first words of the story, the artist has shown lighted windows. She has used yellow in differing shades to create the effect of light coming from the windows. The light is also reflected in the water (also covered in *Ping* and in *Grandfather's Journey*). Let your student try to paint a building with windows, using yellow for the effect of light. Remember, in order for the yellow to be effective, the surrounding scene must look at least somewhat dark.

Math: Counting and Pairs

Count the shoes on p. 17. If this picture shows only one of each pair, how many shoes would there be if each had its mate? If needed, line up small manipulatives to represent each shoe. Then put another beside it making groups of two. Count them all. Talk about the concept of pairs and name things that come in pairs. (Socks, pants [why?], scissors [why?], twins, shoes, earrings, etc.)

For high counting practice try counting all the windows from the beginning of the book to the end. (Notice that in Venice there are flowers boxes hanging in the windows—where else would their gardens be, with streets of water and no yards?)

Science: Human Body - Peripheral Vision

On p. 11 Papa sees something "out of the corner of his eye." Talk about the concept of peripheral vision. Peripheral vision is the ability to see objects to the side while looking straight ahead. Have your student look straight ahead while you move a pencil from around behind her head toward the front. Let her determine when she can first see the pencil using her peripheral vision.

Science: Types and Breeds of Cats

The cat pictured on pp. 17-18 is a purebred Himalayan, which looks somewhat like a long-haired Siamese. In any certain breed there are common characteristics like the blue eyes and patterns of coloring. The kittens, Papa, and Caesar are not purebred cats but have specific patterns of coloring. The kittens are called calico (black and orange spots on white) and tabby (striped).

Teacher's Notes

The *Five in a Row* lesson options for each unit in the manual are all you need to teach your child. The additional resource area provided below is simply a place to jot down relevant info you've found that you might want to reference.

PAPA PICCOLO

Date:
Student:

***Five in a Row* Lesson Topics Chosen:**

Social Studies:

Language Arts:

Art:

Math:

Science:

**Relevant Library Resources:
Books, DVDs, Audio Books**

Websites or Video Links:

Related Field Trip Opportunities:

Favorite Quote or Memory During Study:

Papa Piccolo

Color Wheels
Primary, Secondary and Complementary

With your help, have your child color in the ring around each color wheel with the appropriate colors in each area, blending colors as you move around the circle. For a younger child, simply draw lines inside the circle and have them color pieces of the "pie."

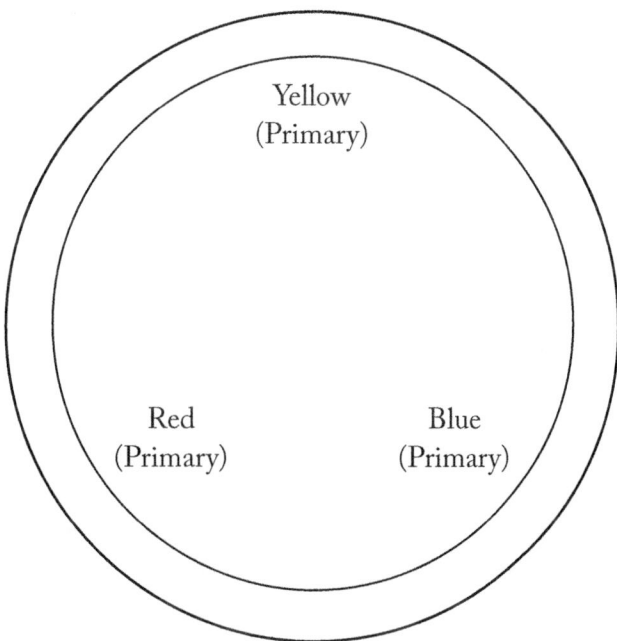

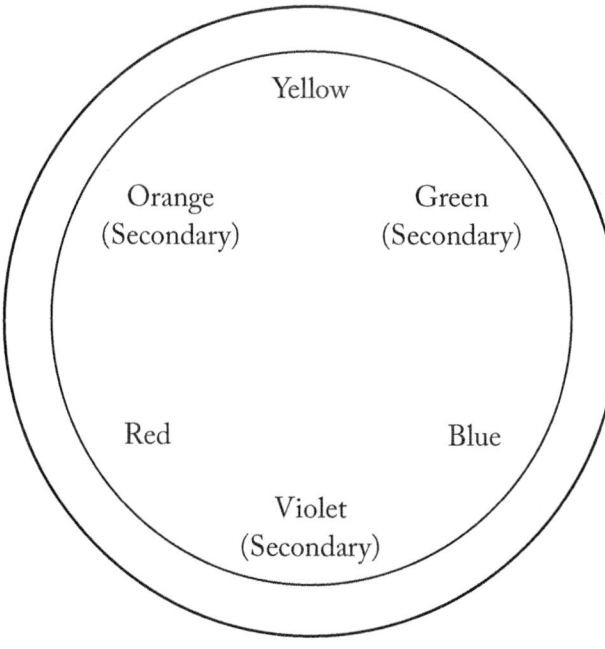

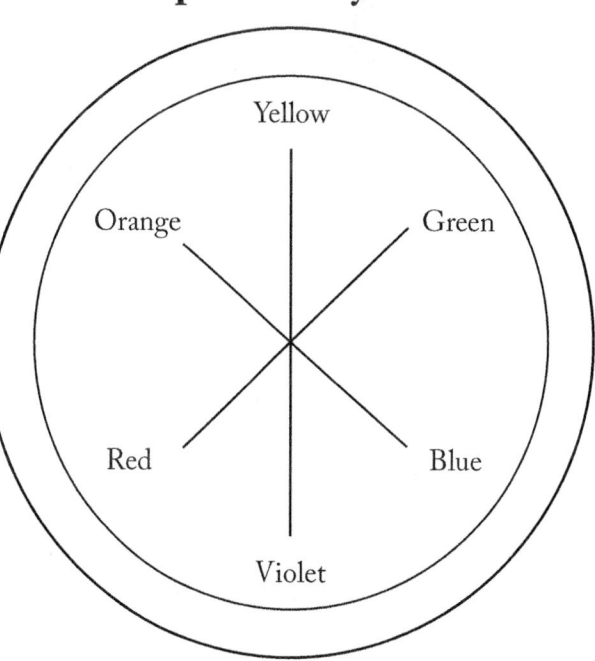

Name:

Date:

Geography: **Italy Flag**

The flag of Italy is a tri-color flag with 3 equal vertical sections. Green is on the hoist side, white in the middle and red on the fly end. *For more information, see Parts of a Flag on page 222.*

Color in the Italy flag below.

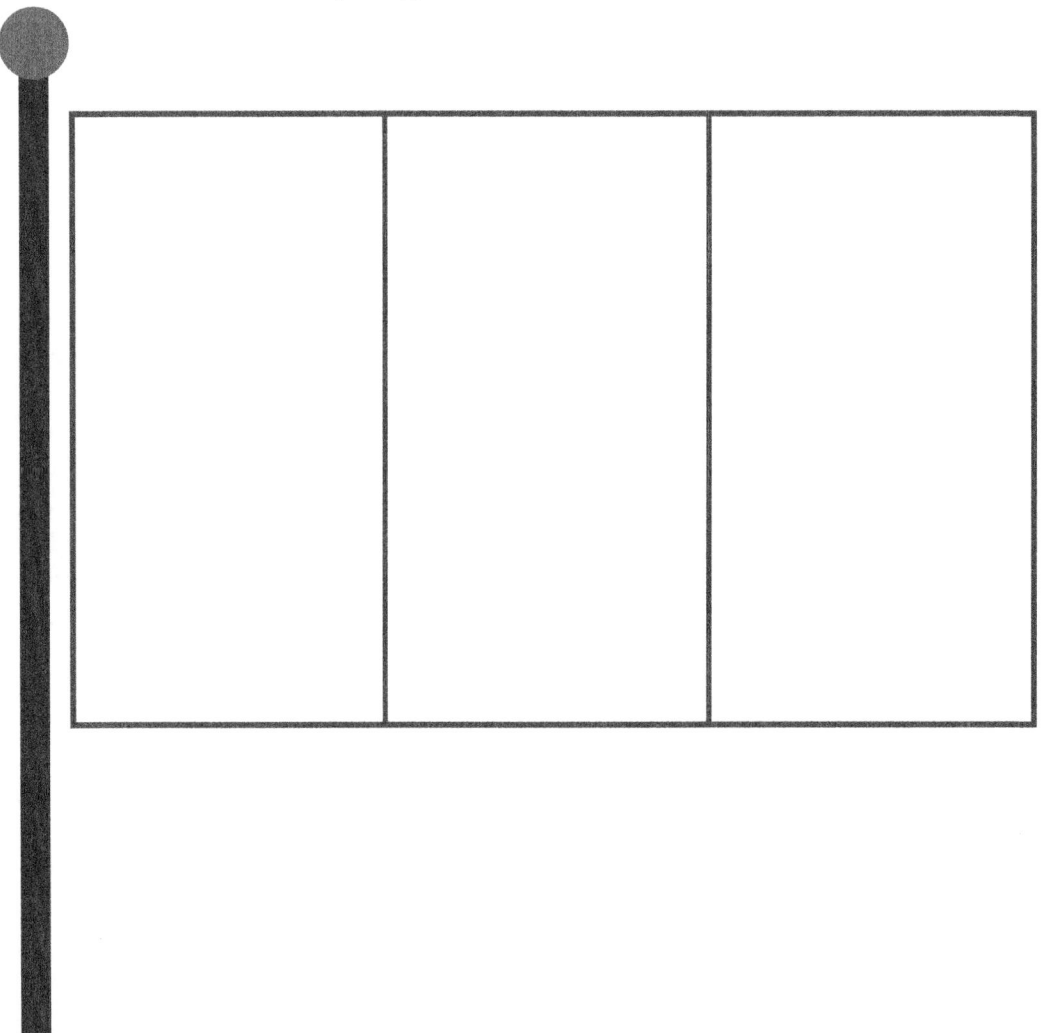

Papa Piccolo

Name:
Date:
Language Arts: **Drama and Exercise**

Charades Game

Copy this page then cut out and shuffle the action vocabulary words. Have your student pick one to act out. Your student can also add more action words to the back of the cards.

It's a good idea to laminate the page before cutting out the cards, to make them more durable.

Curled Up	Sliding	Leaped
Worried	Tumbled	Perched
Awoke	Puzzled	Gasped

Very Last First Time

Title: *Very Last First Time*
Author: Jan Andrews
Illustrator: Ian Wallace
Copyright: 1985
Summary: A little girl embarks on a long-awaited privilege and finds it wonderful and frightening, but in the end, rewarding.

Social Studies: Geography

Very Last First Time is set in Ungava Bay (un GAY vah *or* un GAH vah), Northern Canada. Say Ungava Bay several times. Ask your student if he likes the sound of the name and say it a few times together. This bay empties into the northern Atlantic Ocean, not far from the Arctic Ocean. Use blank story disks to label the Atlantic and Arctic Oceans. Locate Ungava Bay on a map or globe and place the story disk there. Point the disk out each day as you read the story, or see if your student can remember where to place it each day.

Ask your student what he can tell from the pictures and story about the land and climate of northern Canada. It is obviously cold, has jagged rocks, and it is close to the water. This area also has fur-bearing animals, scrub trees, and beautiful sunrises and sunsets. The land type is tundra (nearly level, treeless plains of the Arctic). Key to this book's plot is what occurs when the tide goes out in this frigid climate: the bay's *surface* freezes but as the deeper water recedes with the tide, it leaves an open space for the native people to walk on the bottom of the sea beneath the ice.

Social Studies: Inuit Culture

There is a great deal to be learned about the culture of the Inuit (IN you it) people by examining the story's illustrations, especially the first and second picture. The first picture shows sled dogs, snowshoes, furs being stretched and dried, a church, and colorful clothes. The second picture reveals a modern kitchen, with running water and electricity (not found in the stereotypical igloos), cornflakes, perhaps oatmeal, and even paper towels. Ask your student if he thinks the kitchen looks inviting and enjoy his reasoning.

Talk about the cold temperatures and about the protection of fur boots and parkas (coats with fur hoods). The average temperature in Ungava Bay in January is negative 10 to negative 20 degrees Fahrenheit. The fur-trimmed parkas are made from animal skins. These skins or hides are stretched on doors and the sides of houses. Discuss trapping and tanning, if there is interest. These are traditional activities of the Inuit. Also ask your student why Eva is searching for mussels. (The people of Ungava Bay eat mussels and they must enjoy them to work so hard for them.)

Social Studies: Family Relationships

What sorts of things does your student do with his mother? What sorts of things do children do with their mothers in other cultures? Find pictures of children doing various activities. Eva traditionally (ever since she could remember) had walked on at the bottom of the sea *with* her mother. It was what they did when they wanted mussels to eat.

Talk about the enjoyment of doing things together. Ask your student if he thinks that when Eva was a very young girl, she was glad her mother hadn't just sent her off from their house to search for mussels by herself. When you are young it feels safe and good to be with your parents while doing difficult or new projects. Later when your are older there is more desire to do some things by yourself.

Social Studies: Relationships - First-Time Experiences

Eva walks alone on the bottom of the sea for the first time in her life. Ask your student if he thinks Eva is excited. Does he think gathering food this way sounds like fun? Does he like to try things alone once in a while?

It is a special day when one is finally old enough to be allowed to do a certain new thing for the first time alone. When there has been a process of growth, a maturing, becoming ready for the next adventure or responsibility, then there is a desire for some independence. Discuss activities that your student has had to wait for: walking to a friend's house, taking care of a pet, running an errand alone, etc. How many can your student think of? Was there something you remember waiting for? Was it difficult to wait? Share with each other. Is there something your student is presently waiting to do? (Ride a horse alone, etc.)

Yonie Wondernose, written by Marguerite de Angeli, is a story with a similar incident where seven-year-old Yonie is given responsibility. He then gets to do something he's been waiting for. It is a delightful story about Amish life on a farm.

Language Arts: Story Writing - Good Titles

Discuss the importance of choosing a good title for a story. A creative title often draws you to a book. Jan Andrews thought carefully about the title for *Very Last First Time*. That title is a wonderfully mysterious invitation to the story. How can a first time be last? (Because there is only one first time and after that there will never be for that particular thing another first time.) Your student, too, can think carefully about the titles he chooses for his stories. Add "good titles" to your List of Choices a Writer Can Make.

Language Arts: Vocabulary and Drama

Act out the following words: dragging, shoveling, heaving, peering and fearfully peering, grinning, prying, scraping, singing, humming, scrambling, stumbling, groping, skipping, and squeezing. In acting out the words, your student will increase his vocabulary and remember more difficult words like prying, heaving (lifting or throwing something heavy), peering (looking very intently) and groping (reaching for something that cannot be clearly seen).

Art: Colors and Artistic Style

Ian Wallace used a full palette of colors for this book: warm oranges, yellows and browns, and also cool-toned blues, greens and purples. Your student can see the difference in the picture of Eva first stepping into the ice hole. Her mother says, "Good luck," and the picture is predominately yellows and warm orange. Contrast with the picture of Eva coming out of the ice hole and squeezing her mother's hand. This picture, while containing both warm and cool colors, is mostly made up of cool tones: purples and cool blues.

The illustrations are somewhat **pointillist** (made up of hundreds of tiny dots of paint) in artistic style. You'll also note the strong use of complementary color: purple with orange, blue with yellow, etc. Your student may enjoy imitating the pointillist style with a fine-tipped brush or a cotton swab dipped in watercolor or acrylic paint. Younger students can use colorful markers instead, or even their finger (using finger paints). Try a simple subject such as a house or tree at first. This activity requires patience (many, many dots!), but the result is a unique painting to be proud of!

Art: Detail

Look for detail in Ian Wallace's paintings. Notice the picture behind the last picture of the story: Eva is sitting at a table eating mussels. She is reaping the rewards of her bravery. Discuss being brave, keeping calm, trying new things at the *right* time and feeling proud and happy with new accomplishments. Ask your student if he thinks these mussels that she gathered by herself taste better than any others? She looks very satisfied. (Maybe because she was allowed the responsibility of helping to gather the family food.) Also see if your student can spot the shadow wolf, bear and seal sea monster in the picture where Eva has dropped into the ice hole and has lit her candle.

Math: Ordinal Numbers

If you have not already taught ordinal numbers (numbers that name the order in which objects appear or are counted), use *Very Last First Time* to begin the instruction: Teach about first, second, third, etc. For practice use people in line at the water fountain, grocery store, etc. (Who is first? The man in green. Who is second? The little girl with the doll.) Or line up a row of blocks and ask your student to hand you the third block or the fifth block, etc. For an additional math lesson (or a lesson for a younger student) you can have them count candles, barnacles, mussels, etc.

Science: Safety and Crisis Thinking

Does Eva find out why younger children aren't allowed to go under the ice alone? Eva discovers that her mother has waited for a reason. Eva is old enough not to let panic (sudden uncontrollable fear) cause her to lose her way. If she let fear take over, she might forget the matches in her pocket. Discuss the importance of learning and practicing "crisis thinking:"

CALM DOWN
DON'T PANIC
BE QUIET
THINK CAREFULLY!
WHAT AM I SUPPOSED TO DO?

In following the rules of "crisis thinking," many times people will recall these significant instructions that will help them to safety. In calmness they will be able to make a good plan. There are many different situations in which "crisis thinking" can help: remembering where a door is, or to stay low in a smoke-filled room, or knowing what to do in the first panicky moments of discovering that one is lost or separated from their party. Discuss dangerous predicaments and the safety rules that apply. (There are often free picture brochures of safety tips at the fire stations and police stations.) Consider having your student memorize these steps, using simple hand motions as a memory aid. See the activity sheet at the end of this unit for suggested hand motions.

Science: Health - Dressing for Conditions

Discuss dressing for weather conditions. Dressing in shirt sleeves for 10-degree Fahrenheit weather is dangerous. So is wearing a parka in a 100-degree jungle. Learning to be more independent (doing things without being told) means learning to dress for the weather conditions of the day and even to pay attention to forecasts of changing weather. Draw (or find pictures for) the proper clothing for different weather conditions and in different seasons. Listen to weather forecasts together, and teach your student how to search online for current information.

Science: Subjects for Exploration

Very Last First Time provides an introduction to these topics:

Tides - The water level on the beach becomes more shallow as the tide goes out. The lowering tide allows Eva and her mother to walk under the ice. *Tide* is defined as the alternate rise and fall of the ocean and its inlets, caused by the attraction of the moon and sun. The tide occurs twice in each 24 hours and about 50 minutes. Discuss tides and tide pools (where often small animals are left behind in pools when the tide goes out). If there is interest, find children's books on the topic.

Biome - Biomes are large geographic areas having a similar climate, including the plants and animals that live there. Some different types of biomes are: tundra, coniferous and deciduous forests, deserts and tropical rain forests. Ungava Bay is a tundra-type biome (cold and without trees).

Echo - An echo is the repeating of a sound produced by the reflection of sound waves from a surface. Talk about where you might hear an echo. Echoes are commonly heard where the sound waves are not absorbed but rather reflected, as in a cave, a long, empty hallway, in the mountains, etc. In *Very Last First Time* Eva's song echoes around under the ice. It sounds interesting to her so she sings louder.

Ocean Life - Eva sees the blue-black mussel shells, small shrimps and pinky-purple crabs that live at the ocean. These animals are shellfish. She also sees anemones and seaweed in wet, shiny heaps. There are tide pools left when the tide goes out. In these pools many ocean plants and animals can often be seen. Explore ocean life and make a poster or by drawing some of the subjects you've studied.

Sea Salt - Sea water contains salt. It makes swimming easier because the salt helps the swimmer float. The amount of salt is similar in every ocean because the waves cause a mixing action. Eva could smell the salt in the ocean air. Stir some salt into a small glass of hot water. Can you smell the salt, like the sea? (Obviously, the ocean is not hot water, but the ocean spray does carry the scent of salt.)

Science: Simple Machines

Eva uses her knife as a **lever** (and the rocks or shell as a fulcrum) to pry the mussels off the rocks. Teach (or review) the use of simple machines and how they make life easier for us. Other simple machines include: the **inclined plane**, the **wheel and axle**, the **pulley**, the **screw** and the **wedge**. The wedge and the lever are also studied studied in the lessons for *Who Owns the Sun?*

Teacher's Notes

The *Five in a Row* lesson options for each unit in the manual are all you need to teach your child. The additional resource area provided below is simply a place to jot down relevant info you've found that you might want to reference.

VERY LAST FIRST TIME

Date: _____

Student: _____

***Five in a Row* Lesson Topics Chosen:**

Social Studies:
_____
_____

Language Arts:
_____
_____

Art:
_____
_____

Math:
_____
_____

Science:
_____
_____

Relevant Library Resources: Books, DVDs, Audio Books
_____
_____
_____
_____
_____
_____

Websites or Video Links:
_____
_____
_____
_____
_____
_____
_____

Related Field Trip Opportunities:
_____
_____
_____

Favorite Quote or Memory During Study:
_____
_____
_____

Name:
Date:
Geography: **Canada Flag**

The flag of Canada has a red field with a white square at the center. Within the white square is a red, 11-pointed maple leaf. *For more information, see Parts of a Flag on page 222.*

Color in the Canada flag below.

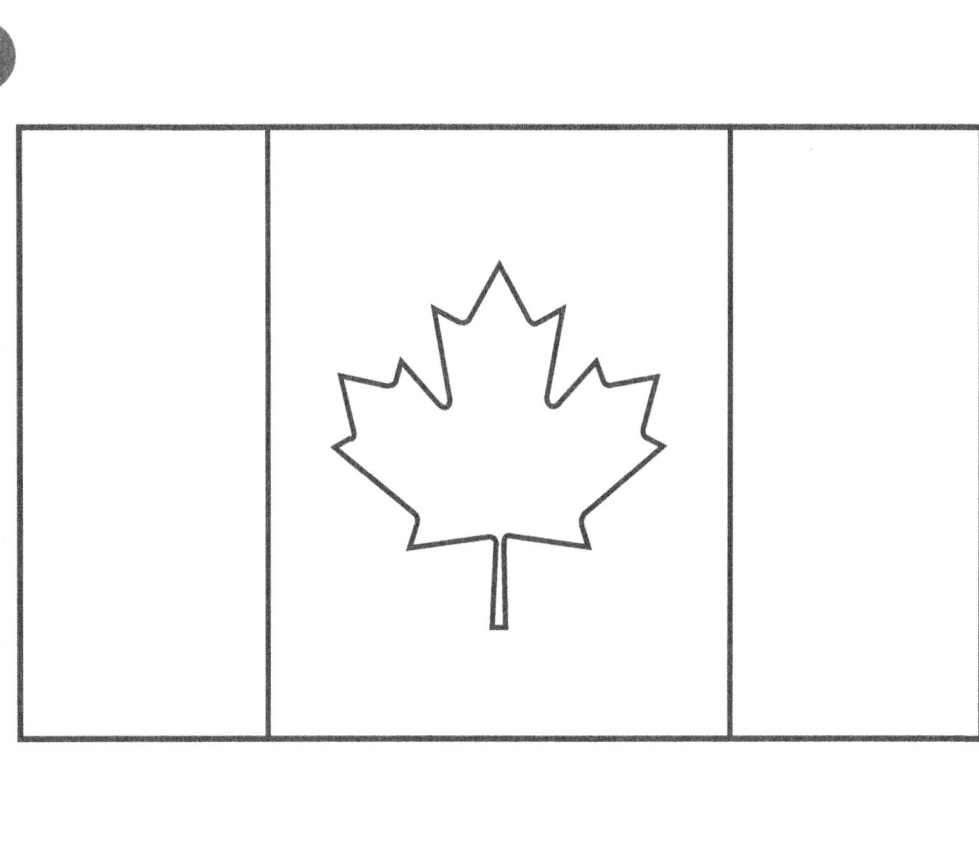

Very Last First Time

Name:

Date:

Science: **Safety and Crisis Thinking**

Memory Aids for Crisis Thinking

The five steps of Crisis Thinking can help calm your student when they're faced with a difficult or scary situation, as well as lead them to a calm, safe solution to their problem. Practice these hand motions as you help them memorize the list and review this lesson when you read other FIAR books that involve difficult or crisis situations.

CALM DOWN

(hands palm-down in front of body, bouncing downward twice)

DON'T PANIC

(shake first finger twice as if saying "no-no!")

BE QUIET

(first finger tapping twice against closed lips, as if saying "shhhh!")

THINK CAREFULLY!

(first finger tapping one temple twice, as if "thinking")

WHAT AM I SUPPOSED TO DO?

(both hands palm-up in front of body, bouncing downward twice; opposite of "calm down," as if saying "what now?")

Name:
Date:
Health: **Dressing for the Conditions**

Draw a line matching the clothing choice to the correct weather/temperature.

COLD

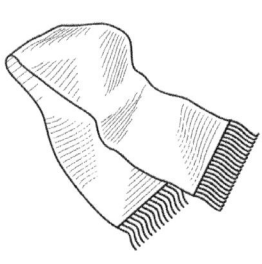

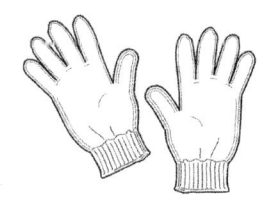

HOT

Very Last First Time

The Clown of God

Title: *The Clown of God*
Author: Tomie dePaola
Illustrator: Tomie dePaola
Copyright: 1978
Summary: *The Clown of God* is the retelling of an old legend, a story of a "gift for *the* Child."

Social Studies: Geography - Sorrento, Italy

The Clown of God is set in Sorrento, Italy. Sorrento is an actual Italian city. Let your student know she could still visit there although it would not look the same as the early Renaissance setting of this story. Nor would the people be dressed in the same way, but she might still see a monastery and a Franciscan monk. Italy is the long, high-heeled, boot-shaped country that appears (on a map) to hang down in the Mediterranean Sea. Using a map or globe, place your story disk on Italy.

Social Studies: Foreign Language - Italian

Review the Italian words previously studied from *Papa Piccolo*. Add these Italian words and Italian names: arrivederci (ah-reeva-dair-chee) means goodbye, grazie (grat-zee) means thank you, signor (seen-your) denotes Mr., and fine (fee-nay) means the end. The names are Giovanni, Arlecchino, and Colombina.

When you say "goodbye" to your student, when you end a book or activity, and whenever you say "thank you," say it in Italian!

Social Studies: Renaissance

The Renaissance was a period of time in European history during the 1300s, 1400s, and 1500s. At this time there was a great revival of learning and art.

When teaching young students about subjects like the Renaissance, try using pictures of clothing, foods, and activities. Gather these and show them to your student and ask her what is different from the way we live today. Let her point out things that are different and then say, "There is a word we use for this time in history, when clothes, etc., were like what you see here—it is **Renaissance** (Ren-ah-sahnce)." Let her enjoy the sound of that word and say it with her several times. Some students will not memorize now, but they will have been introduced to the pictures and the words—a good beginning!

The Clown of God pictures the early years of the Renaissance. Notice the clothes, the lunch of bread, cheese and fruit, going to market with woven baskets, no shopping carts, being entertained by jugglers, traveling actors, no television, movies or electronics, and horse-drawn transportation.

Social Studies: Orphans

The story provides an opportunity to explain the term "orphan:" a child without mother or father. In this story Giovanni has no parents and no one at all to take care of him. Throughout history, due to plagues and wars, many children have been left alone. You can discuss the ways these children are cared for.

Arleta Richardson has written a series of books that tell of the **orphan train** in America called *Looking for Home* and *Whistle-Stop West*. The orphan trains took thousands of orphans from America's eastern cities across the midwest to find new homes with rural families during the last half of the nineteenth century.

In the *Samantha* books of the American Girl series, Samantha meets an orphan and befriends her. These are excellent read-alouds.

There is also a wonderful series about a family of children who run a farm and have countless adventures after having lost their parents. The stories read like the Little House books and are most enjoyable. The reader sees the children accept responsibility and keep a warm family life. These books are called the *Hannah's House* series. They were written by Rhoda Wooldridge. The series includes: *Han-*

nah's Brave Year, Hannah's House, Hannah's Flood, Hannah's Mill and Hannah's Choice.

Social Studies: The Elderly

Giovanni grows from a child to an elderly man in the course of this story. In his case, the people do not show him respect nor do they feel any compassion or desire to help him. Discuss with your student the respect that is due older people. Sometimes older people need encouragement that they have value even if they cannot contribute in the same way that they have in the past. They can be recognized for the wisdom, skills and knowledge that they can pass on. Ask your student if she has any elderly friends and talk about them. Does your student have any grandparents that she sees regularly? Try one or more of these books that showcase older people and their relationship with a child: *Mrs. Katz and Tush* by Patricia Polacco, *Gramma's Walk* by Anna Grossnickel Hines, *Storm in the Night* by Mary Stolz (these three are FIAR titles), and *Uncle Jed's Barber Shop* by Margaree King Mitchell.

Social Studies: Thankfulness

Take the time to remind your student that there are many things for which to be thankful. By reading about people like Giovanni who had a hard life, the student may identify with certain aspects of life's difficulties, and yet realize that she has many things for which to be greatful. Make a list and illustrate it, or make a timeline of the student's life and add all the events and people for which she is thankful.

Social Studies: Relationships - Difficult People

"And wherever Giovanni went, the faces of the crowds would be all smiles, and the sound of laughter and cheers would ring through the towns." But as the years passed, people no longer stopped to watch and they did not respect the old clown who had entertained them. When he dropped "the Sun in the heavens," they first laughed, and then threw vegetables and stones at him. Ask your student why the people acted this way. Discuss the fact that some people, thinking only of themselves, want to be amused. That is all that is important to them. Your student will meet people like that and it helps to understand why people act the way they do.

Wise people enjoy entertainment but also care about the people that entertain them. Discuss the fact that when someone is popular and then falls out of popularity they may experience a loss of self-worth. Having people who care can make a real difference. Is there someone your student knows that needs to be encouraged? Discuss the ways she might do that.

Social Studies: Occupations

From the very beginning of this story, Giovanni is happy because there is something wonderful he can do. In juggling, Giovanni finds a purpose (to entertain) and a way to make his living. And one day the monks even tell him that by doing what he is able to do he gives happiness to people and glory to God as well!

Discuss with your student that it is important to discover what things he can do. It is also important for people to know the value or contribution of their job. Giovanni said, "I used to make people smile." Giovanni thought that seemed valuable. Here are some other careers and some of their possible values. Can you and your student think of more?

Five in Row Volume One

A newspaper man might say, "*I help people know what is going on.*"
A cook: "*I feed people to make them healthy and to make them happy.*"
A house painter: "*I paint houses to make them beautiful.*"
Giovanni: "*I juggle to make people smile!*"
A doctor: "*I treat people to help them get well and to comfort them when they are sick.*"
An artist: "*I paint, etc., so that the beautiful and meaningful things can be preserved.*"
A farmer: "*I grow food so that people will have potatoes and corn to eat.*"
This is how I help the world; *this* is what I do!

Language Arts: Legend

Legends are stories that sometimes have elements of truth but that have been embellished (made greater) by many additions which are not necessarily true. They sometimes glorify a person or an event in which a miracle happens.

In England, King Arthur has become a legend because many stories naming him have been handed down for generations. In America, men like Davy Crockett and Johnny Appleseed have reached epic, legendary proportions.

According to Tomie dePaola, *The Clown of God* is an old French legend. Yet, the author says that following the tradition of storytellers, he adapted the story to the setting with which he was most familiar: Italy.

Language Arts: Vocabulary

juggle   To toss several objects (more than two) in the air, keeping them moving in an arc (portion of a circle) until you want to stop.

eggplant   A purple vegetable (point it out at the grocery store).

zucchini   A long, green vegetable. Can your student tell it apart from a cucumber?

famous   Well-known.

amazement   Wonder.

serious   Without humor or silliness.

magnificent   Marvelous, wonderful, great.

arrangement   Items grouped in a certain way.

troupe   An artistic group of people; a dancing or acting group who work together.

maestro   An Italian word that means a master of any art.

ragamuffin   A ragged person, young or old.

companionship   Being with people.

torches   Sticks that are on fire.

violet   A bluish purple; a mixture of red and blue.

brothers (monks, monastery)   Monks in a monastery, a place where these men seek God as they live a cloistered (isolated) life.

Language Arts: Reading Comprehension

After reading the story, ask your student why Giovanni goes to the vegetable stand every day. (He goes so he will have objects to juggle.) What is the arrangement he makes with Signor Baptista? (Giovanni will juggle and draw a crowd. Signor Baptista knows the crowd will stop and buy his vegetables and fruit. In exchange for the help of drawing the crowd, the Signor's wife will feed Giovanni—a very good arrangement!)

It is helpful to know if your student is picking up the facts as you read a story. It is also good to notice if she is able to infer ideas from what you read to her. Be on the lookout for ideas that are inferred. See if the student has understanding. Reading, ultimately, is more than just looking at the words and being able to say them. It is understanding the meaning of the words, sentences, paragraphs, and ideas that are inferred from the text. Reading often to your young student will have a positive effect on her reading readiness. (Your older student will enjoy hearing you read to her as well.)

Language Arts: A Balanced Story

The Clown of God is an exceedingly well-crafted tale. One of the literary devices Tomie dePaola uses is **balance**. Notice the story beginning with Giovanni, the orphan, who is begging and who then meets the monks (little brothers). Toward the end of the story, Giovanni is begging again and happens upon the monastery, the very one the little brothers are from. The story beginning soon reveals Giovanni as a happy juggler, and also ends with him as happy juggler, doing what he was meant to do.

Try working together with your student to create your own story, balancing opening and closing scenes as Tomie dePaola does in *The Clown of God*.

Language Arts: Repetition

There are repetitive lines in *The Clown of God*. One series of repetitions is the order in which he throws up the colored balls. He throws a red ball, an orange ball, then a yellow ball, a green ball, blue ball, and violet ball. Finally Giovanni throws the Sun in the Heavens (the gold ball). This "order" of action is repeated as he juggles at the monastery.

There is also a repetition of subject (rather than words) as Giovanni begins the story needing to beg for food, and is poor again at the story's end.

Language Arts: Contrast

There is a contrast of emotion between Giovanni the happy child juggler, and the defeated old Giovanni. Can you and your student think of story ideas that would have great contrast of emotion or action? (For instance, imagine a person who is vecy sleepy. Then something exciting happens. He is now completely awake! You might think of someone who appears quite fearful but something happens and they find they are brave. Or, imagine someone who boasts he can do something and finds out he cannot.) When you create story scenarios of this type you sharpen literacy skills while exploring the world of emotions.

Language Arts: Story Endings

What keeps the ending of this story from being *too* sad? How has the author accomplished this? (Giovanni is very old and has lived a hard life. It is a thrill to watch him put on his face and juggle better than he ever has before. It is also a shock to realize that he has given the performance everything he has left. Yet the miracle of the smile on the face of the child and the hand holding the golden ball inspire us and leave us in awe.)

How a story ends is very important. Remember the Afterword in *Who Owns the Sun?* that helps ease the sorrow of the ending. Remind your older student that in crafting a story, she gets to choose an ending that will express the message she has to tell.

Art: Juggling

There is an art to juggling. There is a rhythm, a timing and a way of tossing by which Giovanni brings entertainment to the people. If you, or someone you know, can juggle, let your student see in person the wonder and excitement of this entertainment form. Let her try. If your student wants to learn and be great, then like Giovanni with his juggling and Lentil with his harmonica, she will discover that she must practice. If she decides to make a serious attempt to juggle, have her stand with her waist against a bed (so she doesn't have to bend over so often to pick up the balls) and situate herself with a plain, solid color wall behind the bed so there are no visual distractions. Make or purchase three small, round bean bags to practice with. (Don't stuff them too tight and they'll be easier to catch.)

If you should happen to go to a circus, be sure to watch for the jugglers!

Art: Medium

Tomie dePaola has used pencil, ink and watercolor on hand-made watercolor paper to illustrate *The Clown of God*. His figures are flat and often in profile (seeing a face from the side). Notice that the trees are not all the same. There is variety. Have your student try drawing, painting, or even modeling (with clay) some trees like those in the drawings.

Art: Recalling Venice, Italy

Giovanni travels with the acting troupe. He then begins to perform on his own. Cheers ring through the towns. One of the towns he visits is Venice, Italy. Perhaps you have covered the lessons for *Papa Piccolo*. If so, when reading *The Clown of God*, give your student time to recognize for herself the picture of gondolas, the gondoliers, waterway streets, and striped poles. All of these sights appeared in the illustrations of *Papa Piccolo*. If your student doesn't recognize Venice, share with her and compare these pictures with the illustrations from *Papa Piccolo*.

Art: Symbolic Detail

There is a picture of a dove on the title page. Opposite the first words of the story, "Many, many years ago in Sorrento …", the dove reappears. Find it in the picture where the discouraged old juggler washes off his face and goes back to begging. In this picture, the dove is hiding its head. The dove may symbolize (stand for) Giovanni's talent or his career, for it sits atop the stage on the title page and sits opposite a juggling ball on the next page. On the page where he gives up his career, it hides its head. Or it may just represent Giovanni's sorrow in losing his feeling of being valued (sense of self-worth). In any case, it is enjoyable to notice and appreciate such artistic detail.

Art: Architecture

The Clown of God provides marvelous architectural examples to be introduced and enjoyed. Eventually, your student will begin to recognize familiar styles in books and actual buildings around her. Note the massive stone bridge with people walking on top and the shops above the bridge. (There is a terrific book for children on bridges: *The Bridge Book* by Polly Carter. This book is fun to read, has understandable illustrations and shows an example of the kind of bridge found in *The Clown of God*.)

Notice the columns with the different types of statues at the top. Your older student might enjoy researching architecture and the various columns of Venice. If she is interested, look online for an introduction to the classical types of columns (Doric, Ionic and Corinthian). She may want to discover when and where they originated. If she is observant, she will probably see many examples of these three column types in the architecture of her town or city. Maybe she will also notice columns with animal figures on top of them as illustrated in this story. Your student may want to draw these three types of classical columns for her notebook.

The arches pictured throughout the story are Roman arches. These are rounded at the top, rather than pointed like Gothic arches. Even the arches in the monastery are the Roman type, including the massive arched doors and the windows.

The round window (called a rose window; can your student think why it is called this?) on the front of the monastery is often seen in churches today. Notice that you can see part of this round window from the inside of the monastery as well as the outside. Ask your student if she has seen this type of window and have her be looking for them (especially on churches). (**Note:** There is an informative book on windows called *Let There Be Light* by James Cross Giblin. This book tells the history of windows and contains many fascinating facts that can be shared from time to time with your student. And a memorable learning experience for the teacher!)

Art: Appreciation - Sequencing

The double-sided picture where Giovanni is juggling at the monastery is a thrill to view. The reader nearly holds his breath as across four identical arched spaces Giovanni juggles first six balls, then all seven, higher than he has ever juggled before! These pictures appear in a sequence, much like a cartoon strip. The repetition of the arches provides a rhythm for the juggling.

Math: Grouping and Pre-Multiplication

Use the picture of Giovanni juggling three eggplants. Ask your student how many different groups of eggplants Giovanni can juggle if Signor Baptista has twenty-one eggplants in his vegetable stand. Take twenty-one small manipulatives and make groups of three until they are all accounted for. Now count the groups. (There will be seven.)

Gear this lesson to the level of your older student. At this time you may want to introduce the "x" multiplication sign. You can say, "You will be learning a faster way to know how many groups of 3 there are in 21. By using the 'times' sign, we learn the number fact that 7 groups of 3 (7x3) equals 21. It is always the same. That's why we call it a fact."

Continue using the picture of Giovanni juggling four oranges, five torches, and seven balls to make more grouping lessons for your young student. For your older student who is learning her multiplication tables, have her make multiplication fact flash cards and decorate them with the colored balls that Giovanni juggles.

Math: Counting Practice

For simple counting practice, have your student count the total number of colored balls pictured in the story. For higher counting, have her count all the objects that Giovanni juggles. You can also count trees or people.

Science: Mixtures - Cooking

Giovanni was happy to have his bowl of soup from Signor Baptista's wife. He probably didn't think about the fact that his soup was a mixture. In chemistry, the term "mixture" means a combination of substances held together by physical, rather than chemical, means. An easy way to explain this term is to make soup. Make soup by taking meat, vegetables, water, and spices, and cooking them gently together creating a soup "mixture." Have your student look at the soup. She will see soup, but she still will be able to recognize carrots, potatoes, etc. This is because the ingredients are still there, but they are now held together in the liquid. If your young student finds this lesson hard to grasp, never fear, she will recognize the terms as she is reintroduced to the topic at a later time, and the soup making is fun!

Science: Aging

As people get older, many have a harder time seeing as clearly as they used to, or hearing the faint sounds they once did. They may also have difficulty doing things with their hands and fingers that they could once easily accomplish. What they do have, that they did not when they were younger, is experience in many areas of life and the wisdom (the accumulation of insight, knowledge and experience) which comes from living a long life. When a student is reminded of the importance of respect for the elderly people she knows, an avenue is opened for friendships that can be enriching indeed.

An advanced science lesson would be to research the elderly and the reasons for the aging process.

For your young student, it is enough for her to be aware that an older person might not be able to hear as well as she can, or that they might drop something, wear dentures, etc. By discussing these ideas with your student, she will begin to have compassion and tolerance born of knowledge, rather than ridicule born of ignorance and surprise.

Tomie dePaola has written several other books for children that depict aging adults. You might want to look for *Now One Foot, Now the Other*, which tells the story of a young boy coping with his grandfather's disability, and *Nana Upstairs and Nana Downstairs*, which tells the story of a young child and the loss of his great-grandmother, who lives upstairs from him.

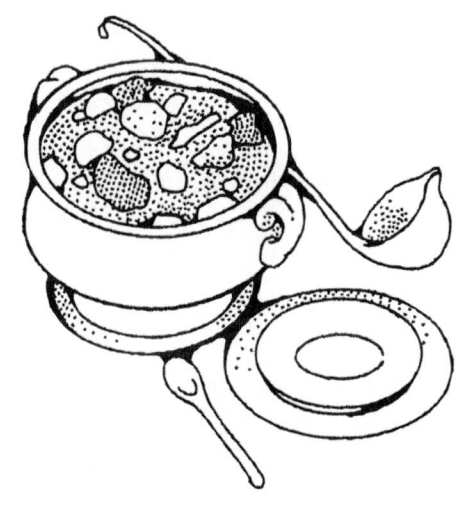

Teacher's Notes

The *Five in a Row* lesson options for each unit in the manual are all you need to teach your child. The additional resource area provided below is simply a place to jot down relevant info you've found that you might want to reference.

THE CLOWN OF GOD

Date: _____

Student: _____

Five in a Row Lesson Topics Chosen:

Social Studies: _____
_____
_____

Language Arts: _____
_____
_____

Art: _____
_____
_____

Math: _____
_____
_____

Science: _____
_____
_____

**Relevant Library Resources:
Books, DVDs, Audio Books**
_____
_____
_____
_____
_____
_____
_____

Websites or Video Links:
_____
_____
_____
_____
_____
_____
_____
_____

Related Field Trip Opportunities:
_____
_____
_____

Favorite Quote or Memory During Study:
_____
_____
_____

The Clown of God

Name:
Date:
Language Arts: **Repetition**

One of the repetitive lines we read in *The Clown of God* is referring to the order in which Giovanni throws the colored balls that he juggles. Color each ball in the order we read: red, orange, yellow, green, blue, violet and finally the Sun in the Heavens (or gold ball). Draw Giovanni under the balls, if you like!

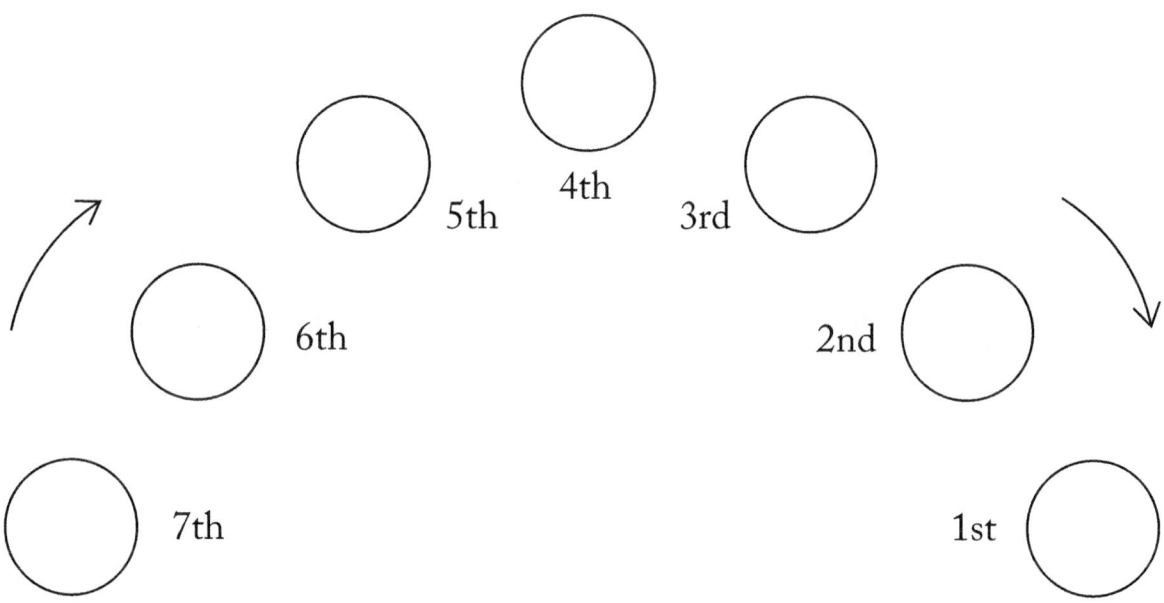

Storm in the Night

Title: *Storm in the Night*
Author: Mary Stolz
Illustrator: Pat Cummings
Copyright: 1988
Awards: ALA Booklist Children's Editors' Choice
Coretta Scott King Honor Book for Illustration
Summary: Grandfather addresses Thomas' fear of thunderstorms by vulnerably relating a story of his own childhood.

Social Studies: Relationships

Thomas and his grandfather have a close relationship. What things does your student notice that show how Thomas and his grandfather feel about one another? Perhaps your student will mention some of the following reasons that he feels they are close:

1. Thomas loves his grandfather's stories. He loves them so much he asks for them again and again. His grandfather explains things to him. He sits close to his grandfather in the pictures. Thomas admires his grandfather for being able to tell "a truth like *that*."

2. Grandfather loves Thomas. He spends time with him and helps him admit his fear by telling Thomas his own vulnerable story. Grandfather is not judgmental or preachy regarding Thomas' fears, but says, "Perfectly natural."

Does your student have someone with whom he shares stories and spends time? Have him describe the relationship. He might say something like, "I spend the weekends with my grandfather. He makes me fried potatoes and we go for long walks."

Social Studies: Emotions - Fear

Thomas says, "*I'm* not afraid of *anything*." Ask your student if he thinks this might be a boast and why? (Most everyone will admit to fearing *some* things.)

Grandfather helps Thomas know that all people are afraid of something, some time, and that it's "ok" to admit it. He also teaches that fears can be overcome. Sometimes people are afraid of the dark, storms, or of experiences that are new or unfamiliar. Discuss with your student things that have made *you* feel afraid, and ask him if there is something that bothers him.

Grandfather tells in his story that he forgot that his parents had gone out for an hour or so, because he was afraid. He says, " ... fear does strange things to people ... makes them forget everything but how afraid they are." This is why learning and practicing Crisis Thinking (studied in *Very Last First Time*) is important.

This story has a happy ending when the electricity is restored. Is it Thomas' hand that willingly turned off the lights when Thomas and his grandfather go to bed?

Language Arts: Contrast

Look at the contrast in descriptive words between the opening lines of the story, describing the fury of the storm, and the lines near the end when "the storm was spent."

Beginning:
Thunder like mountains blowing up
Lightning licking the navy-blue sky
Rain streaming down the windows

Ending:
mutterings of thunder
flickers of lightning
little patter of rain babbling in the downspouts

Let your student hear the contrast and try to imitate a series of descriptions with a contrasting series. For instance:

Horses, galloping like rifle fire
Snorting, sides heaving
Screaming wildly

horses stepping quietly
breathing softly
whinnying gently

Language Arts: Literary Device - Italics

There are several examples of using italics for emphasis. (If you did the Italics lesson in *The Glorious Flight*, you have already introduced the use of italics for the names of boats and ships.) In *Storm in the Night*, italics have been used to show emphasis. In a handwritten story, these words would be underlined. Examples from the story:

"Were there *automobiles*?"
"*I'm* not afraid of *anything*."
"I want to own a *tiger*!"

Help your student recognize that italics is a different type of print from the rest of the text. Your student will be able to tell the difference in the types of print even if he cannot yet read. Mention that one use of this type of print is to *emphasize* the word that is italicized. Make sure you read the italicized word with voice emphasis each day. An older student may want to experiment with using one or two emphasized (<u>underlined</u> or *italicized*) words in a story.

Language Arts: Punctuation - Quotation Marks

Storm in the Night is an unusual children's picture storybook because of the amount of dialogue it contains. Try reading Thomas' dialogue in a certain voice and Grandfather's dialogue with a different voice. Then your student can easily follow who is doing the talking. Because of the great amount of dialogue, this story may be better appreciated on the second or third reading. (Explain that dialogue is conversation: when two or more people are talking to one another.)

When you read dialogue in a book you can see that each time a person speaks, what he says is placed inside quotation marks. Show your student how quotation marks look. When one person stops speaking and someone else begins, a new paragraph is formed. This is to help the reader understand what is being said and to know for sure *who* said it.

Let your young student dictate to you a simple story with some dialogue. Show him how you are using quotation marks. Let your older student try writing a story with dialogue, too.

Language Arts: Vocabulary

mandarin   In this story—orange colored; from mandarin oranges which are small, spicy-sweet oranges with a bright orange peel. Enjoy some fresh or canned mandarin oranges for a snack while you read.

bough   A branch of a tree.

errand   A short, quick trip for a specific purpose, such as to buy something.

Language Arts: Poetic Device - Onomatopoeia

Mary Stolz writes a prose story that has poetic elements. One such element is the use of **onomatopoeia** (ahna-mahta-PEA-uh); a word that makes the sound of the object when you say it. The clock striking ping, ping, ping-a-ling; or tick-tickticktickety; or bong, bong, bong, BONG! are examples of onomatopoeia. (Also see *The Glorious Flight*.)

Remind your student that using onomatopoeia is like writing in sound effects and adds variety to his stories. Have him try a short story using some sound effects.

Language Arts: Poetic Device - Personification

Personification is a poetic (or literary) device that gives human attributes to non-human things. Speaking of the heavy rain, Mary Stolz describes it as "whooping wildly" and "brandishing branches." There is also the phrase, "horns ... hollered," and a clock that is "excited." (Also see *Mike Mulligan and His Steam Shovel*.) With your student, look and listen for other examples of personification in stories.

Language Arts: Poetic Device - Simile

Mary Stolz has included a striking **simile** (sim-uh-lee) in this story. Simile is a statement that one thing is like another, using the words "like" or "as." "That man was seven feet tall and had a face like a crack in the ice." What does that kind of face look like? Ask your student to draw or describe his impression. Similes are used to create greater avenues of description by likening one thing to another. Remember Thomas' voice, *like* a penny whistle, while Grandfather's was described as being *like* a tuba? Even though their voices are not musical instruments, by knowing the characteristics of those instruments, you now have a poetic description of their voices.

Language Arts: Setting and Scenes

The setting for *Storm in the Night* is Thomas' grandfather's house. But, within this setting, the scene changes from the inside of the house to the outside and finally back inside once more. This variety of scene, even within a very small setting, is interesting and something worth pointing out to your student.

The setting itself, and when to change the scenes, can be added to your student's list of Choices a Writer Can Make. Writing is like being in charge, like being the boss. All the choices for a story are waiting to be made. Remind your student *he* can make those choices when *he* writes a story.

Art: Medium

Pat Cummings has used oil or acrylic paint to illustrate *Storm in the Night*. Notice the white rain slashes on the title page. Look for them on the other pages. Observe the white highlights around people and objects and watch for brush strokes (especially visible in Grandfather's sweater when Ringo the cat jumps onto Thomas' lap) in many of the pictures.

Oils or acrylic paints allow white to be applied *over* color, unlike water color where you usually leave, without paint, any spaces you wish to be white. If you have access to acrylic paints, a canvas, a medium wide brush and a very long, thin signwriting brush (or any long thin paintbrush), try painting a dark blue background in different intensities (strengths) of the same blue. This is accomplished by adding varying small amounts of white to the same blue. Let it dry and add the rain slash marks with white, like the title page. Try some dots and splashes too! If it isn't possible to work in this medium, a simple lesson can be accomplished with the sharp edge of white chalk on dark navy blue paper. Try to use dark blues for night (rather than black) as Pat Cummings did in this story.

Art: Expressing Darkness and Light

With the exception of the last half-page of the story, *Storm in the Night* takes place in the dark! How does the artist show the darkness of the night? (She uses blues of many intensities with white and yellow highlights.)

There are different sources of light. The sun is our primary source of light but it does not appear in this story. However, there *is* light in the story. Where does it come from? Ask your student if he knows. Three sources of light in this story are lightning, the woodstove fire and electric light bulbs. Pat Cummings has painted the light from the lightning as white. Notice the pictures where the highlights are white. You know the lightning is flashing. She has portrayed the woodstove firelight with yellow and orange. Find the pictures lit by the light of the woodstove. There is a yellow glow is from the electric light bulb on the last page of the story. On the page where the boy asks his grandfather if there were automobiles when he was a boy, notice how light the room is. Compare this illustration with the picture without the flash of lightning, where the boy says his grandfather knows more stories than a book.

Pat Cummings also uses white outlines in many of the pictures to contrast with the dark blue night.

Art: Reflections

There are several examples of reflections in this story. There is the reflection of the cat in the window where the boy says, "I like cats. I want to own a tiger!" There is a reflection of the grandfather (when he was a boy) in the window as he tells his story. Reflections of faces are difficult, but an adventurous art student can try a picture that includes a reflection. Remember that reflections come from smooth, shiny surfaces. Windows, mirrors, eyeglasses, a shiny kettle, water, a pond or a raindrop can all reflect images.

Art: Facial Expressions

In the picture opposite the words, "There were clocks," Thomas is looking out the window. He is looking sideways. You can tell because the iris of his eye is over to the side and you can see more of the white of his eye than when he is looking toward the reader. It is very easy to draw faces with the characters looking different directions. Let your student try drawing faces with eyes like the ones shown on the next page.

Art: Contrast

The last illustration shows a half-yellow and half-black picture. The contrast is used by the artist to make a dramatic statement. When you want to make a dramatic statement, you use complementary colors (or colors close to them). These

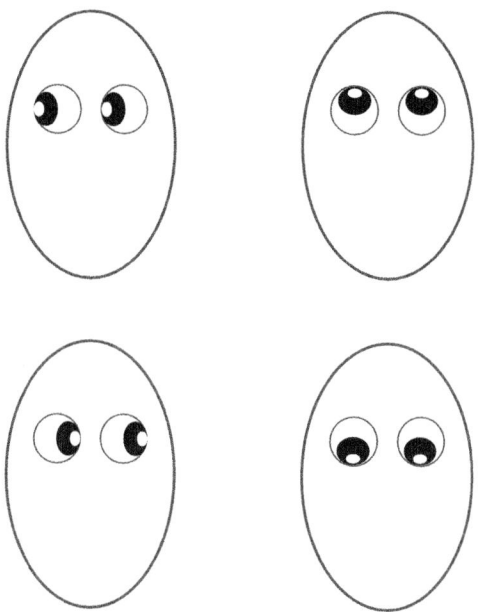

are sometimes called "opposites" on the color wheel. In this case, the yellow makes a strong contrast to the bluish-black. A dark blue next to the bluish-black would have been less striking.

Art: Profiles

A profile is a view of a face from the side. The cover illustration is an excellent example of faces in profile. You can see the cat's face, then Thomas' face and finally his grandfather's face placed in profile from smallest to largest. This illustration is truly a triumph of balance, repetition and beauty. Take a toy animal or doll with a definite profile. Let your student try drawing it, and if possible, try repeating the pattern at an angle across the page. Or find pictures of faces in profile online and print them. Let your student paste them on paper in a repetitive pattern.

Math: Geometry - Quilt

Grandfather tells the story of the night he heard the thunder and hid under the bed. Look at the quilt on the bed. Ask your student what shapes make up the quilt pattern. Maybe he will recognize the triangles (three-sided polygons whose angles add up to 180 degrees). These look like equilateral (equal-sided) triangles. The center is a small, white circle surrounded by a yellow pentagon (five equal-sided polygon). Try making the some equilateral triangles and pentagon with your geoboard. (See *The Rag Coat* Mathematics lesson for instructions on making a geoboard.) You can also use stick pretzels to make various shapes with equal sides.

Science: Sources of Light

Make a list of the light sources that you can think of: sun, moon with reflected light from the sun, stars, lightning, fire, lightning bugs, moonjellies and other sea creatures, flashlights, light bulbs, neon tubes, etc. Discuss that a very small amount of light can dispel darkness. Fnd a very dark room. Give your eyes time to adjust to the darkness. Light a match or switch on a tiny flashlight. Notice with your student how very bright the room becomes with just a small amount of light.

Science: Safety

Your student will enjoy learning about the safety precautions he can make use of during a storm. He might also like setting up a "storm survival kit." (There are free brochures on weather and what to do in case of severe weather at your local police station, television weather station or online.) A "storm survival kit" could consist of a flashlight (keep fresh batteries, especially during storm seasons), or candles and matches. Also, a small first aid kit and a transistor radio with fresh batteries in order to hear severe weather reports, could be included as well. (If you don't own a transister radio or weather radio, it's wise for a parent to have a weather app on their phone or mobile device.) Ask your student if there is anything else he would like to include in the kit. Help him decide on a special place to keep the kit. He needs to remember where the storm kit is kept and practice finding it in the dark! Taking these steps might one day prevent panic, should your student find himself home alone. Remember Crisis Thinking *(see Very Last First Time)* and practice.

You could role play this situation: Your student is home alone. He hears a loud clap of thunder, the lights go out, and two more very loud thunder-boomers split the air. It sounds as if the house will be next! What should he do? (Calm Down, Don't Panic, Be Quiet, Think Carefully, What Am I Supposed to Do?) Maybe he will say after the above steps, "I need to make my way to the place where we keep the storm kit and get the flashlight. If the radio says I need to get to a place of safety [or if he hears outdoor weather sirens], then I know where to go. Otherwise, I will enjoy the storm, knowing that I have everything I need and my parents will be home soon." This kind of training gives your student a feeling of security and responsibility and can prevent many traumatic experiences. Use it for other safety procedures: fire drills, swimming precautions, tornado or hurricane warnings, etc.

Science: Five Senses

Thomas discovers that he can hear better in the dark and also that his sense of smell is enhanced. Ask your student if he thinks this is so and why. (Grandfather explains that your senses are sharpened when you're not trying to use all five at once.) Try sitting in a dark room and listen carefully for sounds that you have not noticed before. It may seem as if each sense is magnified in isolation (used alone.) Go outside. Cover your eyes tightly and concentrate on various smells. You and your student will both be surprised at what you discover.

Science: Aging

Thomas tries to imagine Grandfather as a boy, but it is difficult. List the things he finds different between his aging Grandfather and himself. (Thomas' voice is like a whistle while Grandfather's is like a tuba. Thomas doesn't have a beard, but Grandfather has one, and Thomas is short, while Grandfather is much taller.) Add to the list things your student observes about elderly people, such as being retired, doing volunteer work, walking with a cane, having trouble hearing, having grandchildren visit, or having skin that is wrinkled. Remind him, though, that many people have begun new, successful careers and accomplished wonderful things even in their mature years. Just one example of this is Grandma Moses (Anna Mary Robertson Moses) who began her famous painting career at age 78!

Find several photographs showing the same person at various ages. Perhaps the student has several photographs of a grandmother or grandfather as a young child, young adult, and senior citizen. You might also locate photographs of movie stars from forty years ago and their current photos today. Let your student carefully compare the images, noting the changes which occur in the aging process. (The dark hair has turned white, the skin has wrinkled, teeth may have been replaced by dentures, etc.) You'll both find this a fascinating project! If you can, go back and look at the paintings in *Grandfather's Journey*, and notice the changes in Grandfather.

Science: Clouds

There are different cloud types. Begin to teach your student what they are and the weather they may bring. He may enjoy making use of this type of information throughout his life.

Clouds that are in flat layers are stratus clouds (strato means "in layers or sheets"). Stratus clouds can be associated with rainy weather. Cumulus clouds are white, piled up, billowy masses (cumulo means "heap or pile"). They often appear on sunny days and signal fair weather. Cirrus clouds are delicate, curly, thin upper altitude clouds (cirro means "curl"). They are made of ice crystals and are sometimes called mares' tails. These high clouds signal cold air at high altitudes. Nimbus clouds are gray and dark, often bringing rain (nimbo means "rain").

A combination of cumulus and nimbus clouds are called cumulonimbus clouds, which tower in columns. These clouds often bring violent thunderstorms.

Science: Thunderstorms

Thunderstorms are characterized by high winds, lightning, heavy rains and sometimes hail. They are caused when warm, moist air meets cool, drier air. Although most common in the spring, thunderstorms can occur any time of year—even in winter when they become *thundersnows*!

If you have thunderstorms in your part of the country, the next time you experience a thunderstorm with your student, discuss it while you watch and listen.

Encourage your student to smell the air during a thunderstorm, and again afterwards. Have him try it with his eyes closed! Sometimes people can smell an approaching rain shower before it arrives. This is because small water molecules (not drops but more like a spray) are carried ahead by the wind before the actual storm begins!

Story disk note: You and your student can decide where in the United States the story disk will be placed for *Storm in the Night*. There is no "right answer," but be sure to place it in an area that would experience strong thunderstorms. You may also want to note the types of plants, trees, and other clues in the story to help narrow down your choice. Have fun determining the location with your student!

Teacher's Notes

The *Five in a Row* lesson options for each unit in the manual are all you need to teach your child. The additional resource area provided below is simply a place to jot down relevant info you've found that you might want to reference.

STORM IN THE NIGHT

Date:

Student:

Five in a Row Lesson Topics Chosen:

Social Studies:

Language Arts:

Art:

Math:

Science:

Relevant Library Resources: Books, DVDs, Audio Books

Websites or Video Links:

Related Field Trip Opportunities:

Favorite Quote or Memory During Study:

Storm in the Night

Name:
Date:
Science: **Clouds**

Copy this page, then cut out the cloud viewer and the inside rectangle. Then show your student how he can hold it up to the sky and use it to identify the various types of clouds he sees.

Katy and the Big Snow

Title: *Katy and the Big Snow*
Author: Virginia Lee Burton
Illustrator: Virginia Lee Burton
Copyright: 1943
Category: Classic
Summary: Katy becomes a heroine as she finally gets her chance to work and fulfills her responsibilities.

Social Studies: Running a City

Katy and the Big Snow gives a detailed look at city life and the departments necessary to keep that life moving along. On pp. 6-7, you will find that in the margins Virginia Burton has already illustrated thirty places in Geoppolis. Talk about the different buildings and occupations and how each contributes to the city. Match these numbered pictures to the numbers on the map in the center of the page. Can your student name other types of businesses and occupations necessary to running a city?

Virginia Burton named the town Geoppolis. Ask your older student if that name sounds like any word she knows (*geography*, *metropolis*, etc.). The author symbolized city life everywhere with this name because "Geo" means earth, and "polis" means a city-state in ancient Greece. Thus, Burton's Geoppolis stands for a typical city anywhere on earth.

With your student, make an imaginary city out of blocks or boxes or just a draw a large map. Think up a good name for it. Include the businesses and buildings that your student thinks are important. If she forgets critical services such as doctor's offices or fire stations, etc., ask her if she thinks it would be good to include them. Explain the consequences of not having a particular business or service available. You'd have to drive to another city for your mail or groceries!

If you have an old white bed sheet, you could draw your student's own town using magic markers for the streets, etc. Remember that markers can bleed through the fabric and take protective measures.

Social Studies: Relationships - Responsibilities

Each building or farm represented in Geoppolis has people running it. Each of those people has a job to do in order to keep the town running smoothly. What if the firefighter decided not to work today and a house burned down? What if the mail carrier just didn't feel like delivering the mail? Each person has a responsibility to do his work faithfully (on time) and honestly. If he fails, other people will suffer.

Ask your student what would happen if Katy does not clear the snow. (The schools, factories, stores, railroad station, and airport will have to close. The mail cannot be delivered, the police will not be able to protect the city and the telephone, electric and water lines cannot be repaired. The doctor will not reach his patients and the fire department will be helpless.) Katy has a large responsibility.

Ask your student if she has responsibilities. Does she do them faithfully, sometimes heroically, like Katy? If she does, she needs to know that it makes a difference to those around her, just as Katy's contribution made a difference in Geoppolis.

Social Studies: City - Street Signs

Pages 4-5 show street signs in the margin border. Some of these signs are still used today, but there are some that need to be added. Check online for pictures of street signs; you'll also find some provided at the end of this unit. Have your student make a chart to place in her notebook. Many of our signs today are symbolic (wordless) signs. Teach these signs to your student, along with the reasons for the picture symbols. She will enjoy pointing them out as she notices them along the road. You may want to make miniature signs. You could place them on sticks with clay bases and use them in the town you made in the Running a City lesson on the previous page.

Social Studies: Map Skills - Directions

An introduction to points of the compass and map skills flows naturally from the story *Katy and the Big Snow*.

The most basic lesson begins with an introduction to the directions north, south, east and west. Most maps show north at the top. To make sure of orientation, always check the map's legend, which will point out which direction north is on that particular map. In *Katy*, the compass points are at an angle. This orientation renders north to be in the two o'clock position. If your student is interested, have her follow this slanted compass view on pp. 24, 26, 28 and 30.

If possible, obtain a compass for your student to examine. Explain the directions. (The metallic needle aligns itself with the magnetic poles of the earth, and always points toward north.) Make a simple treasure hunt with an enjoyable object at the end; perhaps a new book, or lunch, etc. Help your student follow a series of clues based on turning certain directions. The directions might start on the west side of the building and instruct your student to go south to the corner of the yard, and then to turn east and walk ten steps, etc.

Together, draw a map of your student's neighborhood from an aerial (bird's-eye) view. Decide which compass direction will be at the top. Make a legend to inform others. In addition, talk about which way your student's home faces. Sometimes point out the direction you are traveling when on outings. Keep in mind that the sun and moon can help determine direction, also.

Language Arts: Meet the Character - Katy

A great amount of description is given about Katy on p. 1. Not only does the text of the story tell about Katy, but Virginia Lee Burton has graphically shown ten facts about her in the border pictures of that page. Burton said she often put details in the margins or on the end papers, because they were too weighty for the body of the text, and, yet children had assured her that they were often their favorite point of interest.

Ask your student to list what she remembers about Katy from p. 1. Then complete the list by rereading the page. (Katy is red. She is a crawler tractor with 55 horses of power and she runs by a diesel engine. She has five speeds forward, two backward and can turn around in the same place. Katy has country shoes, city shoes, and a hydraulic lift system for her blades. She also has a bulldozer and a snow plow. She is very beautiful, big and strong, and Katy can do a lot of things.) Each day, after reading, see if your student can remember a few more of the characteristics of Katy. Developing a good memory is a lifetime benefit.

Language Arts: Literary Device - Personification

Katy's character is portrayed with human qualities by the use of the literary device called **personification**. Giving human qualities to non-human objects, animals or things is called personification. In *Katy and the Big Snow*, the author has given Katy a feminine pronoun "she" and writes that she "likes to work—the harder and tougher the job, the better she likes it." Also, Burton uses dialogue. When Katy is asked to help, she speaks as if she's a person, and she even gets tired but won't stop. She "hurries" to work and then she goes home to rest. Dialogue, emotions, physical weariness, and heroism (not stopping even when tired) are human attributes. When the author presents Katy in this way, it is as if she has a human personality. With your student, try writing a story giving human characteristics to a non-human object.

Language Arts: Vocabulary

bulldozer   A piece of earth-moving equipment.

steamroller   A piece of road maintenance equipment that presses the road flat; this equipment today is no longer steam-powered but rather it is usually powered by diesel engines.

drizzle   Light rain that may last for several hours.

water main   Underground pipes that carry water.

emergency   A situation that calls for immediate attention.

three-alarm fire   A serious fire that requires three different fire stations to respond.

patient   A person under the care of a doctor.

Art: Detail

Virginia Lee Burton has illustrated this story with exquisite detail. This detail is expressed in bright color, exciting action, oodles of information, and courageous personality.

Color Detail: The colors, especially the red, green and yellow, make a bright display for "getting the work done" throughout the story. The dark aqua-blue represents the blizzard day, as on pp. 14-15, making the white snow stand out in contrast.

Detailed Action: The details of action are continuous throughout the story because city life is active with many people working all the time. Katy works too. The final rush to plow the big snow beginning on p. 16 and reaching its busiest climax on p. 33 shows the action mounting and moving across the page rapidly. Trace the path of Katy's plowing through the pages, but especially pp. 34-35. Have your student rapidly move her finger along Katy's paths. Perhaps she may be able to *feel* the action the illustrator drew as the art of the story translates into *emotion* for the reader.

Detailed Personality: The personality of Katy comes from her headlights, made to look like eyes. (See the cover picture and find other examples in the story.) It also comes from her "nose to the grindstone" method of working and her comments of "Chug! Chug! Chug!" as if she just *has* to complete her work, which Burton draws into the pictures.

Let your student try to draw a picture of something not human drawn with human characteristics. (Examples: a tea pot with a happy face, a chair with a face and arms that hug, a flower dressed up, etc.)

Math: Counting

Your student can count the number of telephone poles on the cover, the number of horses on p. 1, the number of bulldozers on p. 2, etc. There is a great variety of counting practice possible in the numerous illustrations of *Katy and the Big Snow*.

Math: Grouping and Counting by Fives

To represent horsepower, Burton has drawn eleven groups of five horses each. You can give your student fifty-five pennies or small manipulatives (or horses if you have them!) and have her put them into groups of five each. She will be able to see that eleven groups of five make the original fifty-five objects.

Explain to your older student that she can also count items more quickly when she learns to count by fives. If there is great interest, introduce the method of counting by fives. (An older student might also be interested to see the products of multiplication by 11. Show your student that $11 \times 1 = 11$; $11 \times 2 = 22$; $11 \times 3 = 33$, etc., all the way through $11 \times 9 = 99$. Learning the "times 11" multiplication facts is often easy and fun.)

Science: Weather Patterns

Explain that weather is not the same from year to year. There might be several years in a row with heavy snows and then several years without a heavy snow. There are flood years, drought (dry) years and normal years. If your older student is interested in weather, help her research a given area. Learn what kind of weather patterns there have been for that area in the past one hundred years. You'll find this sort of information available at the Weather Bureau, your local library or online.

Your young student might enjoy keeping a weather calendar with weather picture symbols for each day (see the activity sheet at the end of this unit). Weather symbols could include: sun, rain, clouds, snow, wind, fog, etc. Help her keep it for a month and note the resulting weather information. For example, there may have been six sunny days, two days of rain, and so on.

Teacher's Notes

The *Five in a Row* lesson options for each unit in the manual are all you need to teach your child. The additional resource area provided below is simply a place to jot down relevant info you've found that you might want to reference.

KATY AND THE BIG SNOW

Date:

Student:

Five in a Row Lesson Topics Chosen:

Social Studies:

Language Arts:

Art:

Math:

Science:

Relevant Library Resources: Books, DVDs, Audio Books

Websites or Video Links:

Related Field Trip Opportunities:

Favorite Quote or Memory During Study:

Name:
Date:
Science: **Maps**

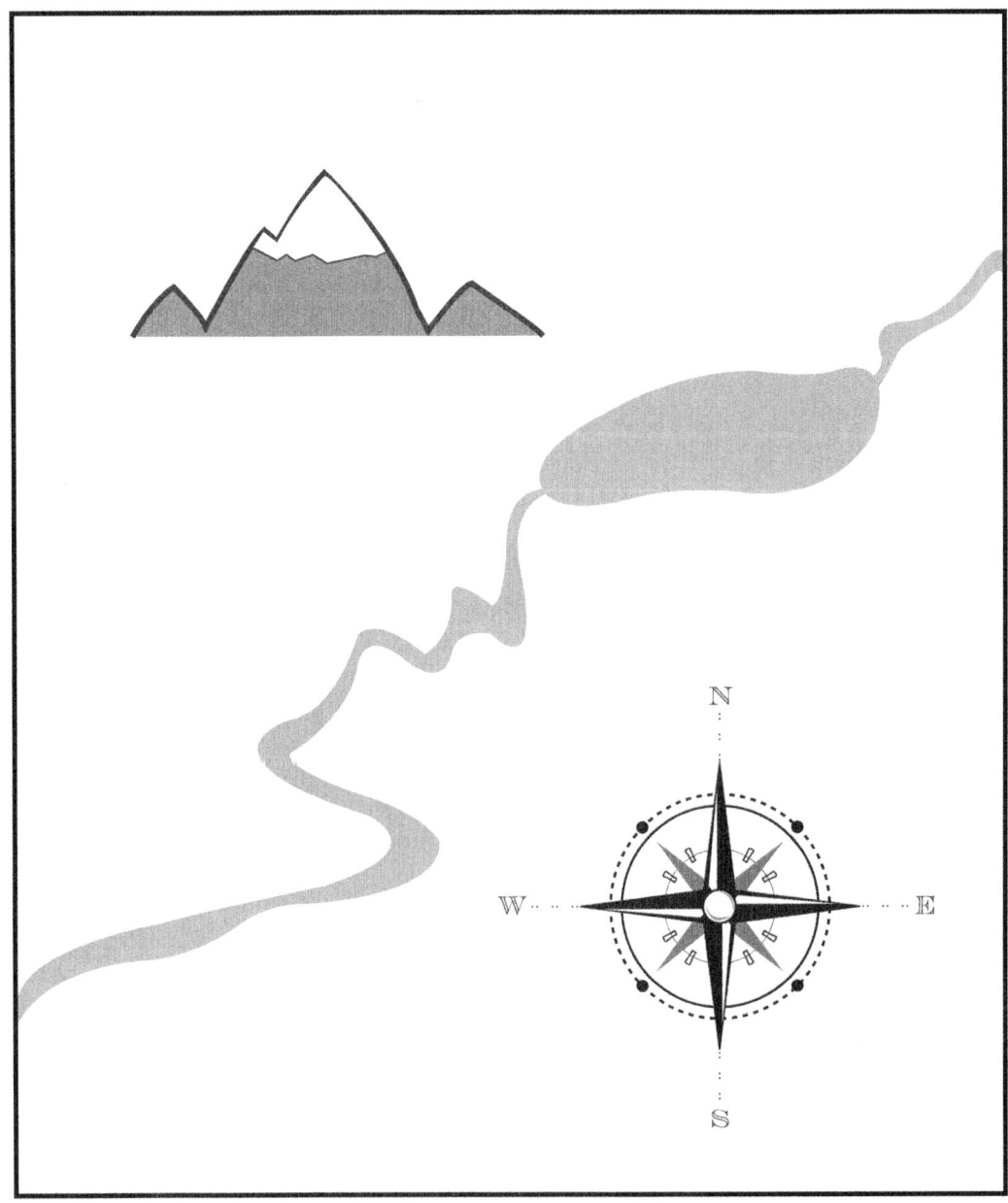

Choose instructions from the list below for your student to complete (there are several options to choose from for differing ages/abilities).

1. Color the stream blue, circle the mountain, and draw a square around the lake.
2. Is the mountain north or south of the lake?
3. Draw a fish in the east end of the lake.
4. Draw another mountain south of the stream.
5. Draw a sun in the northeast corner of the page.

Katy and the Big Snow

Name:

Date:

Science: **Weather**

Copy and laminate this weather calendar, then cut out the cards at the bottom. Using tape, Velcro®, tacky putty or any other temporary adhesive, have your student place the appropriate card on the calendar space representing today's weather.

Today's Weather

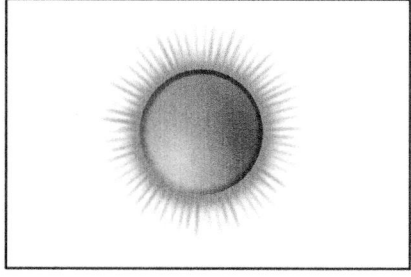

Name:
Date:
Social Studies: **Road Signs**

Here is a grouping of some common street signs. You can discuss these with your student, and even make a copy for them to take on trips in the car.
See how many of these signs they notice as you drive.

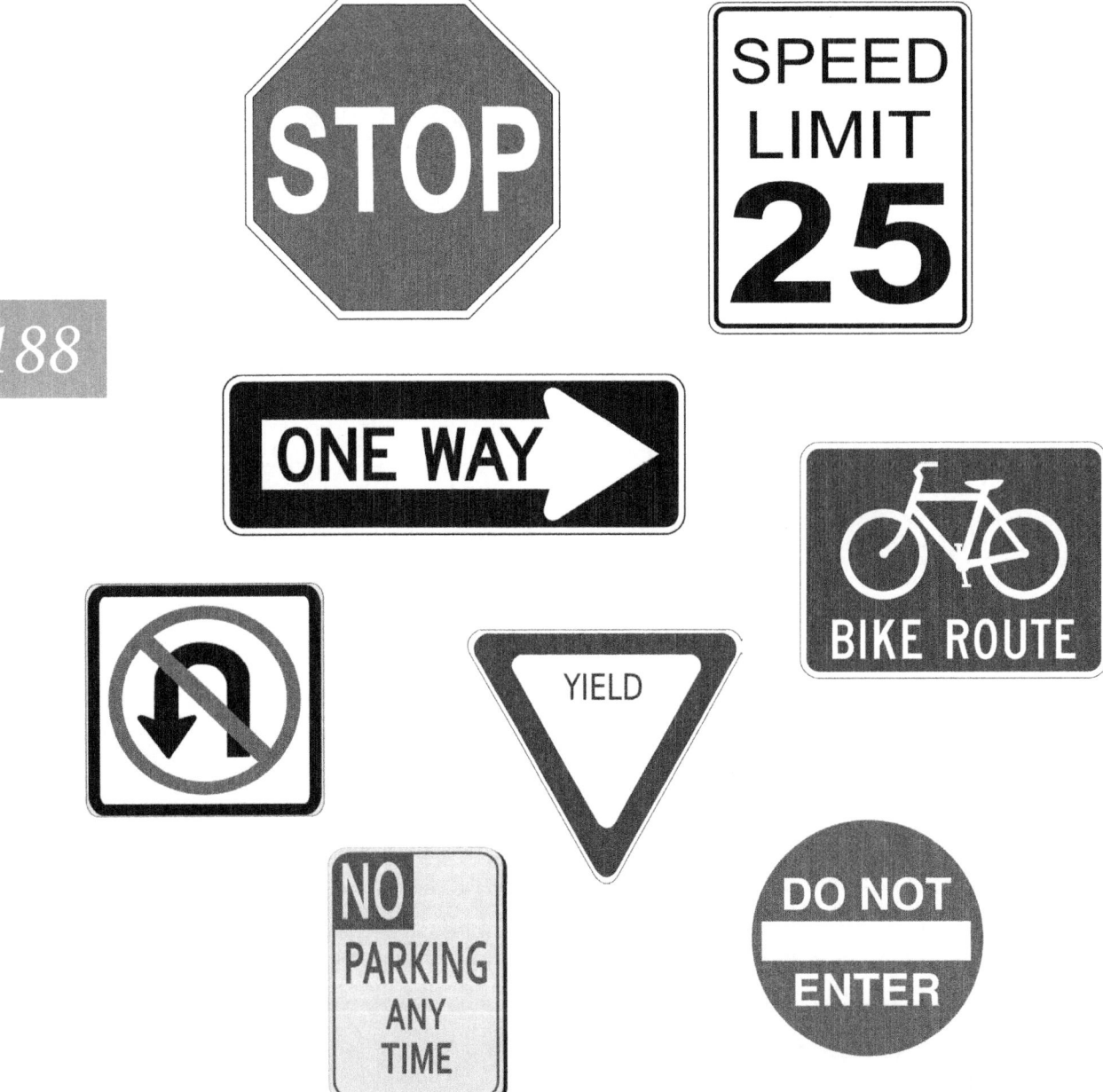

Katy and the Big Snow

Night of the Moonjellies

Title: *Night of the Moonjellies*
Author: Mark Shasha
Illustrator: Mark Shasha
Copyright: 1992
Award: Marion Vannet Ridgway Award
Summary: A seven-year-old boy helps his grandma at her restaurant and she shares a secret with him.

Social Studies: Geography - New England

Mark Shasha has written a book set in a New England town by the sea. Find the states that make up New England: Maine, Vermont, New Hampshire, Massachusetts, Rhode Island and Connecticut. There are many good children's picture books showing the culture and scenery of New England. Place your story disk on New England. If you desire, also find and label the Atlantic Ocean with one of the blank story disks.

You may want to discuss why this area is called New England. The Pilgrims came from England and began to settle in new land. Because they had come from England, they called this new land *New* England.

Social Studies: Introduction to Running a Small Business

In the story *Night of the Moonjellies*, a seven-year-old boy helps out his relatives in their small family-owned restaurant business. These family-run small businesses are sometimes called "Mom and Pop" businesses. What sorts of qualities would be important in running a small restaurant? (Keeping a clean establishment, maintaining healthy food preparation, being friendly, honest, dependable owners, and having knowledge of business affairs.) Small business owner responsibilities may include: purchasing supplies, paying bills (electricity, water, hired help, building payments, supply costs, insurance), cooking and cleaning up, waiting on customers, paying quarterly and annual taxes, etc. Many small business owners enjoy the satisfaction of being the boss. However, the responsibilities can be overwhelming for first-time business owners.

Ask your student to think about a type of business he might like to run and why. Let him imagine being boss. Ask him what kind of people he would hire, and where he would like to have his business (a mall, a corner shop and maybe live upstairs above it, in his own home, etc.) Does he think he would enjoy working at *his* business as much as the boy in this story?

Your student may enjoy pretending to run his own restaurant and take orders from customers. Look for the Guest Check at the end of this unit to help him get started!

Social Studies: Responsibility

Does your student think this seven-year-old boy does well with the responsibility he is given? What is he asked to do? (He is to fill the ketchup, mustard, and relish containers. He is in charge of refilling the straw and napkin holders, and cleaning up the yard [inferred from the illustrations]. He also must stack the hamburgers between pieces of waxed paper, crank open the umbrellas, help with the onion rings, and with drying and putting away the pots and pans.) Do you think he does his job carefully and cheerfully? Can you tell from the pictures? Do you think he *likes* the responsibility? Have your student share the type of responsibilities *he* has at home.

Social Studies: Life Near the Sea

Life near the sea (in *Moonjellies* this means the Atlantic Ocean off the coast of New England) has waves and tides, fried clams and clam chowder, lobsters and lobster rolls. There are lots of other animals near the ocean like starfish, periwinkles, and jellyfish (including moon jellyfish), and sea gulls. There are many kinds of boats including fishing boats, lobster boats and sail boats. The place to dock small boats and buy supplies is called a marina. The air by the seas smells like a mixture of salt and seaweed, and there is lots of sand. There are outdoor shops and stands with many things for sale.

Have you or your student ever been "by the sea?" Share your experiences and memories. If you happen to live near the sea, share stories and memories about a trip to the desert or country instead.

Language Arts: Contrast

Reread the portion of the story where the customers are crowding and the radios blaring, horns beeping, etc. Then reread the description of the thousands of moonjellies stretched along the sea in every direction, as the boy and his grandma stand on the deck and watch the shimmering sea. Look carefully at the accompanying pictures. These scenarios are opposite of each other: one rather frenzied and one more peaceful. Ask your student which scene he appreciates most. Some people love the hustle and bustle of a city with the accompanying noises, sights and smells, while others enjoy a more peaceful country place with the beauty of nature all around them. Either of these preferences is valid, and they also demonstrate contrast!

The variety of scene provides an overall contrast of feeling for the story. Talk about contrast in color like black against white and then about the **contrast** in these **words and feelings** of the story. Let your student try to write a paragraph with contrasting elements such as joy and sadness, or slowness and speed, or heat and cold, etc.

Language Arts: Literary Device - Italics

The names of ships and boats are underlined in handwriting and set in *italics* in printed type. The fisherman in the story that transports the moonjelly to its home has a boat named the *Periwinkle*. Show your student the place in the story where they go to meet the fisherman and his boat. Let him see that the word *Periwinkle* is set in different type. Even if he cannot read the word, he can still recognize that the type is different.

You may have already seen the name of a boat in italics in the story *The Glorious Flight*. Italics are also used for book titles, emphasis in writing, etc.

Language Arts: First Person Point of View

Night of the Moonjellies is written from the first person point of view. That means that the boy writes about himself and those he knows. We see only from his eyes and he uses words like I, me and mine. Try writing a story using the first person point of view.

Language Arts: Vocabulary

marina   A dock for mooring boats and getting supplies; sometimes a service station.

pier   A structure to land and/or tie up boats or ships.

moonjellies   Common jellyfish found on the coasts of the Atlantic and the Pacific Oceans.

Language Arts: List-Making

See how many of the food items mentioned in *Night of the Moonjellies* your student can remember. Make a list and draw pictures next to the words. Let your student add more words to the list each time you reread the story to him.

Art: Medium - Pastels

Pastels are a kind of chalk-like crayon used in drawing. The depth of color is achieved by layering the color and building up the layers. Often when rough-textured paper is used you can see the bumpiness of the paper showing through the chalk pigment. Textured paper can then become part of the overall effect of the drawing. If you have access, try some experiments with pastels. The ocean water on the cover picture would be fun to try to match even if you don't have the same colors. These short, choppy strokes with lots of colors are worth trying to copy. Oil pastels are easier for children to work with since they don't smear as much as chalk pastels. They have long been a favorite of children because of their intense colors. (**Note**: Make sure your student understands the two uses of the word "*pastel*." It can refer to a type of color palette characterized by soft, gentle colors, and it can also refer to a type of artistic medium made of either dry chalks or oil chalks in stick form.) **Caution**: Teacher supervision is necessary with pastels. Your student should not put pastel chalks in his the mouth and he should wash his hands after using them.

Art: Layout

Illustrators and publishers choose how the text and the pictures in a book will be laid out before the book goes to the printer. In *Night of the Moonjellies*, the decision was made to have a single drawing span both pages of the text from the edge of the left side to the edge of the right side. In this story, there are very wide, rectangular-shaped pictures.

Write and illustrate (perhaps even bind*) a small book. Decide if you want a picture under every page of text or one picture spanning two pages of text, as in *Moonjellies*. Decide what medium (watercolors, pastel, pencil, crayon, etc.) you will use. Decide if the pictures will be humorous (as in *How to Make an Apple Pie and See the World*) or serious (as in *Grandfather's Journey*). Remind your student he is the author-illustrator. He gets to make the choices!

*Valerie Bendt's *Creating Books with Children* is a wonderful resource. Along with valuable suggestions to help children with their writing, she carefully explains how to make and bind a book with outstanding results! Seach online to purchase.

Art: Adding Detail Through Illustrations

In *Night of the Moonjellies*, there are a number of details you can learn about the story by looking at the pictures. These details are not mentioned in the text. (The details include: what the boat's cabin looks like inside, a sign that says marina and another sign with the prices of the food, a sign that says diving and fishing charts, a starfish and sea gulls, and the inside details of the boy's grandmother's house, etc.) Talk about the ways a illustrator's detail can help tell much more of the story than is covered in the story text. Have your older student try writing and illustrating a story, or perhaps writing and illustrating a magazine or newspaper type article with this idea in mind.

In addition, the umbrellas that the boy cranks up are not pictured on the page with the text that describes them. See if your student notices that the boy explains his chore before there is any illustration to accompany the text. Point out the illustration on the page that describes the boy and his grandma eating a quick lunch. Remind him that *those* are the umbrellas the boy is responsible for putting up and down!

Art: Viewpoint

The picture on the page where the boy gets his paper hat is drawn from a low viewpoint, as if the artist was sitting on the floor. Look at the cash register and notice how high the little boy looks on the stool. Try sitting on the floor and see how counters, desks, etc., would look if you drew them from that viewpoint. An artist-illustrator gets to choose a different viewpoint for each picture. Sometimes he will draw a picture from high up looking down on his subject, as in the pictures from *The Glorious Flight*. We call this an aerial view, or a "bird's eye view," like in the picture from *Moonjellies* where the boy is running with the broom and pan at the outdoor restaurant. We look down on his activity.

Varying the point of view in the illustrations of a book creates variety and makes the pictures more interesting. Many of the pictures for *Moonjellies* are from a low viewpoint (perhaps to show life from the seven-year-old's perspective), but some are not. Look for other examples of viewpoint in the illustrations of this story.

Remind your student that like this illustrator, he can choose the viewpoint for each picture he illustrates. What viewpoint he chooses to use will depend on the message and information he desires to impart with his drawings and illustrations.

Art: Light and Dark

Find the picture that corresponds to the text, "When the last customers left ..." Hold that place in the book, and find the picture where the boy is filling the catsup container. Now flip back and forth between the two pictures. Note the effect of darkness in one and the lighter rendering of the other. Ask your student how the artist accomplished this effect. (One way is that Shasha has used dark blues in the first picture and light, bright blues in the second. The darkness is not made with black but rather subtle dark shades of blue.) Be looking for other examples of artists illustrating darkness. Note the colors they use to express dark scenes in paintings and books. (Artists rarely use pure black pigments in painting. Pen and black ink, as well as charcoal, obviously utilize pure black.)

Art: Warm Palette

Grandma starts down the pier and stops at the boat. Look at the picture where the fisherman waves. The darkening blue sky gives a feeling of coolness to the night air. Grandma then says, "Let's go in and keep warm." Turn the page and experience the warmth (you can almost feel it!) of the deep orange and yellow colors. This reminds us of the warm, red-orange glow of the fire reflecting off the face of Mako in *A Pair of Red Clogs*. Yellows, oranges and reds (the colors of the sun and of fire) symbolize warmth. These colors are used by artists to help us see and virtually *feel* the heat. Remind your student that when he wants to show warmth in one of his pictures (either of actual heat like a campfire or a warmth of emotion like a loving family scene) he might want to make use of warm colors.

Math: Learning About Money

Night of the Moonjellies provides a chance to introduce the topic of money. Depending where your student is in his studies you could explain the names of the coins and bills. (Let him see real money, touch it, and notice all the differences in color, weight, etc., of the coins, and the different pictures on the bills.) You may decide that it is time to explain coin equivalents, such as five pennies in a nickel, etc.

Making change is another a topic that goes well with this story of a small business. With your student fix hot dogs or sandwiches. Pretend to sell them to each other. (You will need to decide beforehand how much to charge. Ask your student how much they cost to make? What will happen if you sell the hot dogs for that price? It's best to remember to add a reasonable profit!) Then role play paying each other, and make the correct change. Look for the Guest Check at the end of this unit!

Science: Moon Jellyfish

Moonjellies are the most common jellyfish. They are disk-shaped, white or bluish marine animals, and are found along the Atlantic and Pacific coasts—and sometimes at zoos or aquariums. Talk about the fact that the little boy knows that what he finds is alive because he puts it in a bag and adds seawater. What would happen if he had carried it to the restaurant without the water? What might have happened if he had added fresh water? Discuss the fact that the animals that live in water, need water to survive. Those animals that live in salt water need *salt* water, and those that live in fresh water (non-salty rivers, lakes, streams and ponds) need *fresh* water to live.

Science: Biome - Aquatic

A biome is the distinctive group of plants and animals that live in a particular geographic region defined by climate. Scientists loosely recognize the categories of different aquatic biomes. In this story we see or read about starfish, sea gulls, jellyfish, clams and lobsters. Draw a picture of life by the sea and include some of the animals, plants and birds that might be there. If there is interest, find books at the library about the sea and oceans.

Teacher's Notes

The *Five in a Row* lesson options for each unit in the manual are all you need to teach your child. The additional resource area provided below is simply a place to jot down relevant info you've found that you might want to reference.

NIGHT OF THE MOONJELLIES

Date:

Student:

Five in a Row Lesson Topics Chosen:

Social Studies:

Language Arts:

Art:

Math:

Science:

Relevant Library Resources: Books, DVDs, Audio Books

Websites or Video Links:

Related Field Trip Opportunities:

Favorite Quote or Memory During Study:

Name:
Date:
Social Studies: **Working in a Restaurant**

Your student might find it fun to name his own restaurant, create his own menu (with prices!), and then take your order on the guest check below. This activity is enjoyable with either pretend food or real food! An older student can write down actual food items and prices, while a younger child can "write" (scribble) orders on their own guest check, help "cook" or bring food to the table. Make copies before use. This is an activity that your child will enjoy again and again!

Restaurant:

Guest Check

| SERVER | TABLE | GUESTS | CHECK NUMBER |

TAX

Thank You   TOTAL

Night of the Moonjellies

Stopping by Woods on a Snowy Evening

Title: *Stopping by Woods on a Snowy Evening*
Author: Robert Frost
Illustrator: Susan Jeffers
Copyright: 1978 (Jeffers' illustrated edition)
Summary: A counterpoint of verse and illustration draws the reader gently into a winter night.

Note: This is not a "complete" unit because it does not cover Social Studies, or Math and Science in great detail. But even though this unit isn't quite as long as the others, Frost's excellent verse and Susan Jeffers' engaging illustrations are too good to be missed! Since this version of the famous poem is actually a picture book, you'll find it in the children's section of your library.

Language Arts: Poet - Robert Frost

Robert Frost might be the most popular American poet of his time. He was born in 1874 and died two years after reading one of his poems at the inauguration of John F. Kennedy in 1961! His poems are associated with New England and are about common people, working people, country people and the nature around them. With your student, explore other Frost poems. Request a complete collection of his works from the library, or find individual poems online, such as "Blueberries," a story poem of boys picking blueberries, "Mending the Wall," or "A Time to Talk." Your young student will enjoy just hearing the wonderful sounds of the words in these poems, and you can discuss the messages of the poems with your older student.

Five in Row Volume One

Language Arts: What Makes a Poem?

Poetry is as varied as the poets who write it. Robert Frost said, "Poetry is the kind of thing poets write." However, poetry does have certain characteristics. Poetry appeals to the reader's emotions. It often gives a sharp picture (mind's-eye *image*) of the subject. Poets use certain devices in their work including repetition, rhythm, sometimes rhyme, personification, metaphoric language, alliteration (the repetitive consonant sounds in a line of poetry: "silver slivers in the sun"), onomatopoeia, and hyperbole (exaggeration: "he was so hungry he could eat a horse"; hie PER buh lee). These literary devices can be found in prose too, but you *expect* a poet to make greater use of them.

If a *storybook's* author makes much use of these techniques, he is said to have written "poetic prose." Many of the sentences in *Grandfather's Journey* are written with a poetic style even though *Grandfather's Journey* is not a poem.

Stopping by Woods On A Snowy Evening is a poem. Robert Frost has made good use of the various poetic devices, as the reader expects he would.

Language Arts: Poetry - Alliteration

Alliteration, (uh lit ter AY shun) is a repetitive consonant sound in a line of poetry or prose. Usually it is the initial (beginning) sound, but not always. For instance: "silver slivers in the sun." The letter "s" at the end of the word slivers is also alliterative. The "s" *sound* (not always the letter "s") is alliterative. "Smooth circular seashells" has four alliterative "s" sounds, yet not every word begins with the same letter.

Examples of alliteration in *Stopping by Woods on a Snowy Evening*:

"the woods are lovely, dark and deep"

"The only other sound's the sweep"

For your younger student it is probably enough to simply draw her attention to the "sound" of alliteration. She'll enjoy the repetitive sounds and begin to notice them in other books and poems that she hears. For your slightly older student, you may want to encourage her to try writing alliterative sentences by herself. If you feel that she needs help, you may want to begin by creating together a long list of words with the same beginning sound. Let her select several of those words and create a sentence with them. As she understands the concept she may choose to use alliteration in her writing and in her poetry.

Language Arts: Rhyme and Rhyme Scheme

Frost's poem was originally set (as opposed to the line-per-page format of this book edition) in four stanzas of four lines each, called quatrains. You **name** a rhyme scheme by giving the lines with the same ending sound the same letter:

"Whose woods these are I think I <u>know</u>   A
His house is in the village <u>though</u>;   A
He will not see me stopping here   B
To watch his woods fill up with <u>snow</u>."   A

Thus, this poem has a rhyme scheme of **AABA** (except for the last stanza where all four ending words rhyme: deep, keep, sleep, sleep).

To introduce your older student to rhyme scheme, just point out the patterns of the the ending sounds. Children love the sound of rhyme, as evidenced by the popularity of Dr. Seuss and poems by A. A. Milne of *Winnie the Pooh* fame, as well as many others. For an older student, let her try her own poem, duplicating the rhythm and rhyme scheme of the above stanza.

Also, when this poem is set in stanzas, you will notice the ending word of *each third* line is the rhyming sound for the *following* stanza. "Here," in stanza one, becomes the rhyming sound in "queer, near and year," in stanza two, etc.

Language Arts: Literary Device - Repetition

The ending of Frost's poem is a repetitive line: "And miles to go before I sleep." Repetition emphasizes the thought, and deepens the meaning.

Language Arts: Reading Poetry to Children

Reading a lot of poetry to young children helps them develop an ear for interesting sounds and rhythms, increasing their literary appreciation in years to come. Some excellent books of poems for reading together are:

Now We Are Six and *When We Were Very Young*
A. A. Milne

The World of Christopher Robin
A. A. Milne (This is a volume of the above two titles combined.)

Favorite Poems Old and New
Edited by Helen Ferris

The Moon's the North Wind's Cooky
Edited by Susan Russo

Joyful Noise (Poems for Two Voices)
Paul Fleischman (for older students; *absolutely* delightful!)

Sing a Song of Popcorn
Edited by Beatrice Schenk de Regniers

Also look for children's poetry by Robert Louis Stevenson, Jack Prelutsky and Shel Silverstein.

Language Arts: Memorizing Poetry

"Stopping by Woods on a Snowy Evening" is a good poem to memorize (for the teacher or older student) because of the gentle way the words sound next to one another. The peace and tranquility of the poem are comforting and the appreciation of the beauty of nature is inspiring, while the repetition at the end nearly lulls the reader to sleep.

Art: Medium and Style

Susan Jeffers has used pencil, and pen and ink to fashion an experience in the snowy woods. Her naturalistic style (trees look like actual types of trees; the details of nature are carefully preserved) and her restrained touches of color add to the impression of a dusky winter evening.

Find the color (other than shades of gray) on each page. Ask your student what the artist was doing with her use of color. Notice exactly *what* is colored in each picture and think about what she was trying to accomplish with this use of color. (Perhaps she has separated the woods and woodland creatures from the man and his kind. You might infer this, as the houses in the village have some color too.) Can you think of other reasons the artist may have had?

Remind your student that artists choose carefully where to put color. They have particular reasons for deciding whether or not to use color, and if they do, what color expresses their message and represents their ideas. As your student progresses in her art work, she will have the same opportunity to make choices.

Notice the woodland creatures and how alive they look. Even the dried grasses and flowers are recognizable species that grow at the edge of the woods. In the picture opposite the line "The woods are lovely, dark and deep," animals are hiding in the woods. See if your student can find seven animals (a mouse, two deer, a blue jay, two rabbits and a squirrel).*

There are obviously other animals you can't see in the picture you just studied, because if you turn two pages you see a great many animals coming out of the woods to the man's gift of food. Notice how Jeffers portrays the cautious tendencies of animals by causing the reader to wait a page or two before the large group of animals comes out to eat. Susan Jeffers knows her subjects and draws them well, even to the timing and sequence of her pictures.

*There are other pictures with hidden animals in this book.

Art: Integrating Illustrations With Text

Susan Jeffers has illustrated Frost's poem capturing the poet's awe and wonder at the beautiful scene before him. Look at the pictures that accompany the lines "the only other sound's the sweep of easy wind and downy flake." These pictures poignantly display the man's vulnerability. We see him in Jeffers' drawings (as the poet probably intended) unashamedly appreciating the snowy scene. The man enjoys the beautiful scene even to the point of "childlikeness" as he makes a snow angel! Ask your student to look at these pictures and ask her if she thinks the man is enjoying the snow. What could the man be thinking?"

Yet Susan Jeffers has accomplished something else. Besides faithfully rendering the poet's words and feelings, she has also added her own story in her drawings. Had she done the latter without accomplishing the former, her work would not be true to the poem. If you read the poem carefully, you will see that there is no mention of a man making a snow angel, nor of a man feeding the animals, nor of the man's relatives. Yet Jeffers, without harming the integrity of Frost's poem, has included her elements as a sort of artistic counterpoint melody to his poem. The result is lovely and carries two stories, one in the text of the poem, woven together with the other in the illustrations.

Jeffers said of her work on this project, "I worked on the illustrations every day for six months, but I never tired of the poem." After reading it together with your student for five days in a row, it will be a part of *your* shared experiences. And you will be glad you were allowed to experience, with the man, his time alone in the beautiful woods. With the last line and the last picture, the man disappears into the swirling snow. Do you wish you could follow him?

Art: Viewpoint

Jeffers' drawings are all done from a bird's-eye or aerial view. This makes the reader feel as if he is sitting on a branch of a tree looking down on the scene. The one exception (variation) to this is the picture corresponding with the line "Between the woods and frozen lake / the darkest evening of the year." In this picture, the reader sees from the animal's viewpoint and looks *up* slightly, at the man digging for something in the back of his sleigh. How has Susan Jeffers accomplished the task of making the reader feel as if she is looking up? (She elevates the man high up into the corner of the picture and places the animal subject (through whose eyes the reader is looking), in the lower opposite corner. She also makes the man smaller than the animal, so the man looks higher up and far away.

Art: Mood

The mood of Frost's poem is quiet, like the quiet of freshly-fallen snow that muffles the sounds around it. The mood of Jeffers' drawings corresponds with the poet's writings. The illustrations are as quiet and lovely as Frost's words and the woods themselves. There is calmness in the fact that the man is alone. This is a solitary experience. Can your student think of a special time when she saw or appreciated something when there was no one else around?

Art: Detail and History

Discuss the familiar song "Jingle Bells." In the song, the "jingle bells" are like the bells in Jeffers' illustrations and the "one-horse open sleigh" is like the sleigh in Jeffers' illustrations. Seeing a picture of the subject of this famous song can make a difference in your student's understanding. Then she can understand what a sleigh looks like and won't be confused as one child once was, thinking the words to the song were "a one horse soap and sleigh." If you have an opportunity, take a sleigh ride with your student. Farmers and stables sometimes offer such rides if you don't happen to have a friend with a sleigh! Of course some snow is good too. For areas of the country without snowfall you might enjoy finding some children's movies that show snow storms and sleigh rides. The movie *The Polar Express* has excellent examples of sleigh bells jingling. Search online for "sleigh bells" or "sleigh ride" if you would like to familiarize your student with the sound of jingling sleigh bells or a sleigh ride.

Notice the beauty in the detail of the snowflakes on the page with the line " ...and downy flake." Contrast this detail with the last picture of the snow flurry where no single flake is visible.

Don't forget to enjoy the curled-up fox on the title page. He looks like he's keeping warm. Many times the pictures on the title page are overlooked because the reader tends to turn directly to the story's beginning. Some pictures on title pages are quite beautiful and some give information about the coming story. Remind your student to begin reading at the title page. (Noticing the covers of the book, any pictures on the inside covers, or book jackets is also beneficial to the enjoyment and understanding of the story.)

Math: Flash Cards

Make math flash cards or concept cards using animals or animal tracks to tie them to the story. There are suggestions for making flash cards in the "How to Use *Five In A Row*" Math section at the beginning of this manual, and there is an Animal Track Reference at the end of this unit.

Science: Animal Tracks

In several pictures of *Stopping by Woods on a Snowy Evening* you can see tracks of the man and his horse. Near the end, you can also see the tracks of the sleigh as it glides away. Open the book and look for these tracks.

Let your student know that during times of snow, one can often see animal tracks as well. Maybe she has already noticed cat, dog or bird tracks on snowy days. There are other animals that she might be able to detect with some help. Even in the cities or suburbs, one can often see the tracks of squirrels, rabbits and mice. In the country the list grows: raccoons, skunks, turtles (in the summer!), deer, and many more. Even if your student lives where there is no snow, let her know she can often find animal tracks in dust or mud. This is especially true at the edges of creeks and rivers, etc. Studying the tracks of animals in the snow, dust or mud can be an exciting adventure. Two excellent adult books to help the teacher with such adventures are:

A Guide to Animal Tracking and Behavior
by Donald and Lillian Stokes

A Guide to Nature In Winter
by Donald Stokes

A book that your student would enjoy on this subject is *Crinkleroot's Book of Animal Tracking* by Jim Arnosky

Teacher's Notes

The *Five in a Row* lesson options for each unit in the manual are all you need to teach your child. The additional resource area provided below is simply a place to jot down relevant info you've found that you might want to reference.

STOPPING BY WOODS ON A SNOWY EVENING

Date:

Student:

Five in a Row Lesson Topics Chosen:

Social Studies:

Language Arts:

Art:

Math:

Science:

Relevant Library Resources:
Books, DVDs, Audio Books

Websites or Video Links:

Related Field Trip Opportunities:

Favorite Quote or Memory During Study:

Stopping By Woods on a Snowy Evening

Name:
Date:
Science: **Animal Tracks**

Animal Track Reference

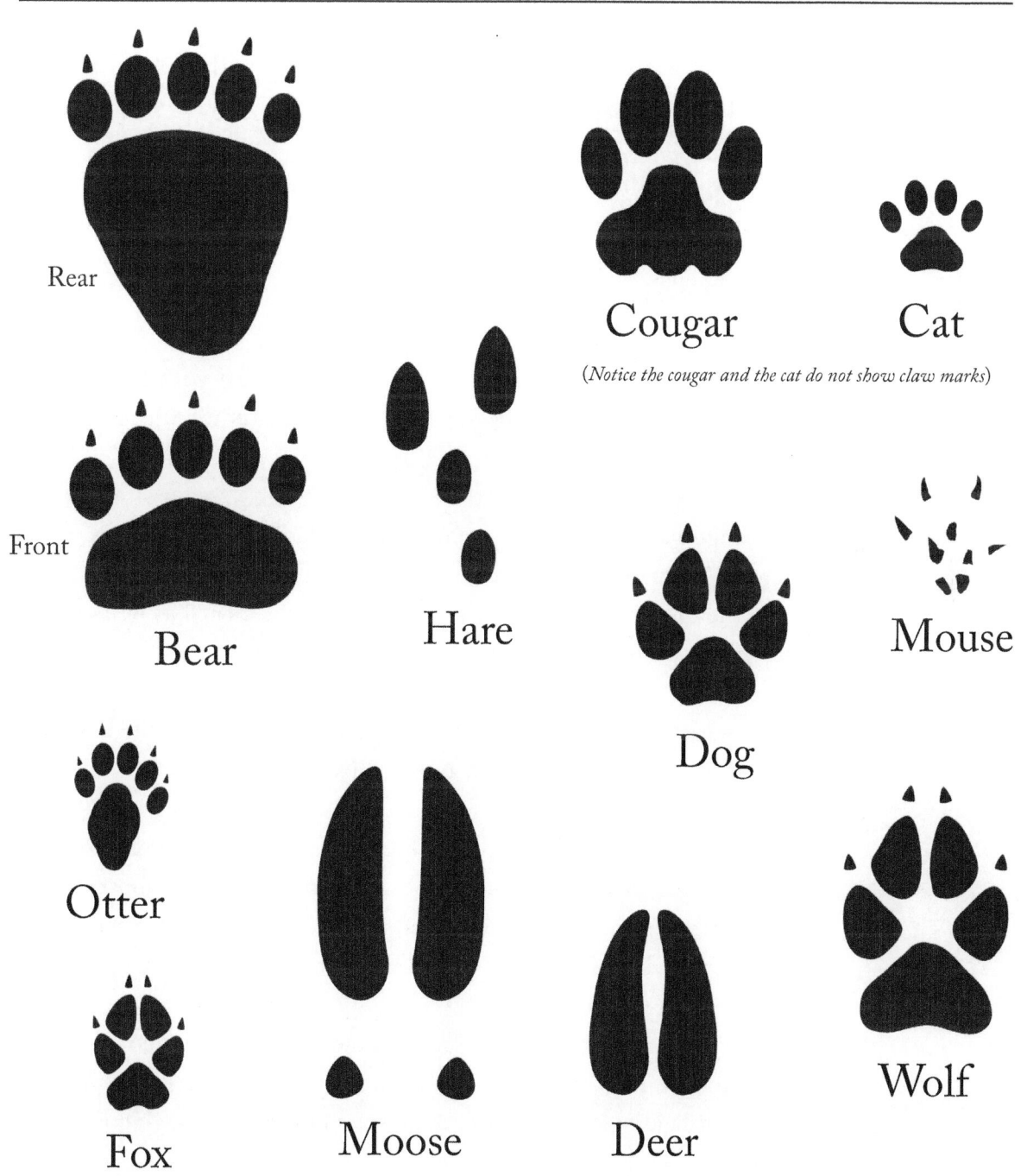

Review Week

Take a week to review the books, authors and illustrators you've studied in *Five in a Row* Volume 1. Recall which titles were award winners. Figure out which book is the oldest, and which book was written the most recently. Discuss the stories you and your student particularly liked and which characters or ideas were your favorites. If you do not own the books, use the colorful story disks to bring back memories of the stories.

Look again at the art work and review the elements of art that you have learned. If you have kept an illustrated chart of art definitions and elements, review it now. Examine your student's art work and point out examples you feel are outstanding. Let her see how much she has learned!

If your student has kept a notebook, leaf through it with her, recalling various projects and reviewing concepts in Social Studies, Geography, Science, and Math.

In Language, review the elements of a story and literary devices. If you have kept an illustrated chart of these items, use it for a comprehensive review. Look over the exercises, stories and poems that your student has written. Point out specific work that was creative or excellent.

Review the vocabulary words using your illustrated list or file box. Recall the stories in which they appeared, and practice using them.

See how many story disks your student can correctly place on the map. If you have studied the continents and oceans, practice placing those, too. Review the lessons in finding directions and compass points on the map. Remember with her the directions she discovered relating to her home and neighborhood.

Thank you for using *Five in a Row* Volume 1. I hope you enjoyed using it with your student. If so, you'll want to continue with Volume 2, which includes 21 more outstanding units that provide inspired learning through great books. And please tell a friend about *Five in a Row*!

Five in a Row Volume One Story Disks

COPYRIGHT © 2020 BY FIVE IN A ROW PUBLISHING • ALL RIGHTS RESERVED

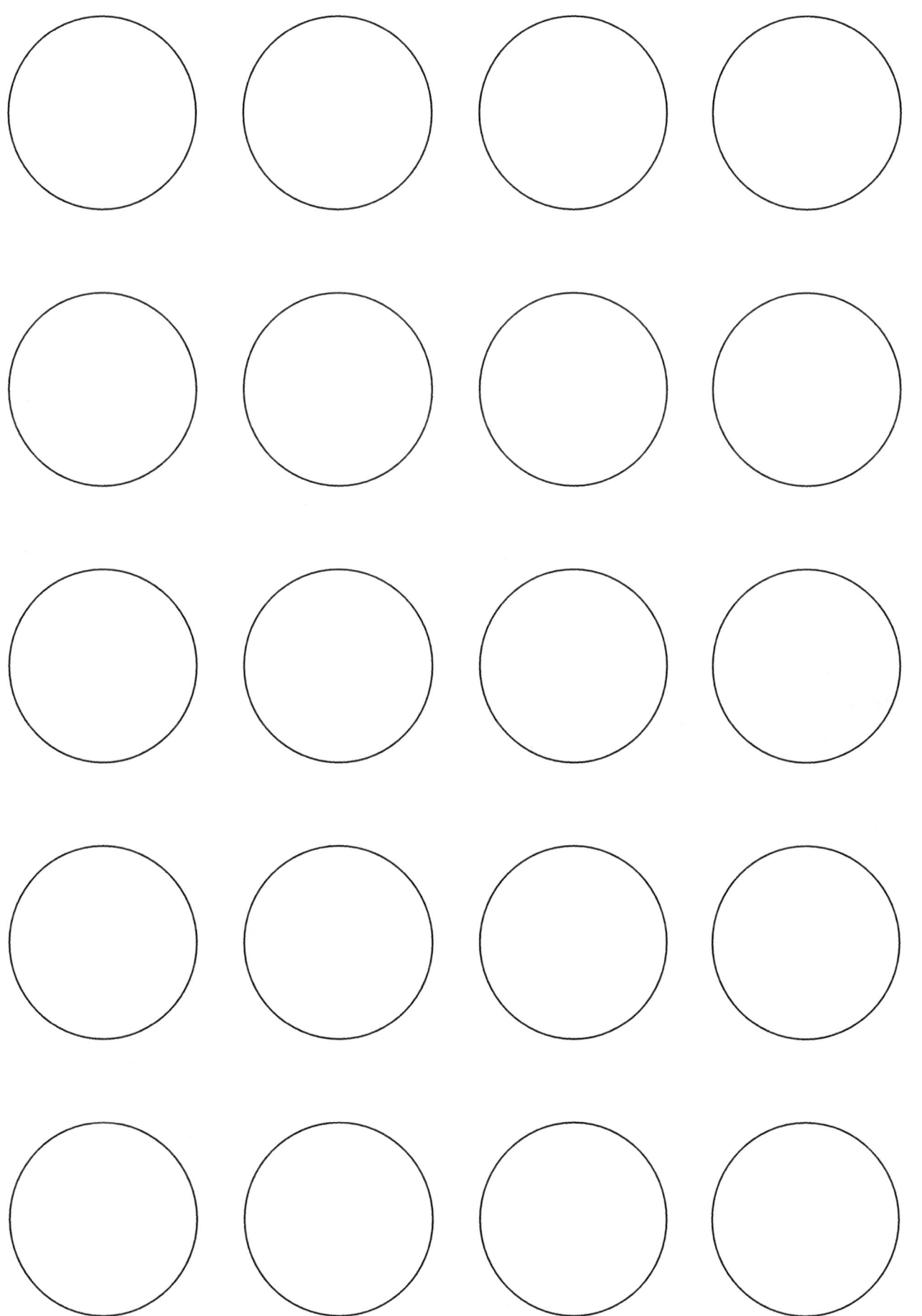

Sample **Lesson Planning Sheet**

Who Owns the Sun? has twenty suggested lessons in the lesson portion of this manual. The sample planning sheet below shows twelve ideas that *could* be chosen for a one-week study for a younger student. You are free to choose *any* of the twenty lesson ideas and keep track of your choices by noting them on the reproducible, blank Lesson Planning Sheet (following pages). For more ideas on making the best use of your *Five in a Row* curriculum, be sure to read the *How to Use Five in a Row* section at the front of the manual.

	Monday	Tuesday
Title: *Who Owns the Sun?* **Author:** Stacy Chbosky **Illustrator:** Stacy Chbosky **Award:** "Written and Illustrated by..." Award	**Social Studies** Read story through, then: Family Relationship Talk about father and son: Father's wisdom Son believes him and admires him Son's labor of love p. 21 Son finds out the hard truth of slavery (how would you feel if you were not free?) Son knows father can't conrtol everything Going on with and making something out of his life	**Language Arts** Read story through, then: List-Making: List the qualities of Big Jim from the reading (What was Big Jim like?) List words on paper as we remember them together Print word with symbol picture beside it: BIG HANDS! (Add to the list as we remember more through the week. Be on the lookout for Big Jim characteristics)

Wednesday	Thursday	Friday
Art	**Math**	**Science**
Read story through, then:	Read story through, then:	Read story through, then:
Discuss the artist, who was 14 years old when she wrote and illustrated this book!	Counting:	Discuss Five Senses from the story and find them on p. 7, etc. Use activity sheet following unit to record them.
Her paintings are simple and strong. Show a picture with fine details to point out the contrast of Chbosky's simpler art style. Filled with strength and emotion.	Count pickets of fence pp. 7 & 21 Count stars on p. 9 Count flowers on p. 17 Count tree stumps on p. 25	smell hearing touch taste sight
How does she do this? (Action and Color)	Use story motif to make cards for addition of twos	Seasons: Spring; story begins Summer; story ends
What colors are on the pages? New colors: chartruese and mauve	2 + 3	Name the characteristics of spring and summer
Do the pictures of the sun make you feel warm? What colors did she use for this? Note also shadows and bright light.	Put answer on back 5	Memory Game: What did Mother pack in Father's lunch?

Lesson Planning Sheet

Title:

Author:

Illustrator:

Award:

Monday	Tuesday

Wednesday	Thursday	Friday

Choices a Writer Can Make

Choices an Artist Can Make

Literary Glossary

Literary Devices

Alliteration
A succession of similar *sounds* (not letters) that occur at the beginning of a group of successive words. "The *d*og *d*ug a *d*eep *d*itch."

Hyperbole
An overstatement or exaggeration: "*I've told you a thousand times!*"

Irony
An event or outcome which is opposite what would naturally be expected: "*It was an irony of fate that the girl arrived just as her date left.*"

Italics
Letters slanted to the right, used for emphasis or to identify book titles, ship names, etc.: "The *Queen Mary* can sail so *fast* compared to ships long ago!"

Mood
The feelings a work of literature brings to the reader: sad, foreboding, buoyant, etc., derived from the particular descriptive words chosen by the writer.

Onomatopoeia
Representing a thing or action by a word that imitates the sound associated with it: *zoom, ping, ding-dong, buzz.*

Personification
Giving a thing, animal or abstract truth human characteristics: "*The moon smiled down on me.*"

Repetition
The repeating of certain words, phrases or ideas throughout a story or poem: "And I will take you home with me; yes, I will take you home with me."

Rhyme
In lines of poetry, where the ending *sounds* (not necessarily the letters) are the same: "Don't blame *me* / go and *see*..."

Simile
The comparison of two dissimilar objects, using the word *like* or *as*. "*When the lights went out, he was as brave as a lion.*"

Symbolism
Writing that suggests more than the literal meaning. "*The innocent girl wore a white dress.*" (White being a symbol of purity.)

Elements of a Story

Characters
A person, animal or thing (wind, for example) that inhabits a story.

Point of view
Who narrates (tells) the story:
>First person: using I, me, etc.
>Third person: using he, she, they, etc.

The point of view is usually the same throughout a short story, but you may find some stories where it changes. Ask, "who is telling this story?" Is the story told from only one character's viewpoint? (first person) Or from the wider view of a narrator? (third person)

Mood
The feelings a story stirs in the reader: calm, happy, sad, fearful, etc. The mood of a story can change; for example, from an ominous beginning to a happy ending. Sometimes there is a pervasive mood throughout a story such as wistfulness, etc.

Plot
The action or story line, which includes:

Conflict - the main problem of the story
Rising Action - events that create rising interest
Climax - the high point of action or tension
Denouement - the resolution or final outcome

Theme
The general idea or insight revealed in the story. The *heart and soul* of the story.

Setting
Where does the story take place: geography, town, a room, etc.? The time frame for the story: an hour, a day, a certain year or period of years, a season, etc.

Style
Someone once said, "Style is the *clothes* the words wear." In other words, how they are dressed—what *fashion* of words and sentence structure a writer uses to *outfit* his story. Many famous writers have distinctive styles. You can often tell by reading only a few paragraphs who wrote a passage. You might say, "Oh, that story sounds like it was written by ...."

Finding the Books

Much has changed in the library system, due to internet access, since *Five in a Row* was first published. Some of the book titles in Volumes 1-3 may be out of print, and your local library branch may not own all the titles that are in print. However, it is easier than ever to search your library's online catalogue and request/hold titles. Even Interlibrary Loan (ILL) is something you can search from your home computer, through your library's website.

Not all library systems are exactly alike, but most online searches work in a similar way. You will sign in to your library system online with your library card number. Your personal account will show books you've requested or placed on hold and books you've checked out. Some systems even have virtual bookshelves where you can place titles for the future or that you've completed. If your online library system has this, it would be convenient to place the FIAR titles on your "future shelf" so that you can quickly go there to request a title or two for your upcoming studies.

When searching your library system's catalogue or the ILL catalogue, here are a few tips. Sometimes a book title won't be found when you search for it. Before giving up or moving on to ILL, try searching the author's name instead. Many times a book can be found listed with all of the author's other books even if it isn't found through a title search. This is true of the ILL catalogue system as well.

Placing several titles on hold every week or two will bring a consistent flow of books cycling in and will allow you to choose which one to use next. By requesting titles online you save yourself the time and effort of searching for books in person. The librarians will locate the book, shelved or misshelved. They will flag the computer to automatically hold the title for you when another library patron returns the book. The ILL requests will automatically happen through the libraries' computer systems. The requested book will be placed on hold for you and shipped to your requested library to be picked up next time you stop by. All of this will save you valuable time and energy!

As your local library collects your requested titles, they will notify you to let you know another book or two is being held for you. What could be easier?

If your library does not carry a *Five in a Row* title, or any book, that you wish they had on their shelves, it's a good idea to request it. The reason for this is that a library will sometimes eventually purchase a book if it's requested often enough. So if the library comes up empty-handed on a particular title, keep requesting it every few weeks. Encourage your friends to request it too! You'd be surprised how many wonderful books end up in the system that way. (Your library may have a quick and easy way to do this: check their website to see if they have an option for "Make a purchase request.")

A personal anecdote: A dear friend who began reviewing *Five in a Row* many years ago obtained *Who Owns the Sun?* via ILL. When she returned it, she suggested the librarian consider purchasing a copy for the local library. The busy librarian brushed her aside saying, "I'm sorry, but we've already spent our budget for this year; it's out of the question." Our friend simply opened the book and began reading it aloud to the librarian right at the check-out desk! Before she was halfway through, the librarian was wiping away tears as she listened to the poignant story, and by the time our friend finished reading, the librarian grabbed the book from her saying, "I'm going to take $15 from our office supply budget and order this book immediately!"

Sadly, many of the most wonderful books being written today, as well as marvelous classics like *The Story About Ping*, are being supplanted on limited library shelf space by books of far less merit. The library system is designed to respond to patron usage and requests. They buy and maintain what the most people are reading. One of our more subtle opportunities is to bless our communities with wholesome, solid books by requesting them, sharing them with local librarians, or even donating a copy of a special title from time to time. Our libraries are what we make of them!

One final note on the titles used in *Five in a Row*. We know that some of the books are difficult to locate or currently out of print for those who wish to purchase them. While we struggled with this issue, in the end, we concluded that we wanted to offer the very best of the more than 5,000 children's books we've explored and examined. In the first three volumes of FIAR, we've supplied dozens of complete unit study lesson plans—more than enough for two, three, or more years of schooling.

For those who are willing to leave no stone unturned in their search for every FIAR title, we're sure you'll be blessed and rewarded for your trouble. Some of the more difficult titles to find are some of the richest! And, since publication of the first edition of *Five in a Row*, many previously out-of-print titles have come back into print, most notably from our friends at Purple House Press. So keep on the lookout for hard-to-find titles by trading with friends, having relatives check their libraries, requesting again and again locally, exploring used bookstores and thrift stores, etc. Many parents find that they enjoy the excitement of the search!

In the final analysis, we've tried to give you the very "best of the best" from the more than 5,000 children's books Jane has explored in the hopes that each one will be a present joy and a lifetime friend for both you and your children. God bless you and your children as you set out on the wonderful adventure of learning with *Five in a Row*.

Integrating Additional Curricula with *Five in a Row*

For teaching very young children, you will find *Five in a Row* to be an exciting and complete curriculum. Once you make the decision that your student is ready to begin phonics, reading and mathematics, you will want to supplement your *Five in a Row* curriculum with these additional materials.

There are many wonderful products available to help you teach phonics/reading and mathematics. You will find helpful descriptions of available products online or through recommendations from other homeschool parents. You may also want to make plans to see and review these materials firsthand by planning to attend a homeschool convention or curriculum fair in your area. Most of these events occur between March and July each year.

Once you integrate your new reading/phonics and mathematics curricula with *Five in a Row*, your teaching day may look something like this:

Morning
Math instruction
Five in a Row (read the story aloud and discuss one of the five subject areas)
Lunch (Nap or rest time?)

Afternoon
Phonics/Reading instruction

Or perhaps you'll want to do phonics and mathematics in the morning and save your *Five in a Row* until after lunch as a sort of reward for the morning's work. Other families prefer to do *all* their work in the morning, leaving the afternoon free for other pursuits. Arrange your teaching day in whatever way works best for you and your student. Don't be afraid to change or rearrange your schedule to provide variety, flexibility or to try new schedules until you find what works best for you. There is *no* right or wrong way to do it!

If you would like to create a chart for your schedule, it might look like this:

Monday	Tuesday	Wednesday	Thursday	Friday
Math	Math	Math	Math*	Math
Phonics	Phonics	Phonics	Phonics	Phonics
FIAR Social Studies	FIAR Language Arts	FIAR Art	FIAR Applied Math	FIAR Science

*You may or may not want to omit your math curriculum lesson on Thursday and concentrate on the *Five in a Row* math lesson instead. We believe it's important *not* to skip the *Five in a Row* math lesson however, because it teaches your student how mathematics is applied in life all around her including measuring, telling time, counting money, sewing, building, etc. This lesson time will stimulate math curiosity and encourage your student that real-life math is fun!

Finally, if you are using *Five in a Row* with older students (third grade and up), consider adding brief grammar and spelling lessons. Workbooks containing these lessons are available through curriculum catalogs, teacher's stores, bookstores, online and even at your local Walmart! One series that we've found useful (and there are many) is the *Brighter Child Series*. One book is entitled *English & Grammar*, available for multiple grade levels. These and other simple, affordable booklets can supplement *Five in a Row* for your older students, supplying the needed sequential learning that's appropriate for language arts.

For Science and Social Studies, you will not need to purchase additional curricula, but you might consider having your older student do additional, self-directed reading and reporting on several of the hundreds of topics you will encounter while doing *Five in a Row*.

By enriching *Five in a Row* using advanced, student-directed research and reporting and by supplementing the curriculum with additional work in mathematics, grammar and spelling, you'll find *Five in a Row* can serve as the educational base for your school-age children all the way through the elementary school years.

Parts of a Flag

Throughout the *Five in a Row* stories, your student will learn about many countries and their flags. This page will help your child learn the parts of a flag.

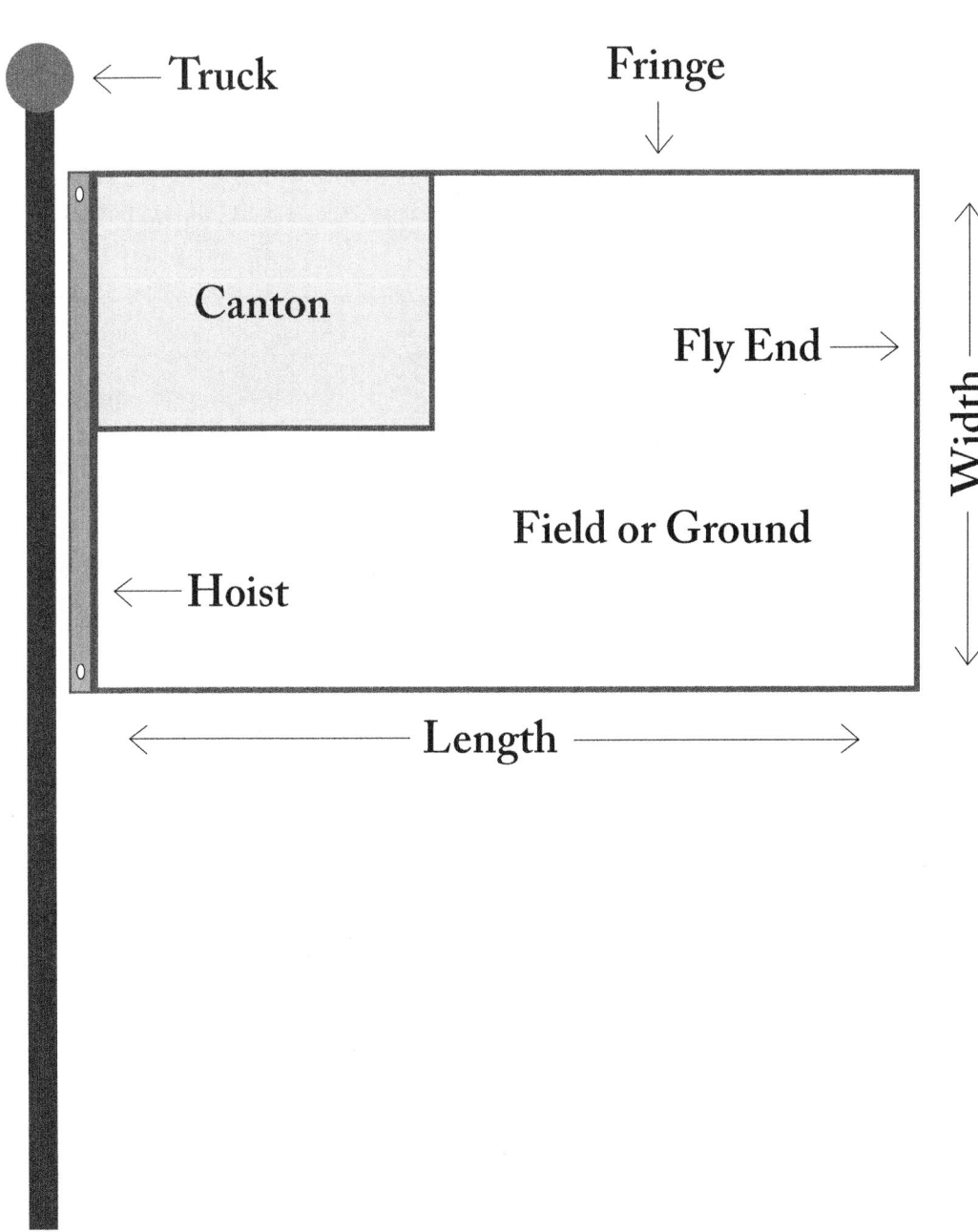

Index

Social Studies
Social Studies, Geography:

Appalachia 66
Arctic 150
Arctic Ocean 150
Asia 111, 141
Atlantic Ocean 118, 150, 189, 190
Cambrai, France 97
Canada 111, 118, 131, 150
China, Chinese culture 28
Compass points (map) 66, 181, 206
Continents 111, 206
Cranberry bog 118
Eiffel Tower 48, 50, 104
England 103, 104
English Channel 48, 97, 98
Europe 89, 103, 111, 141, 160
Flag:
    Canada 156
    China 36
    England 102
    France 54
    Italy 148
    Jamaica 109
    Japan 62
    Russia 138
    Sri Lanka 109
    Union Jack 102
    United Kingdom 102
France, French culture 48, 49, 103, 104
Geoppolis (fictional place) 180
Germany 111
Indian Ocean 104
Inuit culture 151
Island 56, 64, 104, 110

Italy, Italian culture 103, 111, 140, 143
    Language 103, 159
Jamaica, Jamaican culture 103
Japan, Japanese culture 56, 110, 111
Japanese art 113
Land of Make Believe 11
Life near the sea 190
Maine 118, 189
Map 181
Massachusetts 118, 189
Memory game 104, 107, 211
Michigan 104
Minsk 130
Moscow 130
New England 118, 189, 190, 197
New Hampshire 118, 189
North America 110, 114, 118
Oceans:
    Arctic 150
    Atlantic 118, 150, 189, 190
    Indian 104
    Pacific 110
Ohio 38
Oregon 104
Paris 48, 104
Pearl Harbor 111
Popperville (fictional place) 88
Rivers 86, 113, 194, 202
Russia, Russian culture 130, 132, 134, 135
Sea 140
Seine River 48
Siberia 130
Sorrento, Italy 159
South America 111
Southern United States 76
Soviet Union 131

Sri Lanka, Sri Lankan culture 103, 104
St. Petersburg 130
Tundra 150
Ungava Bay 151
Venice, Italy 165, 140
Vermont 103, 104, 118, 189
Washington (state) 104
White Cliffs of Dover 97
Yangtze River 28, 29

Social Studies, Relationships:
Admiration 77
Adoption 142
Ancestors 110
Anger 131
Boasting 87
Compassion 49, 76, 161, 167
Death 67
Deception 57
Devotion 77
Disagreeable/difficult people 39, 119, 161
Discernment 28
Elderly 161, 167, 176
Encouragement 161
Envy 131, 132
Family relationships 28, 76, 151
Fathering 141
Fear 153, 170, 171
First-time experiences 151
Flexibility 87
Forgiveness 67
Friendship 67, 137
Funerals 67
Grandparents 119, 161
Greed 87
Homeless, the 142
Honesty 57
Hospitality 131
Integrity 87, 201

Independence, maturity 151
Jealousy 131
Judging by appearance 119
Love 131, 141, 170
Lying 57
Making reparations 496
Manners 120, 131
Maturity 28, 77, 151
Mothering 151
Mourning 67
Nicknames 119
Occupations 131, 142, 161, 180
Orphans 160
Panic 153, 176
Patriotism 40
Popularity 161
Perseverance 89
Pride 58
Rejecting isolation 67
Respect 131
Responsibilities 181, 190
Sacrifice 132, 141
Self-image 38
Selflessness 67
Stewardship 57, 87
Teasing, taunting 67
Thankfulness 161
Tolerance 111, 120, 167
Traditions 67, 120
Unkindness 87
Wisdom 57, 67, 77, 161, 167

Social Studies, History:
Bleriot, Louis 97
Careers 161, 176
Cities 180
Civil Rights Movement 76
Civil War 76
Cold War 131

Index

Communism 131
Communist Revolution 131
Czarist history 131
Desegregation 76
Directions 181
Discrimination 76
Flag, American 40
Foreign Language:
    Italian 141, 159
    French 48, 97
Funerals, Mourning 67
Geography 38
Gulf War 39
Homeless, the 142
Korean War 39
Map skills 181
Marco Polo 141
Memorial Day 39
Nuclear bomb 111
Occupations 131, 142, 161, 180
Orphans 160
Patriotism 40
Racism 76
Renaissance 159, 160
Revolutionary War 39
Running a city 180
Running a small business 189
Slavery 76
Small business 189
Small town life 39
Steam heat 49
Steam power 86
Street signs 181
Thanksgiving 120
Veterans' Day 39
Vietnam War 39
War monuments 39
World War I 39
World War II 39, 111

Language

Authors of Five in a Row Stories:
    Andrews, Jan 150
    Bemelmans, Ludwig 48
    Burton, Virginia Lee 86, 180
    Chbosky, Stacy 76, 78, 79
    dePaola, Tomie 159
    Devlin, Wende and Harry 118
    Flack, Marjorie 28
    Frost, Robert 197
    Matsuno, Masako 56
    Mills, Lauren 66
    McCloskey, Robert 38
    Priceman, Marjorie 103
    Provensen, Alice and Martin 96
    Say, Allen 110
    Scheffrin-Falk, Gladys 130
    Shasha, Mark 189
    Stolz, Mary 170
    Talley, Carol 140
Awards (for Literature and Illustration):
    Caldecott
    The Glorious Flight 96
    Grandfather's Journey 110
    Madeline (Honor Medal) 48
    Coretta Scott King Honor Book
    Storm in the Night 170
    Marion Vannet Ridgway Award
    Night of the Moonjellies 189
    Written and Illustrated by... Award
    Who Owns the Sun? 76
Characterization 132, 217
Choosing a title 97, 133
Classic literature 29, 90, 180
Climax (element of plot) 40, 41, 79, 88, 122, 217
Comprehension, reading 163
Conflict (element of plot) 40, 88, 122, 217

Contrast 164, 171, 191
Denouement (element of plot) 40, 79, 88, 122, 217
Descriptive writing 98
Drama 105, 133, 143, 152
Elements of a Story:
    Balance 163
    Characterization 132, 217
    Mood 217
    Plot 217:
        Climax 40, 41, 79, 88, 122, 217
        Conflict 40, 88, 122, 217
        Denouement 40, 79, 88, 122, 217
        Rising action 40, 88, 122, 217
    Point of view 191, 193, 217
    Setting 40, 88, 121, 122, 173, 217
    Story endings 164, 217
    Style 217
    Theme 217
Fable 143
Fiction 30
Figurative language 123
First person point of view 191
"Fox and Sour Grapes," fable 143
Humor in writing 105
Italics:
    use of 97, 171
    for emphasis 171
    for names of boats and ships 97, 191
    for names of books 192
Layout, text 121
Legend, 162
List-making:
    Elements of art 113, 206
    Food items 191
    Katy's characteristics 182
    Qualities of Big Jim 77
    Store, list for playing 59
    Things to help people 49
    Things too wonderful to be owned 77

Ways to travel 100
Literary devices:
    Alliteration 121, 198, 216
    Hyperbole 198, 216
    Mood 201, 216, 217
    Onomatopoeia 98, 121, 172, 198, 216
    Personification 79, 89, 173, 182, 198, 216
    Repetition 30, 49, 105, 121, 163, 198, 199, 216
    Rhyme, rhyme scheme 199, 216
    Simile 79, 112, 123, 173, 216
    Symbolism 216
Memorizing poetry 199
Memory games 104, 107
Milne, A. A. 33, 199
Onomatopoeia 98, 121, 172, 198, 216
Pantomime 105
Poetic prose 78, 112, 121, 198
Poetry 198, 49
Point of view, first person 191
Punctuation:
    Question mark 78
    Quotation marks 172
Reading comprehension 163
Repetition 30, 49, 105, 121, 163, 198, 199, 216
Setting 40, 88, 121, 122, 173, 217
Scene 173
Story endings 164, 217
Storytelling 57
Titles:
    A Pair of Red Clogs 56
    Another Celebrated Dancing Bear 130
    Clown of God, The 159
    Cranberry Thanksgiving 118
    Glorious Flight, The 96
    Grandfather's Journey 110
    How to Make an Apple Pie
        and See the World 103
    Katy and the Big Snow 180
    Lentil 38

Madeline 48
*Mike Mulligan and His
    Steam Shovel* 86
Night of the Moonjellies, The 189
Papa Piccolo 140
Rag Coat, The 66
*Stopping by Woods on
    a Snowy Evening* 197
Storm in the Night 170
Story About Ping, The 28
Very Last First Time 150
Who Owns the Sun? 76

Vocabulary:
   amazement 162
   appendix 49
   arrangement 163
   audience 132
   aura 122
   barges 143
   bog 122
   bough 172
   brothers 163
   bulldozer 183
   canal 89, 142
   carnival 143
   cellar 89
   chime(d) 143
   coax 105
   comical 132
   companionship 163
   continue 78
   czar 132
   darted 122
   disaster 49
   drizzle 183
   eggplant 162
   elegant 105, 132
   embraced 132
   emergency 183
   errand 172
   exquisite 122
   famous 162
   forlorn 143
   gilded 143
   glum 132, 143
   gondola 143
   ingredients 105
   jealous 132
   juggle 162
   kimono 111
   ledge 142
   locate 105
   lacquer 57
   maestro 163
   magnificent 132, 162
   mandarin 172
   marina 191
   marvelous 132
   moonjellies 191
   murmured 122
   native 105
   patient 183
   peered 122
   perfectly 57
   persistent 143
   persuade 105
   pier 191
   plantation 105
   pyramid 132
   ragamuffin 163
   regatta 143
   samovar 132
   sardine 143
   scow 143
   serious 162
   signora 142
   situation 142
   skiff 143

solemn 49
squint(ed) 78
starch 122
steamroller 183
superb 105
suspecting 57
three-alarm fire 183
torches 163
trinket 142
troupe 163
turnips 122
violet 163
wander 78
water main 183
wilted 122
windmill 78
zucchini 162

What makes a poem? 198

Writing 77, 151

Art

Action, expression in figures 58, 80, 90, 99
Appreciation 50, 99, 166
Architecture 41, 50, 134, 165
Artistic style 152
Balance 113
Charcoal 41
Color:
    Color theory 144
    Color and contrast 112
    Colored pencil 30, 57
    Complementary colors 144, 174
    Expressing light 123, 145, 193
    Expressing darkness 123, 193
    Mixing, matching colors 143
    Unity of color:
        Theme 58
        Variety 79
    Warm palette 58, 123, 193
    Wheel, advanced color 144

Composition 31
Contrast 106, 112, 174, 183
Creating illusion of speed 145
Detail 41, 134, 152, 165, 183, 192, 201
Drawing:
    Action/expression 58
    Charcoal 41
    Highlights (live eyes) 144
    Motion 90
    Pen and ink 57, 200
    Perspective 99
    Reflections 33, 112, 174
    Silhouettes 123
    Trees 89, 165, 200
    Water 30, 33

Etchings 133, 134
Facial expressions 69, 174
Formal style 113
Highlights 144, 173
Humor 106
Illusion of speed 145
Illustrators:
    Bemelmans, Ludwig 48
    Burton, Virginia Lee 86, 180
    Chbosky, Stacy 76
    Cummings, Pat 170
    dePaola, Tomie 159
    Devlin, Wende and Harry 118
    Garrison, Barbara 130
    Jeffers, Susan 197
    Maeno, Itoko 140
    Mizumura, Kazue 56
    McCloskey, Robert 38
    Mills, Lauren 66
    Priceman, Marjorie 103
    Provensen, Alice and Martin 96

    Say, Allen 110
    Shasha, Mark 189
    Wallace, Ian 150
    Wiese, Kurt 28
Integrating illustrations with text 200
Intensity 113
Juggling 164
Layout 192
Light 80, 123, 145, 193
Live eyes (highlights) 144
Medium 30, 41, 112, 165, 173, 191, 200
Monochromatic 50
Mood 201
Motion 80, 90
Music:
    Dulcimer 67
    Harmonica 42
    "Jingle Bells" 201
    Nutcracker Suite 130
    Practicing 42
Origami 114
Palette:
    Cool palette 152
    Full palette 152
    Limited palette 69
    Warm palette 123, 152
Partial view 123
Pastels, medium 191
Perspective 99
Pictures add detail 41
Profiles 123, 175
Quilts, quilting 69
Reflection(s) 33, 112, 174
Sequencing 166
Shadows, bright light 80, 112
Silhouette 123
Street scenes 105
Style 152, 200
Symbolism 79, 80, 113

Unity of theme:
    Subject 31
    Color 58
Variety 50
Viewpoint 31, 68, 99, 193, 201
Warm palette 123, 152
Watercolor 79, 112, 133, 143, 165

Math

Counting 32, 59, 81, 91, 114, 145, 167, 183, 184
Days in a week 114, 134
Dividing 50
Flash cards 18, 166, 202
Fractions 42
Geometric shapes 70, 90, 175
Geoboard 70, 90, 175
Grouping and counting 184
Grouping and dividing 50
Grouping and (pre) multiplication 166
Hours on a clock 70, 134
Measuring skills 124, 107
Money 194
Multiplication 166, 184
Ordinal numbers 17, 99, 153
Pairs 145
Playing store 59
Relative size and degree 51
Roman numerals 99
Symmetry 51
Subtraction 106
Weeks in a month 114

Science

Acoustics 43
Aging 167, 176
Animal Kingdom:
    Bird 115

    Cat 145
    Cow 105
    Duck 32
    Jellyfish (moon jellyfish) 194
Animal tracks 202
Apples 104
Bacteria 107
Balanced meal 81, 85
Bananas 104
Barometric pressure 59
Biology 115
Biome 154, 194
Boiling point of water 135
Breeds, cats 145
Buoyancy 24, 32
Chemical reaction 125
Chemistry 125
Cities, factory pollution in 115
Cinnamon 104
Cliffs 114
Cloud types 177
Coal and coal mining 70, 71
Cosmonauts 131
Cranberries 118
Creative thinking, problem solving 91
Crisis thinking, safety in emergencies 153, 157, 171, 176
Deserts 114
Dressing for conditions 153
Echoes 154
Ecology (stewardship) 87
Engineering, road building 91
Erosion 114
Evaporation 107
Exercise, Drama actions 51
Exploration 153
Farmlands 114
Flying 100
Forcasting 59

Freezing point of water 135
Fulcrum 81, 154
Health:
    Dressing for conditions 153
    Fresh food 107
    Health habits 51
    Nutrition 81
    Safety rules 153
    Swimming safety 32
Human Body—Anatomy:
    Appendix 49, 51
    Taste buds 42
    Five senses 81, 176
    Peripheral vision 145
Ice 150
Inclined plane 81, 154
Inventions 99
Land types 114
Leavening 125
Lemonade 43
Lever (simple machine) 81, 154
Light sources 33, 175
Machines, simple 81, 154
Memory 81
Meteorologist 59
Mixture 125
Mountains 114
Natural fabrics 71
Nutrition 81
Ocean Life
    Anemones 154
    Clams 118, 154, 190
    Lobsters 190
    Marina 190
    Moonjellies 194
    Mussels 151, 154
    Ocean 154,
    Salt water 107, 194
    Sea gulls 190

Index

    Sea salt 154
    Seaweed 154
    Shellfish 154
    Shrimp 154
    Starfish 190
Patterns, weather 184
Pollution 115
Power, steam 86, 91
Predicting the weather 59
Preserving food 107
Process of invention 99
Pulley (simple machine) 81, 154
Reaction, chemical 125
Reflection of light 33
Road engineering 91
Rock formation 114
Safety 33, 153, 175
Salt 42, 107, 154, 190
Screw (simple machine) 81, 154
Seasons 59, 81, 124
Semolina 103
Senses, five 81, 176
Simple machines 81, 154
Sound and acoustics 43
Starch 124
Sources of light 33, 175
Steam power 86, 91
Storm survival kit 175
Sugar cane 104, 107
Thunderstorms 177
Tides 153
Tundra 150
Wedge (simple machine) 81, 154
Wheat 104
Wheel and axle (simple machine) 81, 154

Supplemental Books Mentioned in the Text:

A Guide to Animal Tracking and Behavior, Donald and Lillian Stokes 203
A Guild to Nature in Winter, Donald Stokes 203
Apartment 3, Ezra Jack Keats 113
Big Yellow Drawing Book, The, Dan O'Neill 69
Bridge Book, The, Polly Carter 165
Christy, Catherine Marshall 67
Drinking Gourd, The, R. N. Monjo 76
Favorite Poems Old and New, edited by Helen Ferris 199
Foxfire Book, The, ed. Eliot Wigginton 67
From Hand to Mouth: Or How We Invented Knives, Forks, Spoons, and Chopsticks and the Table Manners to Go With Them, James Cross Giblin, 57
Gramma's Walk, Anna Grossnickle Hines 161
Hannah's Brave Year, Rhoda Wooldridge 161
Hannah's House Series, Rhoda Wooldridge 161
House at Pooh Corner, The, A. A. Milne 199
How the Tzar Drinks His Tea, Benjamin Elkin 135
I Know That Building!, D'Alelio 41
Joyful Noise (Poems for Two Voices), Paul Fleischman 199
Let There Be Light, James Cross Giblin 166
Lindbergh, Chris L. Demarest, 100
Little Duck, The, Judy Dunn 32
Looking for Home, Arleta Richardson 160
Molly's Pilgrim, Barbara Cohen 120
Moon's The North Wind's Cooky, The, edited by Susan Russo 199
Mrs. Katz and Tush, Patricia Polacco 161
Nana Upstairs and Nana Downstairs, Tomie dePaola 167
Now One Foot, Now the Other, Tomie dePaola 167
Now We Are Six, A. A. Milne 199
Oh, What an Awful Mess: A Story of Charles Goodyear, Robert M. Quackenbush 100
Old House, New House,

Gaughenbaugh and Camburn 41
One Morning in Maine, Robert McCloskey 119
Patchwork Quilt, The, Valerie Flournoy 68
Ruth Law Thrills a Nation, Don Brown, 100
Samatha Books, American Girls Series 160
Sing a Song of Popcorn, edited by
    Barbara Schenk de Regniers 199
Snowy Day, Ezra Jack Keats 113
Stories from Grandma's Attic,
    Arleta Richardson 68
Sweet Clara and the Freedom Quilt,
    Hopkinson 68
Uncle Jed's Barbershop,
    Margaree King Mitchell 161
Under Every Roof, Patricia Brown Glenn 41
Venice: Birth of a City, Piero Ventura 140
When We Were Very Young, A. A. Milne 199
Whistle-Stop West, Arleta Richardson 160
World of Christopher Robin, The,
    "The Mirror", A. A. Milne 199
Yonie Wondernose, Marguerite de Angeli 151

Index

Inspired learning through great books.

Five in a Row is a complete,* well-rounded, literature-based curriculum that takes your child from pre-K through middle school.

Current print products available from *Five in a Row* approved retailers:

For ages 2-4:
Before Five in a Row, 2nd Edition – Available from fiveinarow.com
and Amazon.com

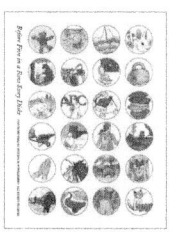

Before Five in a Row Story Disks (full-color, laminated)
– Available from fiveinarow.com

Before Five in a Row Storybook Map (full-color, laminated)
– Available from fiveinarow.com

For ages 3-5:
More Before Five in a Row – Available from fiveinarow.com
and Amazon.com

More Before Five in a Row Story Disks (full-color, laminated)
– Available from fiveinarow.com

More Before Five in a Row Storybook Map (full-color, laminated)
– Available from fiveinarow.com

For ages 5-9:
Five in a Row Volume 1, Second Edition – Available from fiveinarow.com and Amazon.com

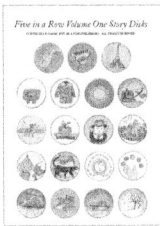

Five in a Row Volume 1 Story Disks (full-color, laminated) – Available from fiveinarow.com

For ages 5-9:
Five in a Row: Volume 2

Five in a Row: Volume 3

Five in a Row Starter Kit: Vols. 1, 2, 3 plus *Five in a Row Bible Supplement*

For ages 8 and up:
Five in a Row: Volume 4 (includes Bible Supplement and Cookbook)

Five in a Row **Supplements:**
Five in a Row Story Disks (full-color, laminated)
Five in a Row Bible Supplement (for Vols. 1, 2, 3)
Beyond Five in a Row Bible Supplement (for Vols. 1, 2, 3)
Five in a Row Cookbook (for Vols. 1, 2, 3 of both *FIAR* and *Beyond FIAR*)

For ages 8-12:
Beyond Five in a Row: Volume 1

Beyond Five in a Row: Volume 2

Beyond Five in a Row: Volume 3

For ages 12 and up:
Above & Beyond Five in a Row

Rainbowresource.com currently offers most *Five in a Row* print products as well as Literature Packages that go along with each of the *Five in a Row* and *Beyond Five in a Row* volumes.

Digital resources available from fiveinarow.com

Visit www.fiveinarow.com for additional digital resources and more information on the products above.

FIAR Notebook Builder
More than 120 pages of notebooking templates for all ages, appropriate for any topic or unit of study.

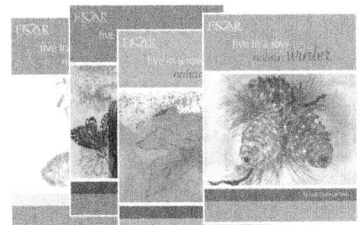

FIAR Nature Studies (Spring, Summer, Fall, Winter)
The *FIAR Nature Study* encourages your entire family to enjoy and explore the outdoors in all four seasons; it is a topic close to Jane's heart. Resources are provided to ensure that you can be a nature mentor to your child! It is a true unit study approach to nature studies; suggestions introduce you and your child to poetry, music, and art that tie in to the season.

FIAR Holiday: Through the Seasons
A treasury of traditions, ideas, and more for making your own special holiday memories.

Homeschool Encouragement Messages (Audio Files)
Inspiring messages from Steve on often-requested topics: Where Do I Begin, I Can't Teach All the Grades at Once, Making Your Children into World Changers, On Becoming Great Teachers, and High School and Beyond.

More digital products available at fiveinarow.com
You'll find other digital products at www.fiveinarow.com, as well, including a *FIAR Planner* and bonus units for Volume 4, as well as other *FIAR* products in digital format: *Above & Beyond FIAR*, the *FIAR Cookbook* and *Holiday* volumes, individual *FIAR Volume 4* units, and *Fold & Learns* for select *FIAR* and *Beyond FIAR* units.

You will need to add math and phonics/reading instruction to **Five in a Row.*

Visit fiveinarow.com for additional information on the latest products.

Printed in Great Britain
by Amazon